THE
EVERYTHING

BABY'S FIRST
FOOD BOOK

Tasty, nutritious meals
and snacks that even the
pickiest child will love—
from birth to age 3

Janet Mason Tarlov

Adams Media Corporation
Holbrook, Massachusetts

An Everything® Series Book.
Everything® is a registered trademark of Adams Media Corporation.

Published by Adams Media Corporation
260 Center Street, Holbrook, MA 02343
www.adamsmedia.com

ISBN: 1-58062-512-6
Printed in the United States of America.

J I H G F E D C B A

Library of Congress Cataloging-in-Publication Data available from publisher.

The information contained in this book is not meant to replace the advice and guidance of your child's pediatrician. Before making changes to your child's health regimen, you should consult your child's pediatrician, who will advise you based on your child's particular needs.

Many of the designations used by manufacturers and sellers to distinguish their products are claimed as trademarks. Where those designations appear in this book and Adams Media was aware of a trademark claim, the designations have been printed in initial capital letters.

This publication is designed to provide accurate and authoritative information with regard to the subject matter covered. It is sold with the understanding that the publisher is not engaged in rendering legal, accounting, or other professional advice. If legal advice or other expert assistance is required, the services of a competent professional person should be sought.
　　　　　　　　　—From a *Declaration of Principles* jointly adopted by a Committee of the
American Bar Association and a Committee of Publishers and Associations

Illustrations by Barry Littmann

*This book is available at quantity discounts for bulk purchases.
For information, call 1-800-872-5627.*

Visit the entire Everything® series at everything.com

Acknowledgments

I am very grateful for the support of many people who helped me as I worked on this book. In particular, I'd like to thank friends who were willing to share their personal stories and advice: Christina Savageau, Susan Ganbari, Kari Worth, Karyn and Scott Miller, Kate Sachnoff, Jane Philipson, Greg Coley, and Leah Sirkin.

I have also benefited enormously from the kindness of strangers who responded to my queries for advice on internet chat rooms and through e-mail missives sent out as I wrote each section.

My agent, Carol Susan Roth, and the editors at Adams Media, especially Pam Liflander, also provided me with the assistance and advice that made it possible for me to write this book in the first place.

The patience and understanding of my coworkers at Market Hall Foods in Oakland and Berkeley, CA, especially Sara Wilson and Ali Jahangiri, was extremely important to me. Many thanks to Lisa Moresco, owner of the legendary Natural Resources store in San Francisco, who provided me with so much support and guidance.

Finally, I'd like to thank my family, especially my husband Richard Tarlov, who helped me to believe that I could undertake and complete such a large project in my first year of motherhood.

Contents

CONTENTS

Introduction

Not long ago, I thought I knew everything there was to know about baby food. As a food writer involved with the specialty food industry for many years, I know a great deal about nutrition, have a good attitude about food, and figured I was fully prepared to provide our infant son Max with a healthy diet.

I began work on this book when Max was eight months old, and he had already proved himself as a chap with a hearty appetite and a healthy appreciation for food. As a new mother, I was proud of the excitement he displayed at mealtimes and the increasing variety of foods he relished. I thought of myself as a "natural" mother, feeding my baby foods I instinctively knew were good for him. And I was right . . . sort of. As I have heard said many times, "I was a much better parent before I had a baby." Subsequent adventures and misadventures in infant feeding and the hundreds of hours spent researching this book have taught me how much I actually still had to learn.

Before I started researching the subject of baby food I thought I had a pretty solid handle on which foods were "good," which foods were "bad," and why. Fresh fruits and vegetables, dairy products, and whole grain baked goods are "good" because they have vitamins and minerals, and no junk. Junk foods, fast foods, frozen entrees, and sugary snacks are "bad" because they have too much sugar, salt, fat, processed ingredients, preservatives, and chemicals. However, what I failed to realize is that no amount of nutritional know-how is going to alter the decisive clamping shut of your baby's mouth when your "good" food is staunchly refused. Suddenly, your confidence may crumble, and the idea of sending your fourteen-month-old to bed without any supper looms as a terrifying prospect after several "good" options have been undeniably turned down.

Going through this process with Max as he rounded the one-year mark taught me how much uncertainty I still harbored with relation to food. Would he be OK without vegetables every day? What if he never ate them again? How can you cure a juice-aholic? Why had he suddenly stopped growing out of all his clothes every six weeks? Fortunately, just as I had settled into the conviction that he would be a permanent picky eater, I realized what was really going on was that he had been holding out for control of his spoon. Suddenly, the adventure of eating was fun again, as he wielded his spoon to his sloppy satisfaction. This is not to say that the

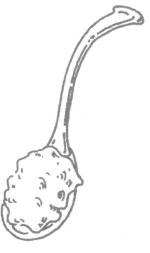

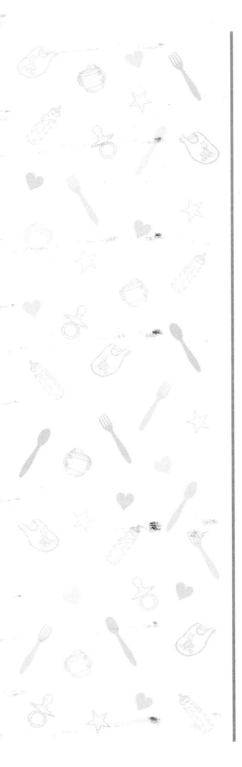

carefree days of introducing a new, readily accepted solid food every two to three days were back, but we were making progress again.

In order to assist parents in the sometimes challenging, often hilarious quest to rear a full-grown adult, I have included many quips and reminiscences from actual parents who are friends, colleagues, acquaintances, or those who have responded to my queries over the Web. These anecdotes, called "Feeding Your Baby in the Real World," are lighthearted complements to the expert advice and scientific research that is also included in the book. *The Everything® Baby's First Food Book* also includes tons of ideas for the new (or returning) parent for different foods at different ages, as well as concrete advice for evaluating your baby's readiness for milestones from the introduction of solid food to drinking from an open cup. There are even a few handy recipes here and there.

In the course of writing this book I have discovered that there is tremendous interest among parents about nutritional information, especially when it comes to feeding infants. The sheer amount of literature and research devoted to infant nutrition is overwhelming, and even a quick search of the Internet will reveal thousands of Web sites offering information and products to help you feed your baby.

It is widely acknowledged that the early years of life are especially critical to children when it comes to intellectual, physical, and emotional development and proper nutrition is an important factor in each of these areas. Parents naturally want to give their children the best they can, and a healthy diet along with a safe, loving, and stimulating environment is a great place to start. As public awareness of the importance of proper nutrition grows, it is inevitable that food service providers, farmers, and manufacturers will begin to offer even more healthful food options for families.

Parenting is a very challenging pursuit, and when it comes to the food you feed your baby, cultural, emotional, and economic issues all get folded into the mixture. You and your partner may go through some sort of process, whether consciously or not, of coming to terms with some of those factors in developing a strategy for feeding your family given your own unique circumstances. It is my goal to take some of the anxiety out of feeding your baby, while providing you with a solid understanding of child development in relation to eating and infant nutrition. Congratulations and bon appetit!

Breast or Bottle?

In the early months, an infant will get all of her nourishment from either the breast or the bottle, and many feed from a combination of the two. However, there is no doubt among experts that breastfeeding is the best choice for nourishing an infant. Indeed, before the beginning of the twentieth century, there was simply no other option available. Breastmilk is the perfect food for human infants. It provides optimum nutrition, hydration, and protection from illness, as well as promoting fast and loving bonding between a mother and her newborn baby. For more information about breastfeeding, see Chapter 2. When nursing is not possible or if a mother chooses not to nurse, her baby will almost certainly grow and thrive on a diet of infant formula, although even the producers of formula acknowledge the superiority of breastmilk. Also, some mothers combine nursing with formula feedings. There are several choices to consider when feeding your baby formula, as we will discover in Chapter 3.

Obviously, breastfeeding was the exclusive method of feeding infants for almost all of human history, but its decline in some cultures began before the invention of formula with the use of wet nurses. Traditionally, a wet nurse was a servant to a wealthy family whose job it was to breastfeed the family's babies. In some cases, these women nourished and cared for babies and children until they were in their 70s! Although the occupation of wet nurse carried with it a measure of respect and stability, many of these women were forced to give up the care of their own children. The practice of using a wet nurse reached its height during the Victorian era, when rules of modesty and distinctions of class were of paramount importance. This was unfortunate in several ways. First, it unnecessarily separated women from their children, which was a tremendous loss to those families and to the society as a whole. Second, the belief that nursing was a task to be performed by the lower class helped to enable quick acceptance of formula feeding just a few decades later.

Formula was first introduced in the United States in 1911, and was increasingly used in the 1930s and 1940s by parents seeking to raise their children according to "scientific" methods

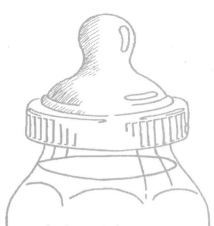

popular at that time. Breastfeeding mothers were increasingly viewed as lower class, and their infants were thought to be deprived of the perceived benefits of modern infant formula. By the 1970s, fewer than one in four babies was breastfed. However, beginning in the 1950s the American Medical Association (AMA) began to acknowledge the health benefits of breastmilk for infants. National programs for promoting breastfeeding were first implemented during the Carter administration. In 1981, the percentage of mothers nursing their babies peaked at 62 percent. Many national organizations such as La Leche League and the American Academy of Pediatrics (AAP) carry on the work of reaching out to mothers to teach them about the benefits and joys of nursing, while helping them through its challenges.

Still, exclusively breastfeeding a baby, with no supplementation of formula, requires a substantial commitment on the part of the mother, which may not work well with her particular situation. Being able to share some of the responsibility for feeding the baby can make a difference. Women today have many more opportunities available to them than their own mothers did. The invention of formula has enabled many women to balance multiple commitments, knowing that their babies' nutritional needs are being met. For some women, this may mean that nursings are supplemented with occasional or daily formula feedings; for others it means that the baby is weaned from the breast early or never breastfeeds at all. For women and babies who have medical issues that make nursing impossible, formula is a literal lifesaver.

Personal Choice

The choice whether or not to nurse your baby and for how long is a very personal decision that only you can make. It is important to realize, though, that doctors, nurses, and midwives place a great deal of emphasis on breastfeeding because of the proven benefits to both babies and mothers. Medical professionals know that if a woman is not given the proper encouragement to try breastfeeding, she may miss an opportunity to have a wonderful nursing experience, and her baby will miss out on the great headstart that

Cultural Support Is Key

In cultures where breastfeeding is the norm, almost 100 percent of women are able to successfully nurse their babies. This is because most women in these societies have unlimited access to support and guidance from their mothers, sisters, and friends. A powerful network exists in these communities where breastfeeding is accepted and honored, and if an infant loses his mother through death, illness, or separation, another woman is usually willing to step in to nourish him until his mother returns or until he is weaned.

breastmilk supplies. Remember that you can always switch to a bottle later, but the opportunity to nurse will be over if you delay too long, so it is usually worth giving nursing a try even if you're not sure it will work for you. Any time spent nursing will be of benefit to you and your baby, and believe it or not, many women who are unsure in the beginning go on to nurse successfully for many months. On the other hand, there can be equally strong pressures placed on a woman by people around her who may not support her efforts to breastfeed. New motherhood can be a time marked by powerful feelings of inadequacy and lack of confidence. Remember that it should be you and your baby who will decide what is best. Learn as much as possible about your options and your concerns, and demand the support you deserve to carry out your decisions.

Early Feedings and Building New Family Relationships

Whether you choose to nurse or bottle-feed your baby, these early feedings are important for your baby's physical and emotional well-being. She emerges from the womb with a powerful instinct to survive by finding food and bonding with the person or people who will provide it for her. Studies have shown that a newborn baby has the amazing ability to "crawl" to the breast and begin to nurse within minutes of birth when placed on her mother's stomach.

When healthy babies are born to healthy mothers, feedings should begin as soon as possible. When the health of either the baby or the mother is compromised, hospital staff are usually willing to make any accommodations possible to allow for maximum parent/infant contact in each given situation. This is because seeing, touching, and feeding your newborn infant are acknowledged as meaningful factors in parent/infant bonding. While an early start is optimal, a newborn baby who is separated from her parents due to medical complications or the process of adoption, for example, has a remarkable capacity for bonding with her special people when they are finally together.

Unparalleled Growth

Your little newborn baby is astonishing. Just nine months ago she was a jumble of genetic information, and now she is a fully formed human being newly separated from everything her body has learned to date. In the coming days, she will most likely lose about 5 to 8 percent of her birth weight. This is because it will be several days before her mother's milk will come in, and also her body will need to metabolize nutrients not delivered through the umbilical cord for the first time. Full-term babies are born with the extra fluid and fat stores needed to cope with this weight loss. If the baby's mother is nursing, she will be getting the benefit of colostrum, the substance produced by a woman's breasts before her milk comes in. Colostrum is a golden, viscous substance that is produced in tiny quantities. It contains innumerable antibodies and nutrients and coats the baby's digestive tract, creating an environment in which healthy bacterial flora can flourish. Babies who are fed formula also typically start with very small bottle feedings, building up to larger feedings after the first few days.

By about two weeks postpartum, most babies will have returned to their birth weight. Pediatricians carefully observe both breastfed and formula-fed babies during this critical period to ensure that the transition to life outside the womb is going smoothly. Your baby's pediatrician will carefully track measurements of his weight, height, and head circumference against a standardized growth chart. If your baby seems to be growing well, your pediatrician will probably want to take these measurements two to three times during the first month, or more frequently if there is concern that he doesn't seem to be gaining weight rapidly enough. Pediatricians and nurses also counsel new parents to keep careful track of wet and poopy diapers, to ensure that babies are feeding and digesting well in the first days. This is especially helpful for breastfed babies, since it is not possible to actually see how much milk a baby takes at each given feeding.

What Is Bonding?

Bonding is a phenomenon that occurs gradually during the first few hours or days after birth, in which a baby and his parents (primarily his mother) become "imprinted" on one another. Research suggests that infants are preprogrammed to respond to one or two caretakers, and that a mother undergoes hormonal shifts simply by seeing, touching, and smelling her baby.

Full-term babies almost always pass quite a lot of meconium in the first 24 to 48 hours after birth. Meconium is a black, sticky, tarlike stool that was in your baby's intestine in the womb. When food is first introduced to your baby, her stools will gradually begin to change. Be prepared for some dramatic greenish, curdlike stools possibly containing mucus as this transition occurs. Although this shift is normal and expected, this strange substance alarms many nervous first-time parents. If you are concerned, there is no harm in saving a diaper to show to your baby's doctor. Within one to three weeks, stools will have settled to a loose yellowish color for breastfed babies, and a more bulky brown for formula-fed babies. Most young babies will have about three, and sometimes many more, poopy diapers every day. After the first day or so, your baby should have at least eight wet diapers every day (some babies pass water as frequently as 30 times in 24 hours). Once urine flow is established, if your baby does not wet his diaper in eight to ten hours, you should call his pediatrician to discuss a possible dehydration.

Tracking Your Baby's First Days

When we brought our baby Max home from the hospital, we felt overwhelmed by the unfamiliarity of our new situation. Like all parents, we were concerned that something might be wrong with our baby (fortunately nothing was), and we worried that we wouldn't be able to tell if there was. My husband, Richard, devised this chart to help us keep track of the essentials: feedings and wet and poopy diapers. I found that having this information in the early weeks was invaluable when talking with the lactation consultant and Max's pediatrician.

Tracking Feedings and Wet and Poopy Diapers

Example: Tuesday 6/11 (3 Days Postpartum)

Time	Feeding (Length)	Wet Diaper (X)	Poopy Diaper (X)	Comments
12:00 A.M.				
1:00 A.M.	15 min? (fell asleep)	X	X	Meconium
2:00 A.M.				
3:00 A.M.				
4:00 A.M.	20 minutes	X		Slept well tonight!
5:00 A.M.				
6:00 A.M.	30 minutes	X	X	Meconium
7:00 A.M.				Awake for a while
8:00 A.M.	25 minutes	X		
9:00 A.M.				
10:00 A.M.	2 minutes			Crying, hard to nurse
11:00 A.M.	35 minutes	X		
12:00 P.M.				
1:00 P.M.				Woke to feed
2:00 P.M.	30 minutes	X	X	Poop more green
3:00 P.M.				
4:00 P.M.	10 minutes	X		Latching problem
5:00 P.M.	10 minutes			Very fussy
6:00 P.M.	10 minutes	X		Nursing again!
7:00 P.M.				Slept almost all day
8:00 P.M.	20 minutes	X	X	Green and slimy!
9:00 P.M.				
10:00 P.M.				
11:00 P.M.	20 minutes	X	X	

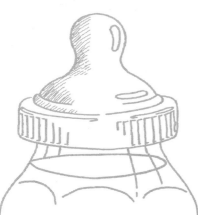

Counting Disposable Wet Diapers

It can be very difficult to detect if a modern superabsorbent disposable diaper is wet, especially since newborns don't always pass a lot of urine. In the hospital, nurses may sometimes even weigh the diaper on a finely calibrated scale to determine if the diaper is wet. Some experts recommend lining the diaper with a tissue in the first days to help detect the actual frequency of urination.

Typical Weight Gain for Bottle- and Breastfed Babies

In the first year, weight gain for most babies follows a pattern of dramatic increase in the first 12 weeks that continues at a steady if rapid pace until it slows down considerably by the end of the first year. Your baby's weight gain may vary from this pattern because of periodic growth spurts and/or illness, or because of her unique body type. Growth in breastfed babies will often slow in weight gain relative to length at about six months, compared to their formula-fed counterparts. This is normal so long as the baby's length continues to increase. If you are at all concerned about your child's growth, consult her pediatrician. Many parents worry that their child is not growing fast enough and are easily reassured by a simple check of their baby's progress using a growth chart.

Pediatric Growth Charts

Pediatric growth charts were developed in 1977 by the National Center for Health Statistics, now a part of the Centers for Disease Control and Prevention. The growth charts track a series of curves called "percentiles" that represent growth rates over time in a large sample of children. Pediatricians, nurses, and parents use these charts to evaluate whether an infant or child is growing within the norm for other children her age. It is a valuable tool for helping to identify children who are at risk of poor growth and overweight. These charts were later adopted for use by the World Health Organization for international use. The National Center for Health Statistics released revised, updated versions of the pediatric growth charts in May 2000, which are included in this book. For more information about growth charts and how they are used, see Chapter 7.

Pediatric Growth Charts

BOYS

Age	Typical Weight Gain	Per Week/Month
2–12 weeks	5–10 ounces	Week
3–6 months	1 pound, 6 ounces–1 pound, 8 ounces	Month
6–9 months	1 pound–1 pound, 1 ounce	Month
9–12 months	10–13 ounces	Month

GIRLS

Age	Typical Weight Gain	Per Week/Month
2–12 weeks	5–8 ounces	Week
3–6 months	1 pound, 2 ounces–1 pound, 5 ounces	Month
6–9 months	13 ounces–1 pound	Month
9–12 months	10–13 ounces	Month

Data obtained from weight-for-age percentiles (25th–75th), boys and girls, birth to 36 months, CDC growth charts: United States

Feeding Schedules and Night Feedings

All newborn and young babies require regular feedings both day and night. Often, a newborn will be very sleepy during his first few days outside the womb, because he will be exhausted after labor and birth. You will most likely need to wake him to make sure he is feeding regularly. Breastfed babies will naturally vary the number and length of feedings each day based on their needs. Nursing babies may also suck for comfort rather than simple hunger if they are allowed to do so. A formula-fed baby

will usually feed about every two to four hours, and a breastfed baby should nurse at least eight times a day. All new babies will need to eat several times during the night for at least a few months. Babies who sleep through the night without feeding at six weeks are rare indeed.

In the past, parents were encouraged to set rigid feeding schedules for babies from birth; a practice now widely disputed. Experts feel that by following an overly strict feeding schedule, babies are encouraged to eat when they are not hungry and/or forced to wait for a feeding when they need to eat immediately. It is believed that this practice sends the wrong message from the start—that food and hunger do not have a strong relationship. Experts worry that this practice may lead to eating problems later in life. It may be helpful to think of your baby's schedule as more of a loose "routine" that will emerge as she develops during the early weeks. This routine should ideally create a compromise between your needs and hers, allowing for you to plan around feedings with the understanding that the schedule may need to be adjusted unexpectedly.

A Feeding Is Not Always the Best Way to Soothe Your Crying Baby

It can be tempting to offer a crying baby the breast or bottle whether or not you think he is hungry, because eating can be very soothing for a young baby. Conversely, a baby who is overly hungry may be so upset by his anxiety over being fed that he literally can't settle down enough to have a proper feed. In this case, you should try other means of calming your baby, such as:

- Walk or dance with the baby in your arms or in a baby sling or carrier.
- Swaddle the baby tightly.
- Sit with the baby in a rocking chair.
- Take the baby out for a walk.
- Take the baby on a car ride.

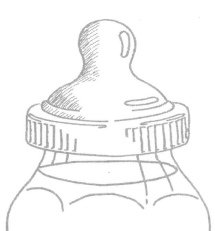

- Put the baby in a wind-up swing.
- Shake a rattling toy in front of your baby's eyes.
- Place the baby directly beneath an interesting mobile.
- Run the vacuum, water tap, or dishwasher.
- Lay the baby tummy-down on your lap and rub his back.
- Change the baby's environment, by stepping into or out of a noisy room for example.
- Give the baby to someone else to hold for a while.

Spitting Up

Some babies spit up more than others, but most will dribble at least a little milk after most feedings. If your baby is a big spitter-upper, you'll know by the constant nagging feeling that maybe she is spitting up too much. There are splatters on the floor and often you and the baby both have to change clothes at some time during the day. If this sounds familiar, you probably have nothing to worry about. What seems a large amount is usually less than a table-spoon. If you spill just a tablespoon of milk, you'll see that it creates quite a mess. However, if your baby is not gaining weight properly, if she is spitting up or vomiting with increasing frequency and forcefulness and/or seems to be experiencing pain while spit-ting up, or if the spit-up consistently contains green bile, you should call the pediatrician immediately.

Why Do Babies Spit Up in the First Place?

Babies spit up because they have very small tummies and they frequently swallow excess air during feedings. Often, this means that gulps of air precede swallows of milk, and according to the laws of gravity, the air rises to the top of a baby's stomach and is belched out, forcing milk along with it. Sometimes, a baby's appetite will simply exceed his small stomach capacity, and he will spit up the excess. Also, parents are frequently to blame if they bounce and squeeze the baby too soon after a feeding.

How Can I Tell If My Baby Is Hungry?

Believe it or not, it's not always easy to read a new baby's hunger signals. Some small babies cry a lot, and some very little, but no baby always cries from hunger. They may cry from gas pain, tiredness, need for comfort, confusion, or any number of other reasons. However, there are hunger signals to look for. Your baby may chew his fists or nuzzle into your chest as if looking for the breast (this is often true whether or not his mother is holding him). This is called the rooting reflex.

The Spit-up Reduction Program

These are some time-tested methods for curtailing the spit-up problem.

- Give your baby plenty of time after each feeding to digest her meal before engaging in more vigorous play.
- Burp your baby frequently before and during feedings.
- Feed your baby smaller amounts at more frequent intervals to accommodate her small tummy.
- Keep your baby in as upright a position as possible during and after feedings.

If none of these measures helps and if your baby is growing properly and seems otherwise well, it may be best to resign yourself to doing a *lot* of laundry. Most babies finish spitting up around the time they can sit. The upright position usually helps keep more milk down.

The Glamour of Burping

All right, burping may *not* be the most glamorous aspect of parenthood, but doing it properly can be tricky and it's important. Giving your baby a thorough burping may not only save your shirt from messy spit-up; it can also keep your baby from experiencing the discomfort of too much gas in her tummy. There are several methods to choose from, and your baby may quickly show a preference for one of them. Other babies are reluctant burpers, and it takes several minutes and some experimentation to coax a satisfying belch out of them. Sometimes a burp happens just because you're changing from one position to another. If a burp doesn't come after several tries, it's OK to give up. She'll probably let it rip in a few minutes.

The Old Shoulder Burp

Of course, the classic burping method is to hold your baby tummy-side-down against your shoulder, patting and rubbing his back. I always found that it helped to pat my baby's back starting at the bottom and working my way up. It also helps to try and position his tummy in such a way that it presses right up against you. Don't forget to use a burp cloth to protect from spit-ups.

The Lap-Sit Burp

This burping method is great for dads who can easily hold a small baby with one large hand. Hold your baby propped forward in a sitting position on your lap, with your hand cradling the entire front of her torso. You'll need to position her head so that it rests on your wrist or forearm if she doesn't have much head control yet. With the other hand, gently pat and rub her back as before.

The Tummy-Down Burp

Some babies give great satisfying burps in response to this method; others almost never burp this way. Hold your baby facedown on your lap, with his tummy draped over your legs. Cradle his head in one hand or turn it to the side and lay it on your lap as well. Pat and rub. The extra pressure on the tummy often does the trick, but there's no help from gravity allowing the gas to rise up as with the other two methods.

Allergies and Infant Feeding

Allergies can pose problems even for the very young, and both breastfed and formula-fed babies may experience allergic reactions. A nursing baby might react to something the mother has eaten, such as chocolate, dairy products, and other common allergens such as eggs, peanuts, wheat, and so on. If you suspect an allergic reaction, try an elimination diet to track down potential sources for his troubles. Once the allergen is identified,

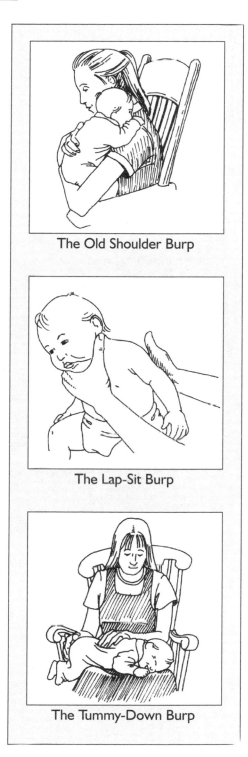

The Old Shoulder Burp

The Lap-Sit Burp

The Tummy-Down Burp

you may have to avoid or curtail your consumption of the offending food either for the first few months or throughout the time you nurse. Formula-fed babies are occasionally allergic to cow's milk or soy derivatives in infant formula, and must be switched to a hypoallergenic formula. If you suspect your baby is suffering from allergies, keep careful track of his symptoms and their timing in relation to his feedings. Before switching formulas or following an elimination diet, it is a good idea to consult your baby's doctor, who may want to examine him to rule out any potential illness.

Signs of an Allergic Reaction in Infants

- Colicky behaviors, such as sustained inconsolable crying, arching and clenched fists
- Excessive spitting up or vomiting
- Frequent watery stools containing mucus
- Very red sore-looking diaper rash around the anus
- An eczemalike rash on the face or torso

Constipation and/or Diarrhea: When to Be Concerned

Breast- and bottle-fed babies have very different patterns when it comes to poopy diapers. A breastfed baby will usually have fairly loose, yellowish stools that change slightly with her mother's diet. Also, breastfed babies are prone to making very loud announcements at the coming of a bowel movement, including flatulence that can be heard across the room. Once you are used to this fanfare you'll probably find it amusing, but you may feel some concern until you realize that this is normal for your baby. It is not particularly common for a baby who is exclusively breastfed to suffer from either constipation or diarrhea. However, the frequency of stools may be extremely variable, from a poopy diaper after each feeding to an occasional several days' passing without any bowel movement at all. If your baby seems well otherwise, you should not be too concerned unless five to seven days have passed.

Remembering to Burp

Sometimes, it's hard to remember to burp your baby, and when she fusses a few minutes after her feeding, you may feel mystified. Burping really is important, so try not to forget about it. Maybe it would help to think of it as a baby chore separate from the feeding, and pass the baby on to your partner for burping after the feeding.

Bottle-fed babies tend to have larger, firmer stools because there is more undigested material left over from formula. Also, formula-fed babies' stools are more consistent, because the formula is always the same, unlike breastmilk. However, formula-fed babies are more prone to constipation. Extra sips of plain sterilized water should help to alleviate this problem. A low-iron formula used to be recommended for constipated babies, but most doctors now agree that this was the wrong approach. Not only is there no evidence that a low-iron formula alleviates constipation, but babies who are fed low-iron formula have a serious risk of dangerous iron deficiency. Bottle-fed babies are also at greater risk of contracting gastroenteritis (an intestinal infection), often caused by improperly sterilized feeding equipment or formula. Diarrhea and/or vomiting, especially in younger babies whether they are breastfed or bottle-fed, requires an immediate call to the doctor; gastroenteritis can be very serious.

A bowel movement may be preceded by a certain amount of straining, which does not necessarily mean that your baby is constipated. If the stool that is passed is hard or pebblelike, or if it causes pain with passing, perhaps even leaving some blood in the diaper, constipation is probably to blame. If simple measures like giving extra water to a younger baby, or providing extra fluids and more fiber-containing foods to an older baby, do not resolve the problem, you should consult your baby's doctor. Similarly, diarrhea is not always indicated when a baby has one or two particularly loose stools. Babies who are suffering from diarrhea have frequent, watery stools that are greenish and/or tinged with mucous and sometimes with blood. A raw, red rash will often appear around the anus. If your baby is suffering from these symptoms, you should certainly call his doctor. Dehydration is of particular concern when a baby has diarrhea, and frequent drinks of a pediatric electrolyte solution may be recommended.

Unfortunately, some babies suffer from chronic constipation or diarrhea. In older babies, this may be caused by something in her diet, such as when a baby has diarrhea from drinking too much juice on

The All-Important Burp Cloth

A diaper, receiving blanket, or dishtowel draped over your shoulder naturally becomes part of the mandatory dress code for new parents. In fact, you can always tell the experienced parents from the novices when you are handing a baby around a group; the ones who "know" will instinctively grab the burp cloth before holding the baby.

Pediatric Electrolyte Solution

Any time your baby is losing fluid through vomiting or diarrhea, you should be concerned that she may become dehydrated, and your baby's doctor may recommend you give her a pediatric electrolyte solution in addition to frequent drinks of formula or breastmilk. Obvious signs of dehydration include the following: infrequent wet diapers, crying with no tears, listlessness, and/or a dry mouth evidenced by less or no drooling. Pediatric electrolyte solution is available at any pharmacy and many grocery stores, and it is wise to keep a few bottles on hand just in case. Your baby's doctor will advise you as to the proper amount of the solution to give her.

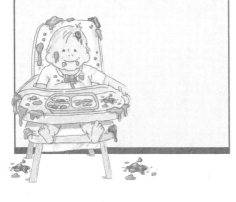

a regular basis. Or, she may have chronic constipation when she is very small because her muscles for elimination have not yet fully developed. There are a host of reasons for chronic constipation or diarrhea. Some cases may be resolved through patient attempts to track down the source of the problem; others may simply require time and measures that help your baby feel more comfortable. Your pediatrician will be invaluable in helping you and your baby through this difficult period.

Combining Nursing with Formula Feedings

Mothers are frequently encouraged to supplement breastfeeding with formula, often when the time comes to go back to work. This is because many people are not aware of the equally practical option of pumping or expressing breastmilk for feedings during separations. The mother simply expresses milk on the same schedule she would normally follow when feeding her baby and this milk can then be given to the baby in a bottle in her absence. Expressing your milk allows your baby to continue receiving the benefits of breastmilk while helping you keep your milk supply high.

Another prevalent reason for combined breast and formula feedings is the all-too-common worry that the baby is not getting enough breastmilk. The truth is that there are many methods for enhancing milk production, and most mothers are able to produce more than enough milk for their babies until they are ready to supplement breastfeedings with solid food. It is important for a nursing mother to understand that once nursings are replaced with formula feedings on a regular basis, her milk supply will naturally decline as her body receives the message that the baby doesn't need the same amount of milk that he previously did. The actual rate of decline can't be predicted, and nursing mothers who regularly supplement frequently wean earlier than mothers who don't. If you wish to continue nursing throughout

Sample Routine for Combining Nursing with Formula

Time	Event	Feeding
6:00 A.M.	Wake up	Nursing
8:00 A.M.	Leave for work	Nursing
Noon		Formula
2:00–3:00 P.M.		Formula or breastmilk in a bottle
5:00 P.M.	Return from work	Nursing
7:00 P.M.		Nursing
9:00 P.M.		Nursing
	Plus one or two feedings during the night	

In this example, the mother might express or pump milk once during her day at work, which would help to keep her milk supply up and allow for only one formula feeding during the day. It is important for the caregiver to make sure not to give the second feeding too close to the time the mother will return from work so that the baby will nurse eagerly, which will also help to keep up the milk supply.

the first year it would be wise to consult your pediatrician or a lactation consultant before making a decision about whether or not to supplement with formula.

Perhaps pumping at work is too inconvenient or difficult. Or, some mothers may find full time breastfeeding simply too draining. This said, many women find that supplemental formula feedings are helpful. If you want to continue nursing throughout the first year or beyond, you'll need to make a conscious effort to keep your milk supply up once formula feedings are introduced. Try to keep the number of formula feedings to a minimum and preserve feedings that precede and immediately follow a separation. Also maintain the bedtime and first morning feedings.

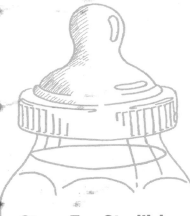

Bottle-feeding Your Baby

Most babies in the United States drink at least some breastmilk or formula from a bottle, whether exclusively, frequently, or occasionally. The exceptions are babies who steadfastly refuse to drink from a bottle and babies whose mothers have made a commitment to exclusively breastfeed until they are introduced to solid food and are drinking from a cup. However, even these parents would be wise to have some bottle-feeding equipment on hand in case of emergencies and to understand some basic information about bottle-feeding.

Bottle-feeding Do's and Don'ts

- Do relax and enjoy feedings. Gaze into your baby's eyes and snuggle up. Maybe sing a song and coo to your baby, but allow for quiet moments also, if that seems to be what your baby needs.
- Don't prop the bottle in order to leave the baby. Leaving your baby alone during feedings is dangerous because of the potential for choking.
- Do hold your baby in such a way that her head is not cocked or thrown back at an angle, which makes swallowing difficult. Also, drinking a bottle while lying flat has been linked to a greater incidence of ear infections because milk can enter the inner ear through the eustachian tube.
- Do warm the bottle of breastmilk or formula in a pan of warm water or under hot running tap water. The milk should be slightly warmer than room temperature, but a bit cooler than body temperature. You can test this by shaking a few drops on the sensitive skin of your inner wrist.
- Don't heat bottles in a microwave oven. This can heat the contents unevenly, causing potentially dangerous pockets of scalding liquid to be swallowed by your baby.
- Do sterilize all bottle-feeding and breast pump equipment thoroughly and store it in a clean environment. Do wash

Stove-Top Sterilizing

Use a large pan with a tight-fitting lid and line the bottom with a clean dishcloth. Fill the pan with cold water to within one inch of the rim, or with enough water to immerse all of the bottles and other equipment. Tilt the bottles to their side to make sure they fill up with the water. Cover the pot and bring the water to a boil, keeping it boiling for at least ten minutes. Using clean tongs, remove everything from the pan while the water is still hot, which will allow for more rapid and thorough drying through evaporation. Drain on a clean towel and store covered.

your hands with soap and hot water before handling any bottle-feeding or breast pump equipment.

Baby-Bottle Mouth

Both bottle- and breastfed babies are at risk for tooth decay as they grow up if they are habitually put to bed with a bottle or fall asleep at the breast. The sugars in the milk collect on the baby's teeth and cause cavities. In serious cases, babies require extensive (and sometimes painful or frightening) dental work years before any dental work should be necessary. However, many parents struggle with this issue because babies fall asleep easily when they are eating from the first days forward. As your baby begins to grow out of middle-of-the-night feedings, try to find other ways to comfort him at bedtime. Rocking, singing, or providing a toy, pacifier, or snuggly blanket may be effective if it is worked into the bedtime ritual. Some bottle-fed babies are just as happy with a little water at bedtime. Still, most babies will need a feeding shortly before bedtime for many months so they can sleep through until morning without getting hungry.

Sterilizing Bottle-Feeding and Breast Pump Equipment

Properly sterilizing bottles, caps, nipples, utensils, and breast pump equipment is extremely important in the early months of your child's life. Basically anything that comes into contact with the breastmilk or formula that your baby will drink is at risk for harboring bacteria that can be dangerous to him (this includes the can opener used to open the formula can). You can buy a sterilizer that runs on electricity or that can be used in the microwave, but I recommend sterilizing in a large covered pot on the stove top. Some experts endorse sterilizing in the dishwasher set for a heated drying cycle if the water temperature reaches 180 degrees Fahrenheit. Whatever

Disposable Bottle Liners

Many parents swear by disposable bottle liners, which are presterilized inserts you can pop into a holder to minimize cleaning. They also have the advantage of collapsing while the baby drinks, so that less air is swallowed with the breastmilk or formula.

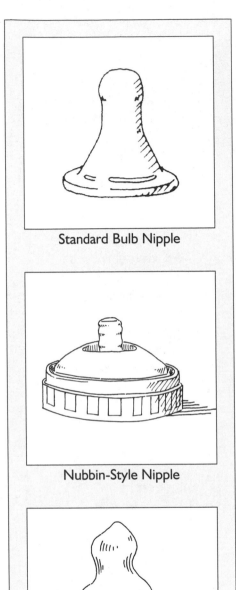

Standard Bulb Nipple

Nubbin-Style Nipple

Orthodontic Nipple

method you use, always wash everything in hot soapy water first, using a bottlebrush to dislodge any dried-on bits of milk. It is best to wash each item soon after you use it, and keep each piece separated until you are ready to do a batch sterilization. Take extra care with the nipples since it can be easy to miss milk that has settled in the tip. Most doctors recommend sterilizing for the first two to three months of your child's life.

Choosing the Right Bottle-Feeding Equipment

Finding a bottle and nipple that is right for your baby may take some experimentation. There are several bottle-feeding "systems" available on the market, and while many have parts that are interchangeable with other brands, some have pieces that will fit only the same brand. It is wise not to make a large investment in any one brand before you know it will work for your baby.

Varieties of Nipple Shapes

The manufacturers of baby bottle nipples all claim that their brand is most like the real thing, but in truth they all fall far short. The oldest design is a simple bulb-shaped nipple with a wide base and a rounded tip:

Standard bulb nipple. This type of nipple may be the simplest to use because it is easy to clean, and babies don't seem to have much trouble latching on to the nipple, usually making a tight seal around the wide base with their mouths.

Nubbin-style nipple. Another popular variety of nipple has a flexible nubbin that is designed to expand in the baby's mouth the same way a mother's nipple would:

In practice, most babies do not suck on the entire nipple the way they are meant to, and easily fall into the habit of latching on to only the nubbin. This is not an ideal nipple to use for the nursing baby, because he may easily become frustrated with having to open his mouth wider for his mother's breast after becoming used to sucking on the nubbin.

Orthodontic nipple. This special type is designed to fit in a baby's mouth the same way a natural nipple would, with an indentation for her tongue to "milk" and a shaped bulb that will fill the roof of her mouth.

This type of nipple also has a wide base similar to the standard bulb-shaped nipple, which encourages the baby to open her mouth wide and allows for a tight seal. The orthodontic nipple is possibly the best kind for a nursing baby and is the one I used. However, I always found myself examining an orthodontic pacifier (which has a similarly shaped nipple), trying to decide which side of the nipple should face up. If it was dark, I was really lost!

Some manufacturers make a special "juice" nipple, with a T-shaped hole, which allows water or juice to flow more quickly and easily. These should only be used when your baby is older than six to eight months, and it is likely that he will be ready to drink from a sippy cup shortly thereafter.

Plastic vs. Glass Baby Bottles

Many people assume that glass baby bottles are a thing of the past, but recently the Evenflo Company reintroduced tempered glass bottles on the market. Why, when plastic bottles are so much lighter and are not breakable? The presence of plasticizers (chemicals used to make hard plastic more pliable) in many plastic food containers and utensils, including many baby bottles, has recently been linked to a class of chemicals known as endocrine disrupters. These compounds have properties that are coincidentally similar to human hormones and are sometimes called hormone mimics as a result. In particular, Bisphenol-A (BPA), found in clear plastic, is suspected of acting on the body

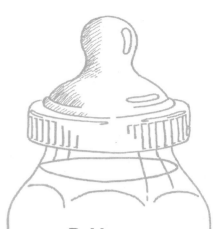

Rubber vs. Silicone Nipples

Silicone nipples, though not as common, do have some advantages over their rubber counterparts. Silicone nipples have no odor or taste, which some babies seem to prefer. They are clear and therefore it is easier to see if they have been thoroughly cleaned. Silicone nipples also seem to stand up better over time and don't develop a gummy quality. Still, many babies seem to prefer rubber nipples, perhaps because they are more pliable and feel better in the mouth. It is also easier to find rubber nipples in many stores.

Nipples: Choose the Right Flow

Most nipple brands are available with different flows for babies of different ages, which is indicated on the package. Small nipple holes will provide a slow flow and are suitable for newborns. Babies will gradually want a faster flow as they reach three to four months and again at about six to eight months. You can add a second or third hole to the nipples you have with a sterilized pin to gradually increase the flow. Check for the right flow for a young baby by holding the bottle up side down. The milk or formula should drip out at about one drop per second.

as a weak mimic of estrogen, which is of particular concern for many parents of developing infants. Some evidence exists in animal studies showing reproductive abnormalities in animals exposed to BPA. However, subsequent studies have disputed these findings. The Food and Drug Administration (FDA) has not given any indication of recalling any brands of baby bottles from the market, and many experts feel that the safety risk has been exaggerated. Clearly the jury is still out. In the meantime, you may want to consider the following measures for reducing the risk of exposure to BPA.

- Use bottles made from milky-colored plastic instead of clear.
- Choose bottles made from polyethylene or polypropylene, which are free of plasticizers.
- Discard any clear plastic bottles that have grown cloudy or cracked with age and use, as these have been shown to leach more BPA than new bottles.
- Heat milk or formula in glass or ceramic containers and transfer to plastic bottles afterward, since heating seems to encourage greater leaching of BPA.

CHAPTER TWO

Breastfeeding: The Best Choice for Your Baby and You

The Many Benefits of Breastfeeding

Experts agree that breastfeeding is the best form of nourishment for infants. The following list explores several advantages of breast-feeding, not only for your baby, but for you as well!

- Breastmilk provides the exact nourishment your baby needs at each stage of her development from birth to weaning.
- Breastmilk contains antibodies important for bolstering your baby's developing immune system.
- Breastmilk contains all of the right enzymes, designed specifically for the human digestive tract, to help babies efficiently absorb the milk's nutrients with a minimum of discomfort.
- Breastmilk contains literally thousands of nutrients designed by nature for human babies. Many of these nutrients and their beneficial properties have yet to be identified. Essential fatty acids found only in breastmilk are particularly important for optimal brain development.
- The health benefits of breastmilk have been well documented in studies that show fewer illnesses and more contented dispositions in babies who are breastfed.
- Children who were breastfed have consistently slightly higher scores on standardized tests than their formula-fed counterparts.
- Hormones released during lactation in the first days and weeks following delivery help the mother's uterus contract back to its normal size more quickly, hastening the recovery process.
- Many women who breastfeed experience a more rapid loss of unwanted weight gained during pregnancy.
- Most mothers find nursing a convenient way to feed their baby, because once a nursing routine is established, a baby can be quickly and easily fed with a minimum of fuss.
- Studies show that breastfed babies are less likely to experience food allergies later in life.

Common Myths about Breastfeeding

- **Women should prepare for breast-feeding by "toughening" their nipples.** Unless your nipples are flat or inverted, you should not need any additional preparation.

- **A woman with small breasts will not be able to produce enough milk to feed her baby.** This is untrue—breast size is completely unrelated to milk production.

- **A woman who experiences sore nipples in the early days of breast-feeding should limit the amount of time she nurses.** Actually, sore nipples are usually the result of improper positioning and are not caused by long feeds.

- **Babies should be placed on a strict breastfeeding schedule from birth.** Doctors and breastfeeding experts now agree that an on-demand feeding schedule is best for babies in the first months. Allowing your baby to develop a natural feeding schedule will send the correct message that eating and hunger are inseparable, which will benefit him later in life.

- **Nursing will ruin the shape of your breasts.** Many women find that their breasts return to their original size and shape when they stop breastfeeding.

- **Unsuccessful attempts to breastfeed are common.** In cultures where breastfeeding is the norm, success rates are near 100 percent.

- **All babies should be weaned within one year.** There is no harm and some wonderful benefits to continuing nursing beyond one year as long as both mother and baby are willing. Indeed, many mothers continue nursing well into toddlerhood. When to wean is a personal decision best left to the mother and her baby.

- Increasing evidence indicates that breastfeeding, decreases the mother's risk for osteoporosis and uterine, breast, and ovarian cancer.
- Formula is expensive! It costs about $100 a month to feed a baby formula in the first months of life. Costs for nursing a baby include only the additional food consumed by the mother.

How Breastfeeding Works

Milk is produced inside your breasts in small milk cells (alveoli) imbedded throughout the glandular tissue of your breasts. The milk then drains through the milk ducts into the milk sinuses located just behind the darker-colored areola surrounding your nipple. When you are lactating, your breasts are always producing varying quantities of milk. Between feedings, milk containing mostly water (called foremilk) will slowly collect in the sinuses, giving you a feeling of becoming fuller as the time for the next feeding nears. When your baby latches onto the areola and begins to suck, nerves are stimulated in your nipples that send the signal to your body to produce and eject milk containing more fat and calories (hindmilk).

A "let-down" (or burst) of calorie-rich hindmilk from the milk-producing alveoli cells to the sinuses will usually happen once, twice, or sometimes more at each feeding, beginning about 30 to 60 seconds after your baby begins to suck. Many women experience a let-down as a tingling, "pins-and-needles" sensation in the nipples. As your milk supply builds in the first weeks of nursing, the let-downs generally become more powerful and you may find that you have milk dripping or spraying from the breast opposite the one your baby is nursing on. Your baby may have a little trouble at first coping with this larger quantity of milk, and may gag or choke on the excess milk. With a little patience though, she will quickly learn how to anticipate your let-downs and will drink more eagerly when they come. Let-downs are experienced differently by each mother and may change at different stages of lactation.

After drinking a few bursts of hindmilk, your baby may feel full and may stop nursing, or when he senses that the supply of rich hindmilk is depleted, he may still be hungry and will switch to the other breast.

Often, breastfed babies will continue to nurse even after the calorie-rich milk is depleted and will enjoy small sips of milk with the continuing comfort of sucking. Bottle-fed babies do not have this source of comfort. The sensation of your baby suckling at your breast stimulates your pituitary gland to produce more oxytocin, the hormone that regulates milk supply. As your baby instinctively helps to build your milk supply in the first weeks, or if he needs extra milk, as when he experiences a growth spurt, you will notice that your baby nurses more frequently and for longer periods. In this way, he is able to regulate your milk supply according to his needs. Your body naturally produces less oxytocin if you are experiencing stress or fatigue. This is why it is so important to get enough help and rest when you are breastfeeding.

Getting Started with Breastfeeding

Ideally, nursing should begin as soon after the baby's birth as possible. This helps to ensure a successful beginning. If you have had an uncomplicated delivery and if the baby is doing well, you should try to breastfeed as soon as you feel up to it. If you or your baby requires medical attention following the birth, this may delay the beginning of nursing. Generally, it is best to have as much practice with breastfeeding as you can before you leave the hospital, because the nurses, doctors, and lactation professionals there will be a helpful resource when questions arise.

Often, as soon as the nursery procedures are completed and sometimes just after the birth, the delivery nurse will encourage you to try breastfeeding. Depending on how you feel, you should go ahead and try it. Hold your baby so that his mouth is level with your breast without either of you being forced into an uncomfortable position (it may be helpful to practice this ahead of time with a baby doll or stuffed animal). Squeeze your breast between your

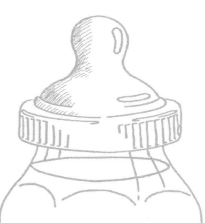

The Rooting Reflex

Before your baby learns to reach with her hands at four months or so, her primary tool for interacting with the world will be her mouth, since eating is her only means of survival. This means that if she senses something near her mouth, such as your nipple brushing against her chin or a pacifier tickling her lower lip, she'll turn her head and open her mouth wide to accept and explore whatever is offered.

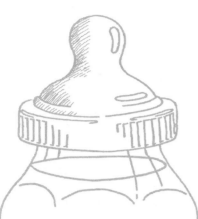

whole thumb and fingers so that the areola is coaxed into a more oval shape to accommodate your baby's mouth. Tickle his cheek with your nipple to stimulate his rooting reflex. If all goes well, he'll open his mouth wide, and you can maneuver your breast into his mouth and begin your breastfeeding career.

Early Lactation

In the weeks before the birth and for the first days after, your breasts produce a thick, yellowish substance called colostrum. Although it is produced in relatively small amounts, it is incredibly valuable to your newborn. Colostrum has many important anti-bodies, sugars, proteins, and minerals that provide a baby with the best possible start. Many mothers worry that this tiny amount of food is not enough to sustain a newborn, and the weight babies typically lose in the first days of life seems to confirm this fear. However, the period of colostrum production is an important step in helping the baby to cope with the "mature" milk that will come later. First, the colostrum coats the baby's intestines, which are unaccustomed to any food, with an immunoglobulin that will prevent germs from entering the bloodstream and harmful bacteria from proliferating in the gut. Also, the smaller quantities of colostrum help the baby practice nursing before he has to cope with swallowing mouthfuls of plentiful mother's milk.

About three to five days after the birth, the composition of the milk will suddenly or gradually transition from colostrum to mature milk. Often this is accompanied by the experience of very full (perhaps even "engorged") breasts. If your breasts become engorged, they will seem hard and the skin may be stretched quite tight, flattening out the areola and nipple. This is where all of the practice and proper technique you have been able to build over the first few days will come in handy. Remember that this is an adjustment for both you and your baby. Your baby may find it diffi-cult at first to get her mouth around the areola to get the milk she so desperately wants, and she may become quickly frustrated and upset if her desires are not met immediately (which in turn makes

Unsuccessful First Feeding

It is not uncommon for either the mother or the baby to be so out of sorts or exhausted after the birth that the first attempt at nursing is not successful. Don't worry about this at all. Immediate breastfeeding is not that important. Try again in an hour or so, when both you and the baby are alert and a bit more rested.

you frustrated and upset). In addition to this new and sometimes unsettling experience, your breasts may feel uncomfortably full, and difficulty in getting your baby properly latched on to the areola as opposed to the more sensitive nipple may make soreness worse. Expressing a small amount of milk before feedings to soften the areola may help make feedings go more smoothly. Initial engorgement usually lessens within a few days.

The Importance of a Good "Latch"

It may seem strange to think that a baby does not really suck milk from your nipples. After all, that is what you have been led to believe all along. Actually, the reservoirs that hold the milk are located *behind* the nipple, under the areola, and the baby doesn't simply suck the milk out, but also uses his tongue to draw the milk from the reservoirs to the nipple. In order for this to work properly (and to save your nipples from unnecessary wear and tear), your baby's mouth must be positioned around the areola with the nipple drawn well back into his mouth. This position is called a latch. Both his upper and lower lip should be spread wide (not tucked under), and you should feel his tongue massaging the areola. When your baby is properly latched onto the breast, nursing will not be painful. Pain is a sign that you should use a clean pinkie to break the suction and disengage your baby from the breast to adjust his position. This takes some practice and can be frustrating (especially if your baby is howling for milk), but remember that a baby who is not well latched will not get the quantity of milk he wants and that a poor latch is the primary reason for sore nipples.

Popular Positions for Nursing

There are three positions most mothers use for nursing: the cradle position, the football hold, and the side-lying position. You will most likely develop a favorite within the first few weeks, but it is best to try them all so that you have practice for later. As your baby grows, you may find that a different position works well for you.

Keep Your Fingernails Short

A newborn's skin is remarkably delicate, and the slightest touch from long fingernails may scratch or bruise her. Also, if you need to use your pinkie to break your baby's suction on the breast, you'll want your nail to be as short as possible.

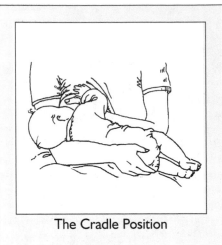

The Cradle Position

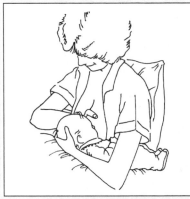

The Football Hold

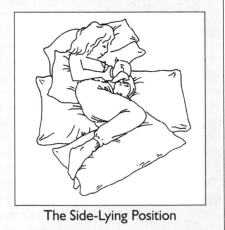

The Side-Lying Position

The Cradle Position

This position is the most common one used, especially when you are out and about with your baby. When nursing a newborn, use the hand opposite the breast to cradle her head and bring it to your breast. This will be more effective than trying to control a wobbly head with the inside of your elbow. You can then use your free hand to position the breast for your baby's mouth. Once your baby is latched on and nursing, you can gently remove your hand and support her head in the crook of your arm.

The Football Hold

This position is especially good if you are nursing a small baby, if your breasts are large, if you are recovering from a cesarean birth, or if you are nursing twins. While sitting, use a pillow beside you to support the baby and your arm. Hold the baby at your side as you would a football. Cradle the baby's head in the hand on the same side as your breast and bring him to the breast. Use your free hand to properly position the breast.

The Side-Lying Position

A favorite among tired new mothers and those recovering from a cesarean birth, the side-lying position can be a lifesaver for those middle-of-the-night feedings. Lie on the side that you want to nurse from, with your arm tucked up out of the way, supporting your head. Turn your baby on her side to face you with her mouth lined up to your breast, and guide her to the nipple with your free hand.

On-Demand Feeding Schedules

In the past, it was often recommended that new mothers impose a strict feeding schedule for their babies from the start. This practice is now widely disputed because experts recognize several important reasons for letting babies set the pace. For example, babies will need to nurse more frequently and for longer periods when they are experiencing a growth spurt, which may happen as often as every two weeks in the first months. Also, it is the frequency and length of feeds that sends signals to the mother's body to produce more or less milk as the baby's needs wax and wane. Your new baby will probably signal that she is hungry by crying, chewing her fists, and "rooting" by butting her head against your (or someone else's) chest. It's not always necessary to try and feed at the first cry, however. If she has already fed recently, perhaps all she needs is a cuddle and a little song. New babies typically feed 8 to 12 times per 24-hour period.

The length of the feeds is also important, because your breasts produce a different kind of milk at the beginning than at the end of the feeding. At the beginning of the nursing, your baby is getting extra fluids in the foremilk, and calorie-rich hindmilk comes at the end of the feeding. This is why you should try to nurse for at least ten minutes on each breast, so that your baby will get both kinds of milk. It is a good idea to let your baby dictate the length of the feed, if you can, to ensure that he is getting adequate quantities of hindmilk to meet his needs. He will most likely stop nursing on his own when he has had enough. It is not uncommon for a new baby to nurse for as long as 45 minutes or longer in a single feeding. You can also end the feeding yourself, by slipping your pinkie into the corner of his mouth to break the suction. If you try to pull your baby off the breast without breaking the suction, you will cause unnecessary trauma to your nipple.

Breastfeeding Challenges and Solutions

There is no doubt that breastfeeding has the potential to be one of the most rewarding mothering experiences you can have, and the advantages for you and you baby are innumerable. Watching your chubby-cheeked six-week-old contentedly nursing while you hold her close and coo is so precious, you want that time to never end. However, the first few days and weeks of nursing are not always that easy, especially for first-time mothers. While you and your baby are wired with many instincts that will help you learn how to

Positioning Your Breast for Your Baby's Mouth

It will take a while for your baby to learn how to open his mouth wide enough to get his whole mouth around your areola, so he will need help from you at first. Using your free hand, you can gently squeeze your breast between your whole thumb and fingers so that its shape is more oval, like the shape of your baby's mouth. You can adjust the position of your hand to anticipate the angle of your baby's mouth. It can be very helpful to practice this maneuver with a baby doll before your baby is born.

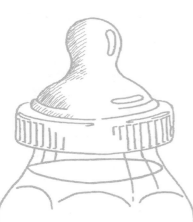

Feeding Your Baby in the Real World

"The best thing I did was to stay as long as I possibly could at the hospital. I felt pretty good after the delivery, and thought I might be OK at home, but I decided to stay an extra night. Having people at the hospital to take care of me while I took care of the baby made a huge difference. My first week breastfeeding was pretty challenging, and I really needed the extra rest."

—Kari, mother of Calem

breastfeed, you should realize that this is a new experience for both of you, and it may take a lot of practice and support to learn the ropes.

It is important to take this time and focus on yourself and your baby exclusively as much as possible. Remember that you are both still exhausted, and you may be experiencing some discomfort post-partum. Trying to do too much can be very detrimental at this stage, because it is possible you will encounter some unanticipated roadblocks and you will need all of your reserves to cope with them. Gather your resources, whether it be help with housekeeping and meal preparations, or the advice of your doctor, a lactation consultant, or another, more experienced, nursing mother. Don't be harsh in judging yourself, and don't let seemingly innocent comments from well-meaning friends and family get you down. There will be a time very soon when you can't believe that nursing wasn't always second nature.

Sore Nipples

Sore nipples in the early weeks caused by breast engorgement and/or inexperience in proper positioning of the baby have caused many women to feel that nursing is not the idealized mothering experience it was made out to be. Occasionally, soreness can be a precursor to painful cracked and sometimes bleeding nipples. This discomfort and accompanying frustration may be enough to make even mothers who are passionately committed to nursing reconsider whether it is worth it. Take heart because this period, while not uncommon, typically lasts only for a few days, and many of the discomforts can be quickly addressed by repositioning your baby's latch on the breast, by expressing excess milk in between feedings, and/or by using a variety of topical remedies. The advice and support of a sister or friend who has successfully nursed can be invaluable during this time. I also highly recommend consulting a lactation professional that may be available at the hospital where your baby was born or whom you may find through a local referral.

Topical Remedies to Relieve Sore Nipples

- Raw cabbage leaves lightly scored with a knife and worn inside your bra for a few hours (sounds weird, but it can be very soothing)
- A bag of frozen peas held on your breasts for a few minutes
- Pure medical-grade lanolin ointment

Thrush Nipples

This sort of irritation to the nipples is not caused by latching problems, but rather by a yeast infection in the baby's mouth that has spread to her mother's breasts. It can be easy to overlook thrush as a cause for sore, red, or cracked nipples, especially in the early days of nursing. A dotty red rash on the nipples may appear and usually indicates thrush. The baby may have white cheesy patches of yeast inside her mouth or a dotty red diaper rash. If you suspect thrush and it is confirmed by your baby's doctor, she may recommend an antifungal cream for both you and the baby to treat it. In addition, you should be careful to prevent the spread or lingering of the infection by changing nursing pads after each feeding; boiling pacifiers, bottle nipples, breast pump parts, and breast shells/shields every day; and rinsing your nipples with water (don't use soap) after each feeding. It may also be helpful to expose your breasts to a few minutes of sunlight two or three times a day.

Inverted Nipples

Inverted nipples affect about 20 percent of women and can present a challenge to getting started with nursing. This can almost always be addressed by taking extra care in ensuring that the baby is properly latched on to the breast during feedings. Keep in mind that the baby is not actually using the nipple itself to obtain milk, but rather the entire areola. It may also be helpful to wear breast shields inside your bra for a short period before feedings. You can also

Finding a Lactation Consultant

Because breastfeeding was not the norm in our society in the middle of the last century, many young women cannot turn to their mothers for help and advice in the early days of nursing. Lactation professionals and expert volunteers are committed women who have themselves nursed and have also received special training in helping women breastfeed their babies. Many times, volunteers can be contacted at any time day or night to help you with unexpected difficulties. To find breastfeeding help, you can call the hospital where your baby was born or contact the local chapter of La Leche League (*www.lalecheleague.org*).

use other measures to help your nipples stand out, such as stimulating the nipples with your fingers, applying suction from a breast pump, or briefly rubbing your nipples with something cold. As your baby becomes a more proficient nurser, these measures should no longer be necessary.

Plugged Ducts and Mastitis

Plugged milk ducts and, less commonly, breast infections can be of concern especially in the early months. Plugged ducts happen when milk solids clog narrow ducts and cause milk to back up inside the breast. It is experienced as a tender lump in the breast, which may be slightly red and is sometimes painful. If a plugged duct is not resolved within a few days, it can lead to a breast infection that should be treated medically. Some women never experience a plugged duct, some do frequently, and some women experience a plugged duct unexpectedly when their baby is much older.

Prevention is the key to avoiding this uncomfortable situation. Drink plenty of water, avoid wearing a bra that is too tight (especially an underwire bra), and be sure to alternate which breast you feed on first, to avoid overfull breasts and to fully drain each breast at several feedings each day. Above all, avoid becoming overtired or emotionally strained, as many lactation professionals believe that this can be one of the causes of plugged ducts.

If you do have a plugged duct, nurse frequently, and drain the breast as much as possible at each feeding. Apply a warm washcloth to your breast for 15 or 20 minutes before each feeding (a hot shower wouldn't hurt either). It can also help to gently massage the area just behind the plug immediately before each feeding in an attempt to dislodge the plug. If you develop a fever or flulike symptoms (fatigue, chills, and achiness), call your doctor. You may have developed a breast infection (mastitis), which happens occasionally and can usually be treated with rest and/or medication.

Medical Problems

Occasionally, a mother may have a condition requiring medication that would be dangerous to her baby if passed through her milk. In this case, it may be possible to give the baby previously expressed milk or formula in a bottle during the course of the treatment. If the mother continues to express, discarding the tainted milk, she will most likely be able to resume nursing once she stops taking the medication. In rare cases, a very young baby introduced to the bottle for this reason will experience what is called nipple confusion and will have difficulty accepting the breast once she has become accustomed to the easier action of sucking on an artificial nipple. This situation can be difficult to cope with, and it is best to consult a lactation professional to help coax the baby into accepting the breast again. If nothing works, the mother may want to consider continuing to express milk to bottle-feed her baby for as long as she can.

Outside Influences

Unfortunately, some mothers are forced to cope with a family member or close friend who disapproves of, is uncomfortable with, or simply does not understand, nursing. Many people do not realize the potency of seemingly innocuous remarks made to a new mother who is struggling with the emotional upheaval associated with hormonal swings and family adjustments during the postpartum period. For example, it is important to recognize that while your mother may have only your best interests at heart if she tells you about her own failed attempts to breastfeed, she is really not helping you. If you can, explain gently that while nursing presents some challenges, you have confidence that you will be able to surmount them and that hearing about worst-case scenarios is not helpful. If you are unable to communicate this point to the unsuspecting offender, try your best to tune her comments out, and seek the support of someone you know who is more understanding.

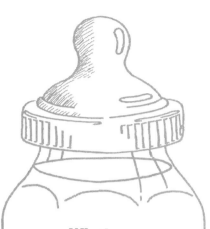

What are Breast Shells?

Also called breast shields or sometimes milk cups, breast shells are worn inside the bra and have a circular base that fits around the areola exerting steady pressure, and a dome that fits over the nipple. Breast shells are often recommended for women with flat or inverted nipples because they may help to correct nipple shape. It may also be helpful to wear breast shells for a half hour before feeding your baby to help soften the areola if you are experiencing uncomfortable engorgement.

The opposite may also be true, and a woman's partner, family member, or friend may be so enthusiastic about the benefits of nursing that his or her encouragement and "helpful" suggestions may actually become annoying. Coordinating all of the elements of positioning, latch, and baby wrangling can be tricky, and trying to incorporate the suggestions of someone who may or may not know what he or she is talking about can be distracting, to say the least. Simply explain gently, but firmly, that what you are doing is not as easy as it looks, and ask your "helper" to buzz off or give you some breathing space.

Handling Unwelcome Comments and Negative Attitudes

Example: At the shopping mall, an elderly lady says, "Don't you think you ought to be doing that in the restroom?" Your response might be, "Do you really think a bathroom stall is an appropriate place to feed an infant? No, thank you, I'm perfectly comfortable here."

Example: Your mother-in-law says, "What? You're feeding him again? But he just ate half an hour ago!" Your response might be, "Our doctor says that little babies should eat as often as they are hungry."

Example: You have just come home from the hospital after giving birth, your hormones are raging, your breasts are hurting, and your baby is crying. You confide in your best friend, "I don't know what I'm doing wrong. I know she's hungry but I can't seem to get her to take the breast right now." Your friend says, "It's OK honey. I couldn't breastfeed either, but she'll do fine with the bottle." Your response might be, "I'm definitely not at the point where I'm ready to say that I can't do this. Can you please just hold her for a minute while I wash my face (or take a shower, or lie down for a minute, or get a breath of fresh air)? I just need a few minutes to gather my wits before we try another feeding. If I'm still having trouble, I'm going to call the lactation consultant at the hospital."

Example: You are nursing your toddler, and a stranger says, "Isn't she getting a little old for that?" Your response might be, "No."

Delayed Appearance of "Mature" Milk

After the first 36 to 72 hours postpartum, most babies begin to feel hunger for the first time. Usually this coincides fairly closely with the appearance of "mature" milk in the mother, but sometimes, for reasons we don't understand, this transition is delayed. Because this problem frequently becomes apparent after the mother and baby are released from the hospital, it can lead to a great deal of anxiety. Many times this spells the end of breastfeeding as a well-meaning mother-in-law stands at the ready with a bottle of formula. However, with the help of a supportive doctor or lactation consultant, many moms and babies are able to ride out this rocky period with the use of a feeding syringe to provide either supplemental formula or a solution of glucose and water while the baby is at the breast. Introducing a bottle at this stage can lead directly to nipple confusion.

Building Milk Supply

Your baby will naturally need only a few ounces of milk at each feeding in her first week or so of life because her stomach is still very small, but she should quickly begin the work of sending the message to your body that she will soon need more. Milk production works on a very simple principal of supply and demand. When the baby nurses, a mother's brain receives the signal to produce milk. The more a baby nurses, the more milk is produced. If a woman chooses not to nurse, her body will get the signal to stop milk production entirely after a few days. A mother's ultimate production capacity is in large part determined by the vigor and frequency of feedings in the early weeks. For this reason mothers of premature babies or babies who have a medical problem after birth

What Is Nipple Confusion?

A young baby is at risk of developing nipple confusion in the early weeks of life if she is offered any kind of artificial nipple before she has become accustomed to suckling at her mother's breast. To avoid nipple confusion, it is recommended that you instruct nurses, doctors, and caregivers not to offer your newborn baby a bottle or pacifier.

are often encouraged to use a breast pump to drain each breast every few hours until the baby is strong enough to nurse heartily on her own.

Tips for Increasing Milk Supply

It is actually your baby who possesses the most useful tool to increase your milk supply—frequent, unrestricted nursing. During the first weeks, he may nurse very frequently to build the milk supply in order to meet his needs. He will also nurse more frequently when he is experiencing a growth spurt. These are some other steps to try:

- If your baby uses a pacifier, encourage him to nurse instead to meet his need to suck, which will build your supply naturally.
- Avoid giving your baby supplemental feedings of formula as decreased nursing will send the signal to your body to decrease milk supply.
- Burp frequently during feedings to reduce the amount of gas crowding out room for more milk in your baby's tiny tummy.
- Get adequate rest, food, and fluid. A mother who is tired, hungry, and dehydrated will naturally produce less milk. Stress is also a well-known milk reducer.
- A lactation consultant may recommend you pump between feedings to build your milk supply.
- Drink tea made with steeped fenugreek seed—an old remedy for low milk production. There are even "mother's milk" tea blends available commercially.

Women Who Are at Risk for Inadequate Milk Supply

The following women may be susceptible to lower supplies of milk, which may or may not be possible to overcome:

- Women whose babies are born more than three weeks premature or are less than six pounds at birth.
- Women whose nipples are very large.
- Women who have had breast enhancement or reduction surgery.
- Women who have unusually shaped or mismatched breasts, especially if they do not experience any breast changes during pregnancy.
- Women whose babies have trouble latching on and sucking vigorously because of a medical condition or a malformation of the mouth such as a cleft palate.

If you suspect that you might be prone to inadequate milk production, discuss this with your baby's doctor before she is born. He may want to schedule more frequent visits to check your baby's growth in the early weeks. I also strongly recommend finding a lactation consultant before your baby's birth. Should you need, many lactation specialists are willing to visit you at home in the early days to help ensure a successful beginning.

Nursing the Sleepy Newborn

You may be amazed at how much your newborn baby sleeps. It seems as if he was never asleep so much when he was inside you. Often, a baby will fall asleep soon after beginning to nurse, even if he had just woken up a few minutes before the feeding. Some babies will keep right on eating after they've fallen asleep, which is good. In this case, you might want to switch to a side-lying position and get a few winks yourself. However, your baby may fall so deeply asleep after three or four minutes of nursing that he stops sucking altogether. It may seem unfair to disturb his peace, but it is extremely important that he has at least eight full feedings a day and that he is not waiting longer than three to four hours between feedings.

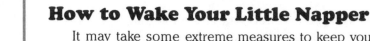

How to Wake Your Little Napper

It may take some extreme measures to keep your sleepy newborn awake long enough to have a good feed.

- Gently blow on her face.
- Rub her forehead with a cool (not cold) cloth.
- Make a sharp clicking noise with your tongue to get her attention.
- If she won't become chilled or anxious, unbundle her, and take off all of her clothes except her diaper.
- Run the tip of your finger firmly up along her spine.
- Burp her after feeding on one breast to encourage her to remain awake while nursing on the other.
- Try to predict when she will naturally waken so you can time feedings to coincide with wakeful periods.

Nursing the Adopted Baby

Incredibly, it may even be possible for an adoptive mother to nurse her baby with the use of a nursing supplementation device that delivers breastmilk or formula from a pouch worn around the mother's neck, through a flexible tube taped to her breast. When using this device in combination with treatment from a doctor, a woman may be able to lactate in some instances. A nursing supplementation device may also be useful in helping a mother increase her milk supply, or if her baby has an inadequate suck.

Women Who Should Not Breastfeed

If a woman is HIV positive, she should not breastfeed a baby because of the risk of passing the infection through her milk. There are a small number of other medical conditions and/or long-term drug therapies that would also make nursing an unwise choice for some women. If you are at all concerned that you may have been exposed to HIV, you should consult your doctor immediately, and, of course, your doctor should know about any medications you may be taking.

How Will I Know If My Breastfed Baby Is Thriving?

Because it's not easy to tell how much milk a baby receives during a feeding, many parents have an uncomfortable feeling of doubt about whether or not their baby is getting enough to eat. This is only natural, especially for nervous first-time parents, but it may be comforting to know that most mothers have no trouble producing more than enough milk to help their baby grow and thrive. And even though you can't see the amount of milk your baby drinks, you can look for any of these signs to help confirm that she is getting an adequate supply:

- She has returned to her birth weight by two weeks postpartum.
- She has at least six to eight wet cloth diapers or four to six wet disposable diapers every day by the fifth day postpartum.
- She is having at least three bowel movements a day during the first month, and they are seedy and yellow in color by the fifth day postpartum (a signal that she is getting calorie-rich hindmilk).
- You can hear several bursts of swallowing as she nurses at each breast during a feeding, which lasts about 10 to 45 minutes.
- She seems to be contented soon after the beginning of a feeding, and is content immediately after the feeding.

- She can wait about two hours between feedings much of the time.
- Your breasts feel full before a feeding and empty immediately after.
- She is gaining weight normally. If you are concerned about whether your baby is gaining enough weight, ask her pediatrician if you can arrange to have her weighed more frequently.

For mothers who are very concerned that their baby is not getting adequate milk, some lactation consultants recommend using a highly accurate digital infant scale to weigh the baby before and after a feeding to see exactly how much milk the baby has consumed. Other lactation professionals disagree with this method however, pointing out that quantities of milk produced at each feeding vary naturally, and a weight measure at a single feeding is unlikely to give a useful indication of milk production overall.

Should I Supplement Breastfeedings with Formula?

Many mothers are advised to supplement nursing with formula feedings at the first sign of trouble, when they may not really need to. If you are considering supplementing because you feel your baby is not getting enough to eat, I encourage you to consult a lactation professional who can be referred to you by your child's pediatrician, the local chapter of La Leche League, or the Lactation Consultants Association. There are many steps that you can take with professional help that may enable you to increase your milk supply and continue with exclusive breastfeeding. After consulting with your child's pediatrician, however, a determination may be made that supplementing with formula is best for your baby.

Other mothers are encouraged to supplement breast feedings with formula as a matter of course. A mother may be told that her baby will have longer periods of sleeping at night if he is given formula. She may be told that feeding with formula will make coping with new motherhood less stressful or that it will

Supplementing with Goat's Milk

Experts agree that babies should not be given cow's milk until the age of one year to prevent allergies and because its proteins are difficult for young babies to digest. On the subject of goat's milk, however, pediatricians, dieticians, and parents are divided.

Evidence shows that the proteins found in goat's milk are more rapidly and easily digested than those from cow's milk. Also, goat's milk contains far less of the allergenic casein protein found in cow's milk. However, neither cow nor goat's milk is nutritionally appropriate for human babies. In particular, goat's milk is deficient in folic acid, and, as a result, some brands are supplemented with this nutrient.

Goat's milk should never be used as a replacement for formula or breastmilk as a baby's main source of food. If you are considering using goat's milk as an occasional supplement to breastmilk, I would suggest you consult your baby's doctor. Your baby's age, propensity toward allergies, and the frequency of goat's milk feedings are all important factors to consider when making a decision about whether or not to give your baby goat's milk.

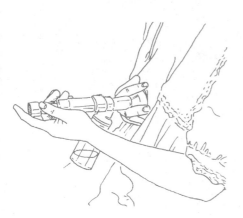

ease a transition back to work. None of these has been shown to be true for all mothers, and in fact what mothers are not told is that supplementing feedings with formula will lead to a premature reduction in the mother's milk supply, which would normally not have occurred until her baby begins eating solid foods.

Returning to Work

Mothers are frequently told that returning to work inevitably leads to giving up breastfeeding. This is simply untrue. Thousands of women handle separations from their nursing baby with no trouble at all. Amazingly, the average American woman returns to work six weeks after her baby is born. Returning this early can make continuing to breastfeed slightly more difficult, but not impossible. If you can, however, wait a bit longer, and return to work when you have established a solid nursing and bottle-feeding routine with your baby. Experts recommend waiting until your baby is about four to six weeks old before introducing the bottle to prevent nipple confusion (see "Introducing the Bottle to Your Breastfed Baby" later in this chapter). If you must return to work sooner, see if you can arrange your schedule so that a gradual transition is possible. Maybe you can work part days for a few weeks, or you can work alternating days. Whenever you return to work or are separated from your baby for another reason, try to nurse him just before you leave and instruct his caregiver to avoid giving him a full feeding near the time of your return, so that you can nurse him right away when you are reunited. During the separation, express milk on approximately the same schedule as your baby's regular feedings. With proper storage and handling, this milk can then be given to your baby by his caregiver. Separations of several days, although more challenging, can be accomplished in the same way.

Expressing Milk

If you will be separated from your baby for more than a few hours, it may be necessary for you to express your milk so that she can have a bottle feeding of breastmilk in your absence and so that you will not suffer from overfull, engorged breasts. Many nursing mothers regularly express milk for their babies when they return to work. Not many women will tell you that expressing milk is fun, but it's usually not a big deal. An electric or manual breast pump is very helpful for most women, but is not always necessary. I have known several mothers who learn, with practice, how to hand express milk into wide-mouthed clean cup.

Choosing a Breast Pump

Whatever method you use to express milk, give yourself some time before your baby will really need the milk if you are separated. It may take some practice to get the hang of pumping. It will be helpful to work expressing milk into your regular daily routine, so that your milk supply remains constant. Additionally, many women find expressing milk easier in the morning, because milk supply is usually more plentiful at that time. With a little planning, you'll be able to stash away a small "milk bank" in the freezer for the time when you start back at work or for unexpected separations.

When choosing a breast pump, consider how frequently you will need to use it and whether or not your milk can be expressed easily. If you will not need to pump every day and if your milk flows easily, a manual or small battery-operated or electric pump may work well. These types of pumps are usually the least expensive. If you know you will be pumping several times each day and/or you've had difficulty expressing milk, you may want to spend the extra money for a fully automated electric pump, which is very efficient and will often allow you to pump both breasts at once.

How to Hand-Express Breastmilk

Many women find they can hand express six to eight ounces of milk in about 20 minutes. Women who are able to express milk in this way are frequently relieved not to have to worry about carting around pumping equipment, and find the experience more natural. When learning to hand express milk, it may be helpful to practice while you are nursing your baby on the other breast (put

Morning and Evening Milk-Supply Disparities

During the longer period of resting at night you relax, enabling your milk supply to build. Also, the periods between feedings at night are typically (hopefully) longer, creating a surplus. In contrast, at the end of the day you may be tired and your milk supply will be lower after more frequent feedings during your baby's active day-time schedule. Unfortunately, evening is often the same time of day when your baby is at her fussiest. If you are expressing milk, this may be a good time for you or your partner to give her a bottle-feeding. This will give you a chance to skip a feeding, allowing you to build up a supply again.

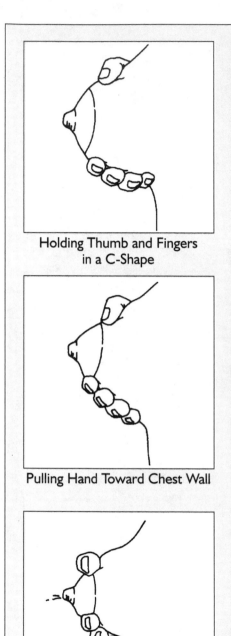

Holding Thumb and Fingers in a C-Shape

Pulling Hand Toward Chest Wall

Pulling Forward

a towel down), because your let-down will help the milk in your breast to flow. Once you are proficient at hand expression, you will notice that you will collect more milk when you are relaxed and unhurried. It can also be extremely helpful to massage your breasts ahead of time and imagine nursing your precious baby.

Techniques for hand expressing milk may be individual from one woman to another, but the main goal is to empty the milk sinuses located about one and a half inches behind and all the way around your nipple (this is usually the size of your areola as well). This is accomplished by holding your thumb and fingers in a C-shape, and placing them just behind the tiny sinuses. Keeping your fingers in the same place on your breast, pull your hand straight back toward your chest wall and then pull forward on your breast with a slight rolling motion. As the milk begins to flow, the let-down reflex will be activated and milk should begin spurting from your breast as you continue this back-forward motion. You can catch this milk in a clean cup or a special wide-mouthed expression funnel to give to your baby later. As the milk in each of the sinuses is depleted, you can adjust the position of your hand so that you empty all of the sinuses around your nipple.

Tips for Expressing Milk

Some women find it difficult to express milk by hand or with a breast pump because they have trouble finding a quiet moment to do so. This makes expressing more challenging because relaxation encourages the let-down reflex, which allows the milk to flow. Here are some tips that may help:

- Before expressing, drink a glass of water. Adequate fluid intake battles fatigue.
- Find a private, comfortable, and relaxing environment. If you are at work, make sure you can lock the door. It's difficult to relax if you think someone might walk in on you!
- Gently massage the area just behind your areola with your fingertips. Making small clockwise circles, slowly work

around and outward on each breast until you reach your armpit. This will help activate the let-down reflex.

- Think about your baby. You may want to look at pictures of her, especially ones of the both of you nursing. Some mothers use headphones to listen to a tape of their baby's voice.
- Practice other relaxation techniques such as deep breathing or meditation. Gently stretch out before expressing.

Safely Handling Expressed Breastmilk

- Always use properly sterilized pumping equipment.
- Always wash your hands thoroughly with soap and hot water before hand expressing or pumping milk.
- Freshly expressed breastmilk will keep in a sterilized closed container at room temperature for 6 to 10 hours.
- If you will not be using the milk within 6 to 10 hours, or if you will be transporting it in a warm car, refrigerate the milk immediately and/or transport it in an insulated container with ice packs.
- Fresh breastmilk can be kept frozen for several months in a well-insulated freezer compartment at a steady temperature. It will keep in the refrigerator for up to five days. Thaw frozen milk in the refrigerator overnight or in a bath of warm water (do not thaw on the stove or in the microwave). Do not refreeze thawed milk. You can store breastmilk in a presterilized bottle or in special sterilized freezer bags available from Medela Inc. (see Resources).
- Always date containers of breastmilk, and store the oldest containers in front of the newest so that they will be used in the right order.
- Throw away any portion of a bottle that your baby starts but does not finish in one day. Store the remaining milk in the refrigerator until use, and do not reheat the milk more than once.

Storing Breastmilk

To safely store breastmilk, your freezer should be able to maintain a constant temperature of less than 0 degrees Fahrenheit. Your refrigerator should stay between 32 and 40 degrees Fahrenheit. To test this, you can buy a refrigerator/freezer thermometer at your local kitchen supply or grocery store. Wait six to eight hours before reading the temperature and adjust as necessary.

Introducing the Bottle to Your Breastfed Baby

Most breastfed babies happily accept feedings occasionally or several times daily from a bottle. Breastfeeding experts recommend introducing the bottle to a nursing baby no sooner than four weeks postpartum to reduce the chance that your baby will develop nipple confusion and refuse the breast after becoming accustomed to nursing at an artificial nipple. On the other hand, they recommend that the bottle be introduced before six to eight weeks of age when your baby may become more attached to breastfeeding exclusively. Babies can be rather particular about this process, however, so don't assume there will be problems if your baby is introduced earlier than four weeks because you have to be separated or later if you change your mind about exclusive breastfeeding. If your baby refuses the bottle on the first few tries, try not to be too concerned. If nothing else, becoming anxious about whether or not your baby will accept a bottle can be detrimental to the process. Everyone has a different story about introducing a bottle to their baby, so try not to anticipate problems that may not occur.

Tips for Successful First Bottle-Feedings

- Choose to introduce the bottle at a feeding time that is typically trouble-free, when your baby is well rested and not too hungry.
- Warm the milk so that it is around body temperature. It should feel only slightly warm on the sensitive skin inside your wrist.
- Tickle the side of your baby's mouth with the bottle's nipple. This will stimulate the rooting reflex.
- Choose a nipple that is most similar to a mother's breast, and make sure it has a slow flow. Babies who are used to the more challenging action of sucking milk from a breast will be overwhelmed by milk that comes out too fast from the bottle.
- Warm the nipple in warm tap water.

- Your baby may be more likely to accept the bottle from someone other than his mother. Your partner, a relative, a friend, or the baby's caregiver may be more successful. It may even be helpful for mom to leave the room or go out on an errand.
- Hold your baby in a position that doesn't suggest nursing. Many babies enjoy being held in the lap facing outward.
- If the bottle is refused, don't push it. Offer the breast, and try the bottle again tomorrow. It may take several days of attempts before the bottle is accepted.
- After a few refusals, try a different kind of nipple on the bottle.
- Once your baby has started with the bottle, try to give him a bottle-feeding regularly. Some experts recommend bottle-feedings every day, others say a gap of three or four days or even a week is no problem.

Breast- and Bottle-Feeding Stories and Surprises

Many mothers worry about introducing the bottle to their breastfed babies. What if the baby won't drink from a bottle? Images of being enslaved to a nursing baby suddenly loom large for a stir-crazy, sleep-deprived new mother who is convinced she'll never again have a moment to herself. In reality, most breastfed babies have no trouble adjusting to bottle-feedings, and the freedom of having a partner or caregiver give feedings to the baby allows many mothers to go to work or to have some much needed time away from the baby. However, sometimes things don't always go according to plan, as you'll see from the stories below. But don't worry—everything always seems to work out in the end.

- Candace was very concerned about bottle-feeding her baby boy, Eli. He was nearly three months old, and every attempt to get him to drink breastmilk from a bottle had failed. Every experienced mother Candace knew had sworn to her

that she would be "the one" to give him his first bottle, but to no avail. Candace had planned to go back to work when Eli was six months old, and she began to wonder if this would be possible. However, when the time did come for Candace to start at work, Eli was happily drinking breastmilk from a sippy cup, which she introduced at five months.

- Mary Ellen successfully introduced Jackson to the bottle right on schedule at six weeks and returned to part-time work at three months. Nursing and bottle-feeding proceeded according to plan until Jackson began eating solid food at six months. By this time, Jackson was accustomed to Mary Ellen's work schedule, which rarely took her away from home longer than four to six hours. As soon as he had an alternative means to satisfy his hunger with solid food, Jackson made it abundantly clear to his parents that he would rather wait to nurse when his mom came home by suddenly refusing the bottle. However, since he was eating well, this arrangement worked fine for both parties.

- Amelia just would not take a bottle no matter what Carol and John tried, and by the time she was three and a half months, they simply gave up. At five months, Amelia began to eat more solid food, and at six months Carol started working part time. When she went back to work, Carol nursed Amelia right before she left and as soon as she came home. She and John began to offer her formula in a bottle consistently every evening, and eventually she accepted it. Since then, Amelia has become a confirmed bottle-drinker, and still has milk in a bottle several times a day at 18 months.

- For myself, Max had no trouble adjusting to taking a bottle in the evenings starting at about eight weeks. We kept on a fairly regular schedule with bottle-feedings for several months. Sometimes I gave him the bottle and sometimes my husband did, depending on if he was home from work in time for the early evening feed. I wouldn't be returning to work for a while, so it didn't really matter much. When Max was about four months old, we began to slack off from giving him a bottle regularly, and he quietly gave up the bottle when he was around six months old. He would occasionally take it, but we realized that in reality we were all half-hearted about the bottle. He started drinking from a sippy cup pretty quickly after this, and whether or not he had a bottle wasn't an issue anymore.

How Your Diet Affects Your Breastfed Baby

Not only is what you eat important for the quality of your milk, but some of the foods you eat can have unexpected effects on your baby. For example, spicy or garlicky foods can change the flavor of mother's milk. Many a mom has a funny story about a sour face made by her baby the morning after she binged on a double garlic pizza. Excess gas or minor tummy trouble caused by something in Mom's dinner is also not uncommon in young infants. Babies may even have an allergic reaction to something their mother ate. Of more concern are harmful substances found in medications or controlled substances, which babies should not be exposed to.

A Healthy Diet for Mom is a Healthy Diet for Baby

It is important to continue eating a balanced and nutritious diet, similar to the one you followed when you were pregnant, while you are breastfeeding your baby. Many doctors recommend that you continue to take a prenatal vitamin as well. Typically, mothers need to consume 500 extra calories (25 percent more than usual) while nursing. Your diet should be rich in complex carbohydrates from whole grain breads, pasta, brown rice, and so on. As always, you should limit the amount of saturated fats found in red meat, lard, and butter, and hydrogenated or partially hydrogenated fats common in margarine, commercial baked goods, and packaged snack foods. Protein and vitamin-rich animal foods such as milk, cheese, and eggs, while containing some saturated fat, are a good source of nutrients and protein and may be consumed in moderation. If you are not already eating the three to five servings of vegetables and two to four servings of fruits each day recommended by the USDA, now is the time to start. Most women are very hungry during the first few months postpartum, so getting the extra calories should not be too difficult as long as you pay attention to proper nutrition. You should definitely not try to lose weight prior to two months following the birth, as it can interfere with establishing milk supply. Additionally, you should be sure to drink eight 8-ounce glasses of water each day in order to keep your body and milk hydrated.

Foods You Eat That May Upset Your Nursing Baby's Tummy

Unlike formula, mother's milk is constantly changing depending on the time of day, how hungry the baby is, the length of time since the last feeding, and not least *what the mother has been eating*. It may surprise you to learn that some flavors and properties of the food you eat can pass easily into your milk. In many ways this is beneficial because your baby will be introduced to many different flavors (albeit one step removed), which might help her to be a more adventurous eater later. However, spicy or gassy foods such as pizza, beans, garlic, onions, or cabbage can cause trouble for an infant's immature digestive system. Acidic foods, like citrus fruits or pineapple, can also pose a problem. If you notice fussy or unusual behavior in your infant, it may be helpful to think back to what you might have eaten in the last 2 to 12 hours. He might be fussing at the breast or rejecting a feeding because of the spicy garlic bread you made for dinner last night. Or, the same burrito that is giving you gas is upsetting his little tummy also. This sensitivity usually doesn't last very long. Avoid suspected foods for a few weeks, and then try again while watching for an adverse reaction.

Breastfeeding Prevents Allergies

Breastmilk contains the immunoglobulin secretory IgA. This substance effectively coats your baby's developing digestive tract, promoting the intestinal lining's ability to break down food proteins into nonallergenic amino acids before they can get into the bloodstream and cause a reaction.

Recommended Nutrient Intakes for Nursing Mothers

Daily Nutrients	Before Pregnancy	During Nursing	Percent Change
Calories	2,200	2,700	+25%
Protein (g)	50	65	+30%
Vitamin A (mcg)	800	1,300	+63%
Vitamin D (mcg)	5	5	0%
Vitamin E (mg)	8	12	+50%
Vitamin C (mg)	60	95	+58%
Thiamin (mg)	1.1	1.5	+36%
Riboflavin (mg)	1.1	1.6	+45%
Niacin (mg)	14	17	+21%
Vitamin B-6 (mg)	1.3	2.0	+54%
Folate (mcg)	400	500	+20%
Vitamin B-12 (mcg)	2.4	2.8	+17%
Calcium (mg)	1,000	1,000	0%
Iron (mg)	15	15	0%
Zinc (mg)	12	19	+58%

From *Feeding Your Child for Lifelong Health* by Susan B. Roberts, and Melvin B. Heyman M.D., and Lisa Tracy. Lisa Tracy, Copyright ©1999 by Susan Roberts, Melvin B. Heyman and Lisa Tracy. Used by permission of Bantam Books, a division of Random House, Inc.

Infant Allergies and Nursing

While breastfeeding your baby has actually been indicated as a strong factor in *preventing* later allergies, an infant who is hypersensitive to a particular food may sometimes have a reaction to the allergen when it is passed through his mother's milk. This is often associated with cow's milk and wheat allergies, and the baby's symptoms are usually chronic and may include a rash, congestion, diarrhea, or colicky behavior. If you have a strong family history of allergies or you suspect that your baby is experiencing allergies from substances in your milk, talk with his pediatrician.

She will most likely recommend that you keep a record of what you are eating and your baby's symptoms. Depending on the severity of your baby's symptoms, it may be necessary for you to avoid or curtail your intake of an allergenic food while you are nursing your baby.

Using an Elimination Diet to Track Down Allergies

Keep a detailed record of the types and approximate amounts of foods you are eating for several days. Carefully read the labels for any processed foods you eat to identify any suspect ingredients. Make notes about the timing of your baby's symptoms and the timing and content of your meals and snacks. Identify suspect foods (such as wheat, eggs, peanuts, soy, and apples) that are eaten two to eight hours before the onset of symptoms. After this task is accomplished, you are ready for the next step.

For three days, avoid all the suspect foods you've identified. If your baby seems much better, it is likely that either his trouble has passed naturally, or one of the suspect foods was to blame. To be sure, reintroduce one of the most likely allergens (often dairy products or wheat) to see if there is a return of your baby's symptoms. More than one food may be the cause, so it is helpful to reintroduce each one to your diet separately to identify the culprit(s). Eat a lot of the suspect food early in the day, hopefully to avoid a difficult night. If your baby has no reaction, go on to the next food in a few days, slowly working through the entire list.

Once the allergen has been identified, it may not be necessary to avoid the food forever. Many babies grow out of these allergies with time or their symptoms are mild enough that drastic changes to the mother's diet are not warranted. Try eating the food again in a few weeks, or limiting your intake. If dairy products are the culprit make sure that you make up for lost calcium by taking supplements and eating other calcium-rich foods.

Substances to Avoid While Nursing

Unfortunately, there are also harmful substances you should be aware of that can be passed to your baby in your milk. Many chemicals are fat soluble, which means they are carried throughout your body by means of fat molecules in your bloodstream; the same fat molecules present in your milk. You should never take a prescription drug when you are nursing unless your doctor recommends it. You should also avoid taking any over-the-counter drugs without consulting your doctor first. If you have a cold or stomach trouble, try to relieve your symptoms without the use of drugs as much as possible. For example, it's amazing how effective breathing hot steam vapors can be in relieving sinus pressure. Also, the saltines and carbonated water you had ad infinitum during morning sickness can come in handy once more to help soothe an unsettled stomach. Just giving up and going to bed can be enormously helpful. Many over-the-counter drugs are made to "keep you going" when you are sick. Maybe you should just rest. Of course, a nursing mother shouldn't suffer in silence when she's sick, but it is important that she acknowledges she is not a superhero. Rest and seek the advice of your doctor if necessary.

Caffeine and Alcohol

Consumption of alcoholic and caffeinated beverages is also on the caution list while breastfeeding because both caffeine and alcohol pass into the breastmilk. Some women choose not to indulge while they are nursing to remove any trace of doubt. As with everything relating to your baby though, you should take into consideration a variety of factors. Your baby's age is particularly important. As she grows, the danger of harmful effects from caffeine and alcohol is diminished. Timing is also a factor. If you have a cup of coffee or tea immediately *after* a feeding, and two hours elapse before the next feeding, less caffeine will be present in the milk. The same is true for alcoholic beverages. And finally, but not least important, your feelings should be taken into consideration. Being a new mother is demanding enough without being made to feel that you must deny yourself every luxury. If a morning cup of tea and an occasional

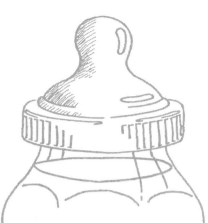

Delayed Reaction

When your baby is receiving primarily colostrum, her tummy is coated with soothing properties designed to prepare her digestive tract for the milk to come. Many mothers who splurge on spicy Asian and Mexican food soon after the birth think they are home free when they see no adverse reaction in their babies. However, once this coating wears off, you may find your baby is more sensitive than you realized.

glass of wine are important to you, consider allowing yourself to indulge in moderation. On the other hand, if a night on the town is really what you need, you can consider throwing caution to the wind, so long as you express and discard the milk from the next one or two feedings. (I once heard a mom call this the "pump and dump" routine.) One more thing: Smoking cigarettes and nursing definitely do not mix, and neither does the use of recreational drugs. This is one indulgence neither you nor your baby can afford.

Breastfeeding and the Introduction of Solid Food

As your baby grows, she will eventually become ready for solid food. When this happens is extremely variable from one child to another. In many societies around the world, infants are not introduced to solid food until after 9 to 12 months. Just a generation ago, our mothers were encouraged to begin adding rice cereal to the baby bottle as early as six weeks (a practice that is now strongly discouraged). Now, some doctors recommend exclusive breastfeeding for as long as one year if the baby continues to thrive on breastmilk alone and shows no interest in solid food. However, most doctors say that babies are ready to eat some solid food at four to six months when their digestive tract is fully developed and when they are beginning to sit without support. Still, breastmilk should continue to be your baby's primary source of nutrition at 12 months.

If you are exclusively breastfeeding your baby you will notice that the introduction of solid food will create a change in your milk supply and nursing routine. Sometimes this adjustment period can become slightly tricky, especially if you find you are pumping milk for feedings that have been replaced by solid food. If you have already begun to supplement breastfeeding with formula, this process will already be under way. Eventually, the consumption of food other than breastmilk will eclipse breastfeeding completely. This is part of the process of weaning your baby, which may be gradual or swift, depending on a number of circumstances.

Weight Loss and Dieting

You need at least 200 extra calories a day while you are breastfeeding (500 if you are not trying to lose weight). However, as few of us are very good at counting calories, be careful not to lose more than one to one and a half pounds per week. More rapid weight loss is not safe for you or your baby, and the more gradually you can lose weight, the better off you will both be. Remember that it took nine months to put on the excess weight your body needed during pregnancy, and it typically takes at least that amount of time for your body to return to normal.

Ten Ways to Calm a Crying Newborn

1. Determine whether the baby is hungry. Sixty percent of the time an empty tummy is what makes a baby cry. Offer a bottle or a breast.

2. Check baby's diaper. Change the diaper as quickly and quietly as you can; making a big fuss over the diaper can actually irritate baby more.

3. Gently rock the baby in a rocking chair. Or standing up, rock slowly back and forth, gently patting the baby's back. Maybe there's an extra burp in there that needs help getting out.

4. Swaddle or wrap the baby tightly in a blanket, just as the nurses did in the hospital nursery. Place the blanket sideways, with a point at the top. Next, place the baby at the top point, and then tuck one side under the baby's body. Pull up the bottom fold, and then wrap the remaining side over the baby's body. You're not cutting off circulation here, but you are providing that feeling of womb-like security for your baby.

5. Give the baby a pacifier. Like them or not, they are often temporary solutions to crying problems. My mother-in-law used to say that pacifiers are more for the mother than the baby, and so what if that's true? At least you've bought yourself a few moments of quiet to collect your thoughts while trying to figure out what's wrong.

6. Try to work out tummy gas. Put the baby on his or her stomach, and gently rub baby's back or pat baby's bottom. Or lay baby on his back while gently moving his legs back and forth. Use gas drops (available over the counter) as a last resort.

7. Give the baby a warm bath. There's nothing so soothing as a warm tub. Many babies calm down as soon as they hit the water. Add an infant massage, and you'll have yourself one calm baby.

8. Give the baby a song and dance. Try singing to your baby, and move around the room as you do so. Babies have short attention spans, and can be easily redirected.

9. Take baby for a walk or a ride in the car. Babies love motion, and the motion of an automobile somehow serves as anesthesia for babies. You'd be surprised to know how many miles are put on a car just for a baby's sake.

10. Put baby to bed. Like all of us, baby can get irritable when tired. Since their bodies are so much smaller than ours, they process food and milk differently and thus get sleepy more quickly than you might think. Put on the baby's lullaby tape or music box, dim the lights, and then walk out. Older babies over six months can be left to cry for at least ten minutes before you return to the room (unless, of course, you're absolutely convinced there's really something wrong). Some crying before falling asleep is normal for most babies.

How Long Should I Breastfeed?

Any time spent breastfeeding, whether it is days, weeks, months, or years, is of benefit to you and your baby. Some women choose to stop after only a few days, when their babies have received the important antibodies and nutrients in the colostrum, which is produced by your body before the milk comes in. The hormones your body produces during these early feedings are also important in helping your uterus contract to its normal size, speeding your recovery from the birth. On the other end of the spectrum are women who choose to nurse their babies until the age of two or three, or even older. Doctors and nutritionists recommend that babies be nursed throughout the first year if possible. After this time most babies will have outgrown infant allergies and breastmilk nutrition can be more easily replaced by other foods. Age of weaning is an especially sensitive topic in our society, and it may be difficult for a woman to tune out the judgmental attitudes of others. It seems unfair that a woman breastfeeding her toddler is just as likely to encounter thoughtless comments from the people around her as one who feeds her newborn formula. Try to remember that how long you nurse your baby is your business and no one else's.

When the time to wean your baby does come, it is best to approach it gradually, phasing out the feedings that seem least important to your baby first. You will know which feedings your baby considers most important by his vigorous protests at their absence and refusal to accept any substitutions like a drink, snack, or snuggle. After a few weeks, you can slowly drop the number of feedings to two or one per day, replacing each dropped feeding with a bottle of formula for a baby younger than 10 to 12 months, and a bottle of formula/milk or a snack for an older baby. Typically, early morning, naptime, and bedtime nursings are the last to go. Breastfeeding as a part of the bedtime routine may be especially important to your baby emotionally, so not only is a replacement bottle or snack important, but special time to snuggle with Mommy and Daddy will help ease the transition as well. For a baby older than one year, it may be more advisable to start a systematic method of weaning in the spring or summer months when the temptation to snuggle up inside with Mommy and nurse on a cold winter day is less immediate. Also, it may be helpful to avoid reminding your baby of nursing. For example, snuggling in the rocking chair where you have always nursed her may lead to more confusion than is necessary.

Many lactation consultants and parenting experts feel that "infant-led" as opposed to "parent-led" weaning is the optimal process for weaning a baby from the breast, and indeed this is the method followed by most cultures throughout the world. Infant-led weaning occurs when a child naturally and gradually gives up nursing as his need to suck for comfort and nourishment diminishes. This can happen anytime between nine months and three years of age, and it is often a seamless passage from one phase to another for many mother-baby nursing pairs.

Nursing Strikes

Sometimes, a baby will suddenly refuse the breast on his own, often between the ages of 8 and 12 months. This may be a natural self-weaning, which is uncommon but not unheard of at this age, or it may be what is called a "nursing strike." A nursing strike can last a few days or even a week, and many babies resume nursing regularly after a strike. Whatever the cause, an abrupt end to nursing can be difficult for both the baby and the mother. For the baby, this is a time he will probably need lots of extra attention from both his mother and father. He may be clingy and whiny, which can be annoying. Don't let this bother you though; it is only temporary. Go ahead and indulge him. A sudden weaning may be even more traumatic for the mother, however. As nursing becomes second nature, you often won't realize just how powerful the instinct to nurse really is. Not only will your breasts become uncomfortably engorged before your body gets the signal to stop milk production, but the resulting hormonal roller coaster can be intense. This is a time to lean especially heavily on your partner if possible. You may need time alone to sort through your emotions before you can present an upbeat attitude for your baby. Remember that the bond between you

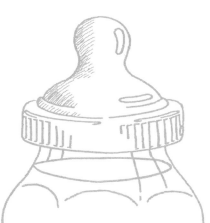

Extended Nursing

More and more mothers are choosing to extend nursing beyond the one-year minimum recommended by health professionals. Although this practice is not widely supported in our culture, the benefits of extended nursing to babies and toddlers cannot be underestimated. The well-known nutritional properties of breastmilk continue to provide older babies with a solid foundation for a healthy diet. Also, many mothers and health care professionals can attest to the emotional benefits of extended nursing to both babies and mothers. Indeed, in many parts of the world, extended breastfeeding is the norm rather than the exception.

and your baby is very powerful, and that nursing is only one aspect of a relationship that is irreplaceable to your baby.

Tips for Handling a Nursing Strike

An illness, teething, or a change in routine often precipitates a nursing strike. Sometimes, a strike will follow an incident when the baby accidentally or through experimentation bites her mother's breast. A strong reaction to a biting incident is understandable, but the baby may be quite startled by it. A baby who clearly wants the comfort of nursing, but who is too upset to attempt it, is likely to strike. If your baby shows signs of a possible ear infection or another illness, have her checked by a doctor. She may simply not feel well and not be hungry as a result. Otherwise, you should keep your milk supply up by continuing to express milk on approximately the same schedule as her regular feedings and try some of the following measures:

- Attempt to nurse in a quiet, dark room when you and your baby are calm and relaxed. You may even want to take a bath together if this is soothing.
- Try a different position. Some women have had success coaxing their babies to nurse while they are walking around the house!
- Try to nurse when your baby is very sleepy. Just after a nap or when she wakes in the middle of the night are good times.
- If your baby is not already drinking from a bottle, this is probably not a good time to introduce it if you really want to resume nursing, since she may develop a preference for the bottle. Otherwise, it may be helpful to offer a small amount of your breastmilk in a bottle to calm and encourage her, and then offer the breast immediately after she empties the bottle.

Tips for Handling a Biting Baby

It can be very difficult to avoid a strong reaction if your baby bites your nipple while nursing. If you do shout or jump, don't blame yourself, just try to be prepared for the next time. Babies bite for a variety of reasons. Often, the urge to bite coincides with a particularly painful bout of teething, but biting can also be simple mischievous behavior by a curious baby. You may be able to predict the times your baby is most likely to bite, either at the beginning or end of the feeding. Or your baby's face may suddenly change expression as the idea occurs to him. Whatever the reasons or circumstances, you owe it to yourself to stop this painful experience from happening.

- Stop the feeding immediately by breaking your baby's suction with your finger and try to stay calm. If you feel it will be helpful, gently but firmly explain to your baby that he should not bite while he is nursing. Use words you are fairly sure he understands, like, "Ouch that hurts Mama, no. Don't bite Mama. Mama has a boo-boo." Remember that even if your baby is not old enough to understand the language you use, he may be dramatically affected by your tone of voice and facial expressions. Be careful not to frighten him.
- Do not try nursing again for at least a half hour.
- Offer your baby a cold teething toy before nursing.
- Try to anticipate when your baby might bite, and stop the feeding at the first sign that he may do so.

Feeding Your Baby in the Real World

"Moses weaned himself at eight and a half months. Perhaps he would have done it anyway, but we made a trip without the children. Allison had pumped bottles for the 36 hours that we were gone. My parents stayed with Moses and our daughter Zula while we were gone. Apparently, Moses liked how easy it was to get milk from the bottle. Until then, he was accustomed to getting a bottle twice a week. Having the bottle exclusively for a day and a half seemed to convince him that it was far superior to nursing. Allison tried to continue nursing, but after a month and a half of difficulty, we have given in and give him formula exclusively."

—Greg, father of Zula and Moses

CHAPTER THREE

Formula Feeding: Options and Insights

Bottle-Feeding the Newborn

If you have chosen not to breastfeed, formula-feedings may begin very soon after birth. Hospital staff will supply formula when it is needed and unless one or both parents have an allergy to cow's milk, they will probably suggest trying a whey-based formula first. Once you are home with your baby, it may take a while to work out a routine for preparing bottles and formula, but within the week, you should feel much more comfortable. It may surprise you how many bottles you need to wash and sterilize in a day, and it may be awkward at first learning how to prepare formula. Planning ahead is essential. Buy bottle-feeding supplies and sterilize them before your baby is born. Think about how and where you will store the bottles, so that they can stay clean and be easily accessible without getting in the way.

Bottle-Feeding Supplies

If you will not be breastfeeding, make sure to have the following supplies on hand before your baby arrives:

- Four 4-ounce bottles with nipples
- Ten to twelve 8-ounce bottles with nipples
- Bottle and nipple brush
- Sterilizer, or large pot with lid
- Tongs
- Large, heat-resistant glass measuring cup
- Long-handled mixing spoon

What to Buy If You're Worried You Won't Be Able to Breastfeed

Usually, fears about an inability to breastfeed are unfounded, and with the proper support and guidance, even the most hesitant new mother is able to nurse for as long as she wants. Be careful that you don't set yourself up for a self-fulfilling prophecy. Buying all of the bottle-feeding supplies, assuming you won't be able to breastfeed, may ensure the outcome. By the same token, unexpected circumstances such as an illness or difficult birth may create a situation where bottle-feeding becomes necessary, even for mothers who planned to breastfeed exclusively. The safest bet is to be prepared with three or four sterilized 4-ounce bottles and nipples and a bottle/nipple brush, so that you can provide your baby with a day or two of feedings, sterilizing and reusing bottles as needed, before you buy the rest of the gear.

The First Feeding

The first feeding should be as quiet and as comfortable as possible. This is your first chance to provide your baby with the reassurance of sustenance, and to begin the bonding process, in which a newborn and his caregivers establish the beginnings of a beautiful relationship. Usually the birth attendant or maternity nurse will suggest a feeding at about two to five hours after the birth, or as soon as the baby is alert and calm. If you are separated from your baby for a time after the birth due to complications, work with the hospital staff to reunite with your baby as soon as it is safe, and to begin bottle-feedings shortly thereafter. Start feedings with a calm baby and a calm mother (or father/partner). If the baby is fussing, the bottle may calm him, but if he is crying hard, it may be better to soothe him with a song and rhythmic walking or rocking first.

Cradle your baby with her head resting in the crook of your arm so that she is in a semi-upright position. Make sure her head is not held at an odd angle. Her chin should not be resting on her chest or tilted to one side. Gently tickle her cheek with the nipple of the bottle, just next to her mouth on the side closest to your body. This should cause her to turn her head, and open her mouth, in a newborn reflex called rooting. Then you can insert the nipple between her lips so that they close around the bulb. At this point, she will probably begin sucking immediately. Tilt the bottle up so that the liquid fills the entire nipple, keeping air out of the nipple and out of your baby's stomach. Don't be surprised if your baby stops drinking or falls asleep after drinking only an ounce or less. Her stomach is very small, and she's most likely

Storage for Bottle-Feeding Supplies

You may want to buy a large rectangular plastic storage container (approximately 14- x 8- x 8-inch) to keep your bottle-feeding supplies in. Choose one with a lid that fits tightly over the top, and line the bottom with a clean cloth. Storing bottle-feeding supplies in this container will keep dust and kitchen grease from settling on them.

gotten all she needs for now. She is unlikely to be very hungry right away; breastfed babies generally do not get milk until the third or fourth day. If she fusses, she may need to be burped, and she might have a bit more to drink after the excess gas is expelled.

If you get off to a rough start, don't be too dismayed. If your baby starts to cry or becomes confused, soothe him as best as you can and try again in a few minutes. He will probably catch on fairly quickly. If you are still having trouble, one of the nurses will be able to help. If your baby is choking or gagging when you give him the bottle, the nipple hole may be too large, and he cannot cope with the amount of formula coming through. Always use a nipple with a "slow flow" designed for babies newborn to three months of age. Check to make sure the flow is right by holding the bottle upside down. The formula should drip out at about one drop per second. If it spurts or flows, it will be too fast, and you should try a different nipple. On the other hand, if your baby seems to be sucking very hard and expresses frustration by crying during feedings, the nipple hole may be too small for him.

Enjoy these early feedings. A newborn baby can focus at a distance of about 10 inches, and his instinct will be to gaze into your eyes, examining your face with a combination of wisdom and wonder. Snuggle up and get comfortable. Your smiles and songs and soft voice will help him to associate eating with pleasure and human company, which will hopefully stay with him the rest of his life. Do not prop the bottle so that you can leave the baby. It is dangerous to leave a baby unattended during feedings at any age.

Keep Feedings to Yourself at First

Although many young babies will happily accept a bottle from anyone who offers, you may want to keep this precious time just between yourself, your partner, and your baby at first. As your baby adjusts to taking his first bottles, he'll need time to sort through this new routine, and feeding time can be a great opportunity for early parent-infant bonding.

Infant Formula Basics

Formula is made by combining ingredients so that its nutritional qualities resemble human milk as closely as possible. Proteins, fats, and carbohydrates are combined in the right proportion with all of the known essential nutrients necessary for infant health and development. The FDA is responsible for making sure that all infant formulas provide all the nutrients babies need. Approximately $1.9 billion worth of formula is sold in the United States annually; the average can of powdered formula costs approximately $10.50. This adds up to approximately 180 million cans of formula annually. About half of the formula sold in the United States is purchased by the federal government to be distributed at a discount to families covered under the Women, Infants and Children (WIC) nutrition program. Currently, three large companies control the majority of the U.S. market for formula: Ross Laboratories (Similac), Mead Johnson (Enfamil), and Carnation (Good Start). Recently, a few generic brands have begun to appear on supermarket and pharmacy shelves.

Is It OK to Buy Generic Formula?

Generic or store brand formulas have begun to make a tiny dent in the formula market as consumers begin to warm up very slowly to the idea of paying up to $3 less per can of powdered formula. Manufacturers of generic brands insist that their products are nearly identical to the national brands but cost less because they are not aggressively marketed through sales representatives and free samples given to pediatricians and new parents. Also, generic brands merely copy specifications and ingredients developed by the larger corporations and do not spend additional money on research and development of improvements. Many experts are suspicious of generic brands, and doctors who feel that breastfeeding already faces enough challenges from formula are actively discouraging a lower-priced product. If you are considering switching to a generic brand, consult your pediatrician first. Generic brands are suitable only for babies who can tolerate standard cow's milk or soy-based formulas, because generic brands are not available in hypoallergenic versions or for babies with specific digestive problems.

Stand Up for Your Right to Bottle-Feed Your Baby

With so many medical professionals keen to promote breastfeeding for public health reasons, many laypeople have decided to jump onto the breastfeeding bandwagon as well. This means that a variety of people may inquire about your method of feeding your baby, including your mother-in-law, your friends and coworkers, and even perfect strangers on the street. While all of these people may have good intentions, they have no business inquiring into your personal affairs, and you are under no obligation to explain your reasons for bottle-feeding your baby. Simply say, "My little baby loves his bottle. Look how cute he is!" and leave it at that.

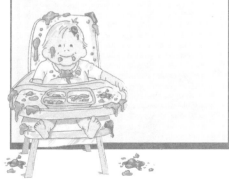

Choosing the Right Formula

When a baby is breastfed, the milk supply and qualities are constantly being adjusted to meet the individual needs of each baby. Formula, on the other hand, is always the same from one feeding to the next, and the choices available are limited to matters of convenience for the parents and to the varieties of formula that will be the most digestible for most babies. Until recently, medical professionals and books were the only sources for information about varieties of formula, and changes were made solely on the basis of advice from a pediatrician. This is still the ideal arrangement, but formula companies now regularly advertise on television and in magazines, often providing free samples to new parents. The AAP feels that it is a mistake to treat formula simply as another food product to be marketed by advertisers and CEOs who may know nothing about infant nutrition. It is always best to consult your baby's doctor about your choice of formula.

Powdered or Liquid?

Formula basically comes in one of three forms: powdered, concentrated liquid, or full-strength liquid. Which type you choose will depend on your need for convenience and how much you want to spend. Powdered formula is the least expensive but requires the most preparation for each feeding. Full-strength formula requires no preparation at all, and concentrated formula is simply diluted with sterilized or distilled water. Many families use powdered formula at home and save liquid formula for outings or trips.

Standard Formula

If your baby was born healthy and at term and if you have no family history of food allergies and/or childhood diabetes, a standard formula will probably be well accepted by your baby. National brands of standard formula are Enfamil and Similac. Most babies fall into this category and continue with a standard formula throughout the first year. Standard formula obtains most of its protein and carbohydrates from nonfat cow's milk that is reformulated to suit human infants and enriched with the essential nutrients found in breastmilk. Fats are obtained from a variety of vegetable oils chosen to provide the essential fatty acids necessary for proper development.

Low-Iron Formula

The AAP recommends against using low-iron formulas. In the past, low-iron formula was sometimes recommended because it was believed that iron in formula caused gastrointestinal irritation and constipation. However, this claim has never been proven, and reducing the amount of essential iron in infant formula raises an alarm among health professionals. Amazingly, low-iron formula is still widely available.

Hydrolysate Formula

This type of formula is designed for babies that have trouble digesting the proteins found in cow's milk. National brands of hydrolysate formula include Alimentum, Nutramigen, and Pregestimil. The proteins are still derived from cow's milk but have been broken down into submicroscopic pieces for easier digestion. Carbohydrates in hydrolysate formula come from corn sugars or fruit sugars, and fats from vegetable oils as with standard formula. Hydrolysate formula tends to be more expensive than standard formula (up to three times as much), but can be a welcome change when the baby is suffering from digestive trouble caused by standard formula. Carnation Good Start is one type of hydrolysate formula that has a whey protein base rather than a casein protein base (both are proteins found in cow's milk) and gets its carbohydrates from lactose. It has some of the benefits of a regular hydrolysate formula but is much less expensive.

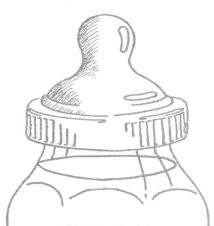

Fatty Acid Controversy

Some critics believe that formulas marketed in the United States are deficient in long-chain polyunsaturated fatty acids such as arachidonic acid and decosahexaenoic acid (DHA), which are thought to be essential for optimal brain development and which are both found in breastmilk. The body can synthesize these acids from the two fatty acids already found in infant formulas, linoleic acid and alpha-linoleic acid, but experts are concerned that more may be needed. This topic is currently being hotly debated among doctors and researchers involved in the development of formulas.

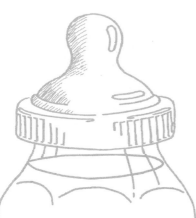

Soy-Based Formula

National brands of soy-based formulas include Atsoy, Somil, and ProSoBee. Soy-based formulas were once widely recommended for infants who have trouble digesting proteins obtained from cow's milk. However, it has since come to light that approximately 30 to 50 percent of infants who are allergic to milk proteins are also allergic to soy-based proteins. Still, about a quarter of American babies are fed soy-based formula, a situation some pediatricians would like to change. There are concerns that human infants cannot derive sufficient amino acids from plant-based proteins, and that soy protein binds with calcium, iron, and zinc, inhibiting absorption of these essential nutrients. In addition, soy-based formulas contain elevated levels of sodium and aluminum, which, while not proven harmful, are not beneficial, either. Soy-based formulas are also thought to increase the risk of allergies to soy later in life. For infants who are intolerant of standard formula, many pediatricians would recommend a hydrolysate formula instead of a soy-based formula. However, some pediatricians still recommend soy-based formula as a matter of course, and certainly many babies thrive when they are given soy formula.

Hypoallergenic or Elemental Formula

This type of formula starts as a cow's milk-based formula, but all of its nutrients are broken down into their most elemental form, which theoretically prevents any allergic reaction. One national brand is Neocate. Elemental formula is only for babies with severely impaired intestinal function and hypersensitivity to many food allergens and is the most expensive formula on the market. Additionally, the intense processing required to break down each ingredient to its elemental form results in a bitter, largely unpalatable product, but is the only option for a small minority of babies.

Well Water and Formula

If you use a well for drinking water, call your local health department or cooperative extension office to have the water checked before using it to make formula for your baby. Some well water contains nitrate levels that are unsafe for babies, and the nitrates are only further concentrated when the water is boiled. If this is the case, you should use store-bought distilled water to make formula for your baby and for drinking in the first years of life.

Lactose-Free Formula

Lactose-free formula is for the extremely small number of truly lactose-intolerant infants. Lactose is found in both breastmilk and cow's milk and is rarely the cause of indigestion in babies (lactose intolerance is more common in children over the age of three or four). One national brand is Lactofree.

Follow-Up Formula

Follow up formulas, such as Carnation Follow-Up, Carnation Soy Follow-Up, and Enfamil Next Step Soy, are made for babies between 6 and 12 months of age. Follow-up formulas are meant to bridge the transition from formula to cow's milk, usually introduced at 12 months, and are less expensive than standard formulas. Many parents choose to switch to follow-up formula at six months or so, but they should be aware that when comparing standard formula to cow's milk-based follow-up formula, lactose is replaced as a carbohydrate source by corn syrup, which accounts for much of the price difference. Babies who are thriving on infant formula will almost certainly continue to do so without switching to a follow-up formula.

Unsuitable Replacements for Formula

Infant formula is the only acceptable substitute for human breastmilk when feeding an infant in the first four to six months. Other milks and beverages do not supply the correct nutrition and may be too high in sodium or other harmful ingredients. Tragic consequences such as severe malnutrition and irreparable harm to the digestive tract have occurred because people wanted to avoid the expense of formula or have the mistaken belief that other options are more natural or healthy.

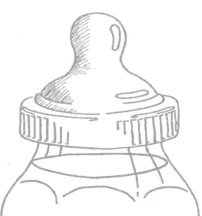

Signs to Switch Formulas

Often, symptoms that are written off as colic may be solved by a switch in formula. If your baby is suffering from coliclike symptoms, you're probably ready to try anything, so consult your pediatrician about using a different formula. Other signs of intolerance to formula are:

- Bloated, distended stomach
- Stuffy nose or wheezing
- Vomiting or diarrhea
- Bright red rash around the anus

- **Cow's milk.** Besides the fact that human infants typically have trouble digesting the proteins found in cow's milk, a diet of cow's milk does not contain enough of vitamins C and E and is critically deficient in iron and zinc. It is fine to give your baby cow's milk after one year, when most milk allergies have resolved and when your baby is getting these nutrients from other sources.

- **Goat's milk.** Deficient in iron and folic acid (although some brands are fortified with folic acid), goat's milk has a reputation for being more easily digested than cow's milk, which is true for some babies. Many parents of babies older than one year swear that their child is able to tolerate goat's milk but not cow's milk, which can be a tremendous nutritional boon, especially if it is enriched with folic acid. However, goat's milk should not be used as a substitute for infant formula. Some doctors will allow goat's milk to be used as a supplement to breastfeeding, but only occasionally.

- **Soy and rice beverages** (commonly known as soy or rice milk). Animal dairy advocates have successfully lobbied for soy and rice drinks to drop the "milk" from their names. Marketers of these drinks are also required to include a statement on the label indicating that they should not be used to feed a baby instead of breastmilk or formula. Amazingly, this mistake still has occurred and a few babies have become very sick as a result. Among other problems, soy and rice drinks do not contain enough fat or protein to nourish an infant who has not been weaned to solid food.

- **Homemade formula.** Although I have seen several recipes for homemade formula during the course of my research, I do not recommend using any of them without prior advice from your baby's pediatrician.

Comparing Formulas

Type	Contents	Uses	Brands
Standard	Cow's milk, whey, and casein for protein, lactose for carbohydrates, and plant oils for fat.	This type of formula is suitable for most babies without special problems or who do not have or have a family history of allergies.	Enfamil Similac
Hydrolysate	Hydrolyzed (broken down) cow's milk casein for protein, corn syrup, dextrose or sucrose for carbohydrates and plant oils for fat.	Although the proteins are obtained from cow's milk, hydrolyzation minimizes the risk of allergic reactions in sensitive infants.	Alimentum Nutramigen Pregestimil
Whey protein hydrolysate	Hydrolyzed (broken down) cow's milk whey for protein, corn syrup and lactose for carbohydrates, and plant oils for fat.	This is a good option for babies who have some sensitivity to standard formula, but seem less sensitive to whey than casein.	Carnation Good Start
Soy	Soy for protein, corn syrup or sucrose for carbohydrates, and plant oils for fat.	Because soy is a potential allergen to babies, many pediatricians recommend hydrolysate formula instead of soy-based formula for sensitive babies. However, this formula is well accepted by babies who have sensitivity to milk, but not soy.	Alsoy Isomil ProSoBee
Elemental	Elemental amino acids for protein, corn syrup for carbohydrates, and plant oils for fat.	This formula is designed for a small minority of babies with severe food allergies.	Neocate
Lactose free	Cow's milk, whey, and casein for protein, corn syrup and sucrose for carbohydrates, and plant oils for fat.	This formula is designed for a small minority of babies with true lactose intolerance.	Lactofree
Follow-up	Cow's milk, whey, and casein or soy for protein, corn syrup for carbohydrates, and plant oils for fat.	This type of formula is designed for babies between 6 and 12 months, and may be used as a replacement to standard or soy formulas.	Carnation Follow Up Carnation Soy Follow-Up Enfamil Next Step Soy

Feeding the Sleepy Newborn

A newborn baby should have a formula feeding about every two to four hours. However, many babies are very sleepy, particularly in the first few days. If your baby has been asleep for longer than four hours, you should try to wake him for a feeding. You may need to gently jostle him or unwrap his swaddling blankets to rouse him. If the room is warm enough and he is still very sleepy, you may need to undress him down to his diaper before he wakes up. If he falls asleep midway through the meal, use your best judgment as to whether you should try and keep him awake until he finishes the feeding. If he has fed well during the last few feedings, he will probably be fine with a partial feeding this time. If, on the other hand, you are concerned that your baby is sleeping too much and eating too little, you should attempt firmer measures for keeping him awake. Blow on his face or make clicking sounds with your tongue. Run your fingertip up and down his spine, or burp him halfway through the feeding. Try to time feedings to coincide with the times you think he will be most wakeful.

How Much Formula Should I Give?

Newborns typically will take only an ounce or two at each feeding during the first week or so. Depending on the frequency of feedings, most babies will have worked up to three to four ounces at each feeding by about six weeks of age. Because formula is more slowly digested than breastmilk and because feedings tend to be about the same quantity each time, formula-fed babies often have a more regular feeding schedule than breastfed babies do. However, be aware that your baby's appetite may still vary from day to day as his growth and activity level change. If your baby is crying and you think he can't possibly be hungry only two hours since the last feed, you might just be wrong. A top off may be just the thing he needs if other measures like a diaper change, a nap, or a change of environment don't do the trick. Similarly, if your baby quits feeding after two ounces, when he usually takes four, resist the

Nighttime Formula Feedings

Preparing a bottle two, three, and sometimes four times during the night might be the biggest drawback to formula feedings, and there are hundreds of products on the market designed to make this task less of a chore. Many parents use some kind of electric bottle warmer, designed to heat a refrigerated prepared bottle to the right temperature in a few minutes' time.

temptation to encourage him to take the whole bottle. Babies have an amazing capacity to regulate their feedings to suit their needs if they are allowed to do so. Because of their small stomachs, smaller, more frequent feedings are best.

A good rule of thumb is that most babies will need about two to two and a half ounces of formula per pound of body weight per day. This means that a 10-pound baby will drink about 20 to 25 ounces of formula each day, which may mean that she will have 3- or 4-ounce feedings six or seven times each 24 hours. Variations do occur, particularly just before or during a growth spurt when she may require quite a bit more than usual. Most babies will have 3 to 4 ounces at each feeding by three months of age, 4 to 6 ounces at each feeding by six months, and up to 8 ounces at each feeding after six months, depending on the intake of solid food.

Preparing Formula

Always follow the instructions on the package *exactly*. Making formula too strong or too weak can have serious consequences. It is a mistake to try and stretch a can of formula by watering it down. Your baby still needs the same amount of food to stave off hunger and will simply be getting more fluid, which will not contribute to her growth. Because bottle-fed infants are at greater risk of developing gastroenteritis from improperly sterilized feeding equipment, you should pay particular attention to hygiene when preparing formula and bottles for your baby. To sterilize bottles, measuring cups, bottlebrushes, and so on, follow the instructions in Chapter 1. If you are using full-strength formula, no further sterilization is necessary. To sterilize powdered or liquid concentrate formula, you should use one of the following methods:

- Boil water for five minutes and cool to room temperature in a covered saucepan. Mix with powdered or concentrated formula in a sterilized measuring cup and pour the mixed formula into sterilized bottles. Screw on caps and store in refrigerator for up to two days.

Too Many Ear Infections?

Studies have shown that babies who are breastfed for at least the first three months have, on average, fewer ear infections than formula-fed babies. One reason is that babies receive infection-fighting antibodies in breastmilk. Also, breastmilk is less irritating to the ears than formula is, should some of it pass from the throat to the middle ear during a feeding. If your bottle-fed baby is plagued by ear infections, try to feed her in an upright position (greater than 45 degrees) to prevent milk from entering her ear. There are also special bottle straws you can buy that will allow your baby to drink from a bottle in the upright position.

- Prepare formula in a sterilized bowl or measuring cup, and pour it into presterilized bottles. Screw the lids on loosely and place the bottles in a wide-bottom pot on top of a rack or dishtowel. Fill the pot with water so that the bottles are submerged to three inches and bring water to a boil. Cover and keep water at a steady boil for 25 minutes. Remove the bottles with tongs and allow to cool. When cooled, tighten the lids and store in the refrigerator for up to two days.

- Boil water for five minutes and cool to room temperature in a covered saucepan. Pour boiled water into sterilized bottles, and screw on caps. When your baby is ready for a feeding, add the specified amount of powdered or concentrated formula to the bottle and shake well to mix. You can keep bottles of sterilized water at room temperature for up to two days.

Other Tips for Formula Feedings

- Always wash your hands with hot soapy water before handling any bottle-feeding equipment.
- Always shake bottles of premade powdered or liquid formula to ensure that the contents are well mixed.
- Don't prop the bottle so that you can leave your baby during feedings. This is a dangerous practice because your baby could choke, and no one would be there to help him.

CHAPTER FOUR

Introducing Solid Food

S tarting your baby on solid food is probably one of the most anticipated events of early parenthood. Unlike most milestones in your baby's development, solids feedings are (almost) completely under your control. You have no say in when your child will roll over or sit up, but you can plan around the big day when you give her the first taste of rice cereal. Before you get the video camera rolling, though, there are some things you should know.

When to Start

It used to be that parents were encouraged to begin solids feedings early, when their baby was as young as a month or even younger. Mothers were instructed to add infant cereal to a bottle with an enlarged nipple hole, which allowed even the youngest infant to eat "solid" food. The belief was that eating solid food would help the baby sleep through the night. There is no evidence to support this theory, however, and doctors now agree that starting a baby on solid food too early can actually have a detrimental effect. For example, too-early introduction of solid food has been linked to weight problems (both obesity and failure to thrive) and excessive diarrhea or constipation. Also, giving a young baby solid food may cause the baby to develop allergies to the food he is given. This is because the baby's intestinal tract is immature and unable to fully digest the food before it is absorbed into the bloodstream, causing the body to have an allergic reaction. So, how can you know if your baby is ready to begin solid food? Current research suggests the following guidelines:

- Between four and seven months an infant's digestive tract completes a maturation process know as "closure," preventing potentially allergenic substances from entering the bloodstream.
- Babies over the age of four months may have stopped exhibiting what is known as the tongue-thrust reflex. Babies younger than four to six months will spit out any foreign object, including food, as an instinctive defense against

choking. For this reason, parents used to feed their babies extremely diluted solid food in a bottle with an enlarged nipple, which doctors now agree was a mistake. If you do this, you are fighting a baby's natural tendency to start food at the right developmental stage.

- Some doctors recommend that parents wait to start solids until the baby weighs at least 13 to 15 pounds or has doubled her birth weight.

- The baby should be able to sit with some support and have control of his head and neck muscles. This will allow the baby to lean forward in anticipation of food he wants and to turn away if he is not hungry.

- It might sound basic, but a baby who is ready to begin eating solid food will often simply *seem* hungry. She might demand to be nursed more frequently than before, perhaps more than 10 times a day. She may be drinking 32 to 40 ounces of formula a day but still want more. She might begin waking in the middle of the night hungry, while she had been sleeping through with no problem for several weeks. Or, she may just be intensely interested in watching you eat.

There Really Is No Rush

Watch for signs of readiness for solid food in your baby, but also be aware that parents, particularly mothers, may be anxious to get the process started for reasons of their own. Maybe a nursing mom is going back to work and is worried that she won't be able to pump enough milk for the time she is away from the baby. Or, she may simply feel drained from exclusive nursing of a quickly growing baby and feels that solid food can give her a little break. Also, family members and friends who inquire about your baby's progress will frequently begin to ask whether or not your baby has started with solid food beginning at about three months and continuing throughout the rest of the first year. While this may be simple polite conversation on their part, you may unconsciously read it as

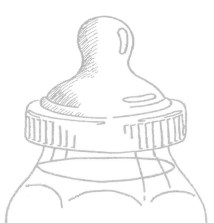

Failure to Thrive

Failure to thrive syndrome may be caused by a feeding difficulty or developmental problem, and is recognized as a significant dropoff in growth or weight gain in an infant under one year of age. Doctors use pediatric growth charts (see Chapter 7) in order to identify infants who may be at risk, and pay careful attention to children whose weight or length fall below the 5th percentile of babies at the same age.

pressure to begin with solids feedings as soon as possible. Not least, mothers will frequently begin to experience some boredom at around four or five months and will simply welcome any change in the routine. While none of these factors is particularly invalid as a reason for starting to feed your baby solid food, it is important that you take the time to recognize them when making a decision.

There's certainly no harm in introducing solid food at four months if your baby shows other signs of readiness. However, you should keep in mind that some parents wait until their baby is nine months or even close to the first birthday before they start with consistent feedings of solid food. A baby who eats later may show interest in food during the second half of her first year. Her parents can let her experiment as she wishes, but they don't actively encourage eating solid food. Often, these babies will continue to thrive on a diet composed primarily of breastmilk or formula, and when left to their own devices will begin to demand more solid food when the time is right. While this approach is somewhat unusual, it seems to work well for some babies, particularly if they are prone to allergies.

First Feedings of Solid Food

It's really quite easy to become excited about giving your baby his first feeding. It seems that for weeks you've been seeing that box of baby cereal on the supermarket shelf, and you finally bought it. In the week leading up to this first attempt, you've been thinking, "Today! No. Maybe tomorrow?" Well, finally, today *is* the day. Even firmly resolved, you may have some lingering questions. What if he's allergic to the food? What is the proper way to mix the cereal? What time should I feed him? Do I have the right kind if spoon? What if he doesn't like it?

Take heart. This first feeding should be fun for both you and your baby. If it's not, you should try again another day. Even with all the anticipation, there's really no rush. First feedings aren't about eating. They're mostly about practicing for eating, and as with any kind of practice, a lot can go wrong before you both get it right. Remember there are many aspects of this new experience for your baby to adjust to before she assimilates solids feedings into her daily routine. She has to learn about keeping the food inside her mouth *and* how to use her tongue to get it to the back of her mouth *and* how to swallow the food once it gets there. Not to mention the fact that she has to learn that this *is* food and not another plaything to explore with her mouth and hands. All babies must go through this process, and while some may get it on the first try, others may need weeks of attempts before catching on. Don't rush, and don't worry if success doesn't come instantly.

What Should I Serve?

Iron-fortified rice cereal is the most recommended first meal because it is easily absorbed by the body and is one of the least allergenic foods. There are many brands of precooked powdered dry cereal to choose from, including a few made from organic brown rice. This kind of cereal is easily prepared mixed with distilled water, formula, or breastmilk until the consistency is very watery, although it should still stick to the spoon. Most doctors recommend breastmilk or formula to mix with the cereal, because the familiar taste will help your baby adjust to eating solids. A few babies don't like the taste of rice cereal, so before you decide that she isn't ready, try another infant cereal (oat or barley, but not wheat), or try finely pureed banana or applesauce (homemade or store-bought are fine). Cereals fortified with iron are best, because babies are susceptible to anemia at this age.

Iron Deficiency Anemia at 9 to 15 Months

Most pediatricians will routinely check babies at around nine months for iron deficiency anemia by performing a simple hemoglobin test with a drop of blood from your baby's finger. It is not uncommon for a baby this age to have a low hemoglobin level, which indicates that the large iron stores that were present in his body at birth have

Feeding Your Baby in the Real World

"We started our kids late on solids. Partly because Mira was a big spitter-upper, and also, our doctor was not into pushing solids. His recommendation was that breastmilk be their primary food up to a year. He said that when they're grabbing food off your plate, they're basically ready to eat. Tano didn't really start on solids until he was 9 months and I nursed him until 13 months when it was still his primary source of food. Mira also had this spit up issue, so I wasn't eager to have her spitting up spinach. It was bad enough with the milk."

—Leah, mother of Mira and Tano

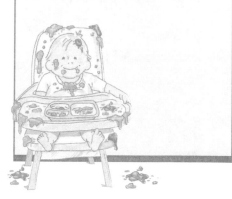

Other Questions You May Have

- *What temperature should the food be?* Be very careful not to serve food to your baby that is too hot, as it can easily burn the delicate tissues in her mouth and throat. Food that is room temperature or very slightly warmed is fine.

- *What kind of spoon is best for first feedings?* Your baby hasn't yet learned to open her mouth wide to receive her food, so the spoon you choose should be quite small with a shallow bowl. You may already have a small spoon that will work well, or you can buy a good baby-feeding spoon in most grocery stores or baby supply stores. Some babies prefer to get their first feedings from Mommy's or Daddy's familiar fingertip.

- *How long should meals last?* Generally, it is best to limit mealtimes to 20 minutes or less. Longer than this will probably try your patience and your baby's patience also.

finally been depleted after many months. Formula and breastmilk are both good sources for iron, and the iron in breastmilk is particularly well absorbed by the body. However, anemia may still occur, which is why it is a good idea to feed your baby iron-fortified infant cereals when he is starting on solid foods. Symptoms of iron deficiency anemia include irritability, poor appetite, slowed growth, listlessness, and a generally pale appearance.

Hooray, My Baby Loves Eating! What Now?

Congratulations! Your baby has started down the road to a lifetime of eating pleasure. In these early weeks, you should expect to feed your baby solid food about once a day. It's OK to skip a day here and there in the first two weeks, but you'll quickly notice that this little meal has replaced a feeding of breastmilk or formula, and your baby will start to rely on it. Your baby will also slowly increase the amount he eats at each meal, but let him decide on the proper amount. In a few weeks, you can introduce an evening meal as well, and then it isn't long before your baby will have breakfast, lunch, and dinner every day with nursings or formula between meals and before bedtime.

Changing Stools

Immediately after the introduction of solid food, you will notice a change in your baby's stools. This is only natural, but after months of predictable diapers, the change can be a shock. Most babies' stools will become much more firm, and the frequency of bowel movements will decrease. Many babies who regularly moved their bowels several times a day may suddenly skip a day or two. You shouldn't be concerned until three or four days go by. You should be aware that the early feedings of rice, banana, and applesauce are quite binding; in fact, these foods are also recommended for babies and children suffering from diarrhea. Fortunately, you can adjust your baby's diet to compensate for this by introducing pureed prunes and cereals such and oat and barley.

As more new foods are introduced, be prepared for even more dramatic diapers. Before you panic, remember the bright red substance you've encountered is almost certainly linked to the beets served at lunch. Other common foods that lead to surprising diapers are carrots, sweet potatoes, and the tiny seeds in kiwi fruit.

Food Allergies

Approximately 3 to 7 percent of adults and children experience allergies to food. You may already know that your baby is prone to food allergies. Perhaps food allergies run in one or both parents' families, or your baby may have even displayed allergic reactions to foods transmitted to her in her mother's milk. However, this is often not the case, and an allergic reaction will take parents by surprise.

If you suspect a food allergy, discuss it with your child's pediatrician. The doctor will probably recommend you keep close track of what your child is eating and its relationship to the onset of symptoms. Keep in mind that all of these symptoms can also indicate an illness like a virus or infection.

Signs of Food Allergies

- Runny nose, watery eyes, sneezing
- Diaper rash or rash around the anus
- Rash, especially on the face
- Swollen lips, hands, or feet
- Hives
- Sores in the mouth
- Headache
- Asthma, bronchitis, or recurrent ear infections
- Nausea, diarrhea, vomiting, or gas
- Poor weight gain
- Fatigue
- Unusual or irritable behavior

The Right Seating for First Feedings

Your baby may be ready for solid food but may not be quite up for the job of sitting in a high chair to receive it. This is a delicate moment of transition, and while it usually lasts only a few weeks, it's worth paying attention to. Here are some options:

- Hold your baby in your lap while you feed him.
- Prop your baby up in a nursing pillow that helps her to sit.
- Feed your baby in a bouncy chair.
- Feed your baby in a high chair, with small pillows to support him, or use a "high chair helper" designed for this purpose.

Food Allergy vs. Food Intolerance

Food allergy and food intolerance are not the same thing, which becomes very confusing since they frequently have similar symptoms, and also, both types of reactions are often grouped together under the name of food intolerance. A food allergy is essentially the immune system's reaction to a foreign substance, usually a protein, such as the protein found in peanuts. In food intolerance, on the other hand, a reaction is most commonly caused by the body's inability to digest a particular protein because it cannot make the enzyme needed for that purpose. If your digestive system does not produce the enzyme lactase, for example, you will not be able to digest the lactose protein found in cow's milk.

Many food allergies can be prevented by delaying the introduction of all solid foods until after four to six (or more) months, and the delayed introduction of potentially allergenic foods until after one year of age. This is because a baby's immature digestive tract is likely to allow undigested proteins to slip into the bloodstream, setting the stage for an allergic reaction. Many food allergies are dose related, meaning that you may be exposed to the allergen more than once or possibly many times before an immune reaction is elicited. However, once an allergic reaction has occurred, even a small subsequent exposure to the allergen will elicit a reaction. Some allergies lessen in severity or disappear over time, and others, especially those that cause severe or even life-threatening reactions, do not.

Most people never outgrow food intolerance, because the body will never have the capacity for producing the enzyme needed to digest the offending protein. However, they may be able to tolerate small quantities of the food in question. Also, it is possible to take a supplement containing the needed enzyme, which will aid in digestion. Many people take a lactase supplement, for example, so that they can drink milk or eat ice cream.

Cautious Introduction of New Foods

Doctors and dieticians recommend that you introduce new foods to your baby slowly in the early months. Wait three or four days after the introduction of one new food before trying another. You should also serve the new food several times, because one exposure may not be enough to elicit a reaction. Once you know that a food does not cause an allergic reaction, you can serve it with other foods that have also passed the test. If you suspect your baby is having a mild reaction to a certain food, you should notice the symptom(s) disappearing within 24 hours of discontinuing the food. Otherwise, call the pediatrician because your child may have a virus or infection.

Steps for Preventing Food Allergies

- Delayed introduction of solid food is one of the most important steps for preventing food allergies. Before the age of four to six months, your baby's digestive system is not mature enough to fully digest food before it enters the bloodstream. The body's inexperienced immune system is then likely to overreact to the foreign substance, increasing the risk for allergy.
- Studies show that breastfeeding your baby in the early months plays a significant role in the prevention of later food allergies.
- Do not feed your baby foods known to be highly allergenic to infants, such as cow's milk, nuts, and shellfish, before the age of 12 months. For a more complete list, see the allergens sidebar later in this chapter.
- Provide your baby with an ever-increasing variety of foods. Sometimes, "overdosing" on one particular food can cause an allergy.
- Avoid feeding your baby processed and packaged foods. Many additives and dyes in these foods are known allergens.

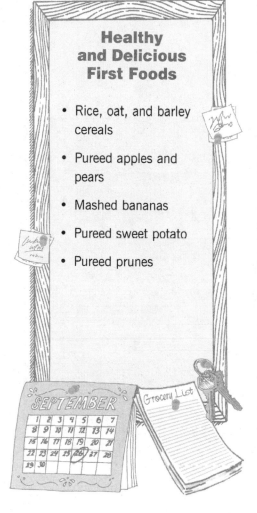

Healthy and Delicious First Foods

- Rice, oat, and barley cereals
- Pureed apples and pears
- Mashed bananas
- Pureed sweet potato
- Pureed prunes

Foods That Are Not Good for Babies

- Babies who are younger than one year should not eat honey, because it contains bacterial spores that may cause clostridium botulism. After a year, the flora in your baby's intestines will be able to defend her body against this threat.
- Any hard or chunky piece of food is a potential choking hazard. Among other things, avoid: popcorn, whole berries, candy, raw carrots and apples, seeds in fruit or olives, or any hard baked goods like pretzels. Also, peanut and other nut butters can cause choking if taken in large bites.
- Before your baby is eight months old you should not feed him home-prepared beets, carrots, green beans, squash, turnips, spinach, or collard greens. These vegetables may contain elevated amounts of nitrates absorbed through the soil in which they are grown. Commercially prepared baby foods that include these vegetables are fine, because they are screened for nitrate content. Also avoid any meats that contain nitrites, such as hot dogs, cured ham, bacon, and salami. Nitrites and nitrates can cause anemia in young babies.

Rare Severe Allergic Reactions

Rarely, a child will have a severe allergic reaction, often to nuts and especially peanuts. Children who are susceptible usually also have a family history of or themselves have asthma, eczema, or hay fever. About 20 percent of the time, a first-time severe reaction is life threatening and requires a trip to the emergency room. However, most first-time reactions are mild or moderate, increasing in severity unpredictably with each subsequent exposure. Symptoms of a severe allergic reaction include hives, wheezing, persistent coughing, a swollen tongue or throat, swollen hands or legs, and sometimes vomiting or diarrhea. The reaction will usually occur in one of two ways: either the food will cause swelling to the vocal cords as it is

Food Introduction Timeline

Age	Foods to Try	Foods to Try With Caution
4–6 months	Fortified rice, barley, or oat infant cereal; mashed bananas; apple or pear sauce; pureed prunes; mashed sweet potatoes	Some finger foods like soft pieces of cooked fruit or easily dissolved unsweetened breakfast cereals, wheat products, egg yolks
6–9 months	All finely pureed: carrots, peas, green beans, asparagus, summer and winter squash, zucchini, broccoli, peaches, prunes, apricots and plums	Legumes, tomatoes, citrus fruits and juices; more finger foods like whole grain pasta, bread, teething biscuits, crackers, plain yogurt, and cottage cheese
9–12 months	Gradually more textured: brown rice, couscous, millet, brussels sprouts, spinach, kale, rhubarb, rutabaga, turnips, beets, kiwi, avocado, pineapple, persimmons, cultured dairy products (not fluid cow's milk), mild cheeses, lamb, veal, tuna, chicken, and turkey	Tahini and almond or peanut butter and finely ground nuts and seeds, whole eggs, whole cow's milk, berries, shellfish
12–18 months	More fully prepared entrees like stews, rice, and pasta dishes; cabbage, cauliflower, tomatoes, cucumbers, artichokes, mushrooms, onions, eggplant, tofu, lentils, chickpeas, lima beans, dried peas and beans; cantaloupe, watermelon, papaya, figs, cherries, citrus fruits, white-fleshed fish, pork. It is now OK to give your baby honey.	

swallowed (laryngospasm), or the food is swallowed and anaphylactic shock occurs any time within two hours. In the emergency room, a doctor will administer an injection of epinephrine to control a severe reaction. Parents who know that their child has a potentially life-threatening allergy of this nature may carry with them at all times a kit with injectable epinephrine prescribed by a doctor, and they are often instructed to administer an injection if they even suspect the child has ingested the allergen. To guard against potential sensitization to peanuts and nuts, it is best not to allow your baby to be exposed to them before 12 months, especially if your baby may be prone to other allergies, asthma, or eczema.

Dealing with Severe Allergies

If your child has a severe allergy of this nature, you can never be too cautious about preventing exposure to the allergen. Unlike other allergies, such as an infant's allergy to cow's milk, children do not grow out of life-threatening food allergies, and there is no method for treating or "desensitizing" an allergenic person with these types of allergies. Sometimes, simply touching the allergenic food is enough to elicit a reaction. Carefully read all food labels, and be aware of the sorts of food that may contain the allergen. For example, nuts are used in baked goods and many ethnic cuisines. Additionally, nut oils and other nut byproducts are an ingredient in hundreds of foods. Tell anyone who might serve food to your child about his allergy; from school administrators to caregivers to the host of a birthday party to the waitress at a restaurant. Keep in mind that avoiding allergens may be particularly difficult when you are eating out, because the waitstaff may not know all of the ingredients in a dish, or

may not know that peanut oil, for example, is just as harmful as peanuts themselves. Also, recipes can frequently change on a daily basis, depending on the ingredients available to the chef. (Your best bet is to stress the severity of the allergy and be vigilant about reminding people who may already know about it.) Given all of these uncertainties, you may simply want to bring food from home when eating out.

Sulfite Allergies

The FDA estimates that about 1 percent of the population has a sensitivity to sulfites, which are widely used as an additive to fresh and dried fruits and vegetables, wine and shellfish, as a bleach for food starch, and as a dough conditioner. They are also used as a preservative in some drugs. Allergic reaction can range from hives, asthmalike symptoms, diarrhea, and nausea to, less commonly, loss of consciousness and anaphylactic shock. Five percent of asthma sufferers are sensitive to sulfites. In extremely rare cases, death has occurred. For a person who is sensitive to sulfites, avoidance can be very difficult because they are so widely used. The FDA regulates sulfites in the following ways:

1. Their use is prohibited in fruits and vegetables that are usually eaten raw.
2. Sulfites must be listed as an ingredient in packaged goods when they are present in quantities greater than 10 parts per million, or if they are used in any quantity as part of processing.

If you suspect your child is suffering from allergies to sulfites, contact his pediatrician, who may recommend seeing an allergist.

Potential Allergens for Babies and Young Children

If your child is prone to food allergies, you may wish to avoid all of these ingredients until after 12 months of age. If you have no family history of allergies, you can go ahead and cautiously introduce the ingredients that only sometimes cause allergies and cultured dairy products like yogurt and cottage cheese after about nine months.

Reading Ingredient Labels for a Child with Allergies

Once you discover that your child has a food allergy, you will need to become familiar with other names commonly used for the allergen on food labels. Depending on the severity of the allergic reaction, you may need to be vigilant about reading every single label. If you notice that a food you regularly buy is suddenly "new and improved," check the label again. Common allergens, and their less common names, include:

- Cow's milk dairy products: whey, casein, sodium caseinate, lactalbumin
- Egg white: albumin, lactalbumin
- Wheat: durum, semolina, farina
- Corn: may be a derivative of dextrose or glucose
- Soy: hydrolyzed vegetable protein

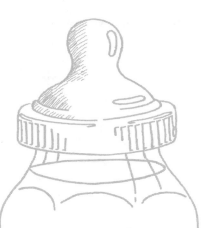

Growing Out of Allergies

If your baby experienced a mild allergic reaction to a certain food before the age of 12 months, you can usually safely reintroduce this food at one to three years. Give your child a moderate amount of the food early in the day, for several days in a row, to be sure that no reaction will occur. If the initial allergic reaction was moderate or severe you should consult your baby's pediatrician before reintroducing the allergen. If your child has a severe allergy, especially to nuts, he will never grow out of the allergy, and should never be exposed to the allergen.

Foods That *Frequently* Cause Allergies in Young Babies

- Beans and legumes, including soybeans and soy products
- Berries
- Buckwheat
- Chocolate
- Cinnamon
- Citrus fruits
- Coconut
- Corn
- Cow's milk and dairy products
- Egg whites
- Food additives like monosodium glutamate (MSB), sulfites, benzoates, and tartrazine
- Mustard
- Peanuts and tree nuts
- Peas
- Pork
- Shellfish
- Tomatoes
- Wheat
- Yeast

Foods That *Sometimes* Cause Allergies in Young Babies

- Cabbage
- Hormone residues in milk, beef, and chicken
- Mango
- Melon
- Mushrooms
- Onion
- Papaya
- Pesticide residues
- Rye
- Strawberries

CHAPTER FIVE

Shopping and Cooking

Commercial Baby Food

Commercial baby food (unlike most other kinds of processed food) has improved in quality immensely over the past few years. Strict governmental and industry standards for safety and hygiene practically ensure the safety of the commercial food you give your baby. Many parents choose to feed their young babies food from a jar, and there is nothing wrong with that. Parents should be sure, however, that the commercial food does not contain any unwanted ingredients. Most food for very small babies has very pure ingredients, usually just the fruit or vegetable and water. Some brands even use organic fruits and vegetables or whole grains like brown rice. However, some brands still use tapioca as a filler, and salt or sugar to make the food more palatable to parents, who may unknowingly buy baby food more for its taste than its ingredients. Be especially careful to read the labels for food designed for older babies. It is not uncommon for these foods to contain sugar, fillers, and hydrogenated or partially hydrogenated oils.

Reasons to Consider Homemade Baby Food

- Homemade baby food is much less expensive. Most of the cost of commercial food is actually in the packaging, and often the first ingredient is water. Why pay for that?
- You can have more control over the way baby food is prepared, using all organic ingredients and whole grains, for example.
- Feeding your baby homemade food helps integrate his meals into meal preparation for the rest of the family, setting the stage for later social development.
- Homemade baby food tastes better.
- Methods for producing commercial baby foods can destroy important nutrients, particularly thiamin and vitamin C.

Methods for Preparing Homemade Baby Food

There are many ways to prepare your baby's food. Pureeing the food in a food processor or blender and fork-mashing cooked food for older babies are probably the most common methods. I recommend purchasing a baby-food mill, which usually costs between $10 and $15 and is available at most good baby supply stores.

Standard full-size food mills, available at good kitchen supply stores, work well also. Using a food grinder is a very convenient way to prepare fresh food for your baby. I used mine as many as three times a day at one point and was still using it almost every day months after my baby had moved on to finger foods and table foods. The food grinder was easy to use and clean, and it allowed me to make nutritious, fresh food for my baby with a minimum of planning or preparation. On the other hand, I've had several friends say that their baby-food grinder saw the most use as a sand toy. I suppose this must mean that the tools you use will most likely reflect your own style of food preparation, which may be hard to predict. For batch production of baby food, a blender or food processor is also very convenient, as are mini–food processors.

When feeding my own baby, Max, I chose to give him mostly jarred organic food at first. Soon though, the limited number of jarred flavors began to seem boring to me and (I assumed) to him, so I switched to making all homemade food. My own program for making homemade baby food was loose and simple. When Max was small, I made sure to have small quantities of one or two of the following precooked ingredients in the fridge: brown rice, pasta, oats, barley, potatoes, sweet potatoes, squash, beans, lentils, or hard-cooked eggs. For each meal, I would usually steam some fresh or frozen organic vegetables until they were soft and mix them in the grinder with one or two precooked grains, legumes, or hard-cooked eggs. The hot food and cold food mixed together usually came out to be about the right temperature. I added water, breastmilk, formula, yogurt, or juice if the food was too dry, and powdered rice cereal or powdered formula if the food was too mushy. Sometimes I would grind up something the rest of the family was eating, like lentil soup

The Baby-Food Mill

There is only one brand of baby-food grinder that I am aware of, The Happy Baby Food Grinder. You can contact the manufacturer, Omron Healthcare Inc., at (800) 634-4350, or visit their Web site at *www.omron.com*.

or stir-fried vegetables, but only if the food wasn't too highly seasoned, and I would usually mix it with another plain ingredient.

As Max graduated to finger foods, and later to eating foods with a spoon and fork, I still used my food grinder to mix together ingredients as part of his meal. For example, my husband makes a fantastic Bolognese meat sauce, which was a particular favorite for Max. Sometimes, I would make pasta for the baby and toss it with the Bolognese sauce ground up and mixed with other ingredients like cooked sweet potatoes, corn, or broccoli. This way, Max would get extra nutrition from the vegetables, and the rich, seasoned sauce would make the meal enticing for his developing palate. Other times, I would use the grinder to make a small batch of apple or pear sauce, which he absolutely loved. I would cook cubed apples or pears, sometimes mixed with in-season peaches or dried fruit, in boiling water for about 15 minutes or until they were soft. Then, I would grind this up and serve it with oatmeal or yogurt or just plain. Yum!

For quick heating of small portions of baby food, you can't beat a microwave oven. However, you should be very careful to stir the food thoroughly after heating and to carefully test it, making sure it is not too warm. If your baby prefers his food warm (not all babies do), it should be warmed to only slightly above room temperature so that it doesn't burn his sensitive mouth. If you accidentally make something too warm, you can pop it in the freezer for a few minutes until it cools down. If you don't have a microwave (I didn't), you can use a small saucepan or butter warmer to heat portions on the stove. I used my little saucepan for everything from tiny portions of oatmeal to boiling pasta.

Getting Organized

There's a lot to keep track of when you make your own baby food. Keeping it all in one place can make things a little easier. We found it helpful to set aside a corner of our kitchen counter, where we kept a small tub to hold all the essentials.

- Baby-food mill
- Baby-food bowl and spoons

- Small strainer
- Small rubber spatula
- Masking tape and marker for labeling food

Syrup of Ipecac

It is very wise to keep a bottle of syrup of ipecac (available at all pharmacies) in your home once your baby learns to stand or crawl. Very often, operators at a poison control center will suggest you give a dose to a child (or adult for that matter) that has ingested a poisonous substance in order to induce vomiting. However, it is sometimes even more dangerous to give syrup of ipecac, depending on the type of poison that has been ingested, so it should never be administered without medical advice. I suggest you keep two bottles handy but out of reach of your child, one at home and another for outings and travel. Tape a piece of paper to the bottle with the phone number for the poison control center and your baby's doctor, and instructions to only use it under instruction from a poison control center or doctor.

Batch Production of Homemade Baby Food

Some parents find it more convenient to make larger batches of pureed food to freeze and serve at a later date. This is usually accomplished by steaming fruits and vegetables until they are very soft and pureeing them in a blender, food mill, or food processor. Freezing the food in ice cube trays and then transferring the frozen food to a storage bag or container is a popular way to easily use the food, especially if you have a microwave oven for quick defrosting. Parents who use this method will defrost three or four cubes of several varieties of pureed foods for each meal. As your baby gets older and her appetite increases, you can graduate to freezing larger portions or freezing complete prepared entrees such as casseroles.

Batch Freezing Tips

- Label and date everything you store in the freezer. Most foods will keep frozen for at least two months. If you're thinking of making more baby food than you'll use in two months, keep in mind that your baby may have moved on to finger foods by the time you are ready to use it.
- Try to get any excess air out of a container to prevent freezer burn. Suck excess air out of a storage bag with a straw. Lay a sheet of plastic wrap over food that doesn't quite fill a container. Note, though, that food expands when it freezes. Don't overfill the container.
- Save on plastic containers for freezing by transferring food to heavy-duty plastic storage bags once it is frozen. Just dip the frozen container in hot water so that the food slides out for transfer.
- Freeze cooked, pureed food in ice cube trays. Transfer to a heavy-duty storage bag or larger storage container after the food cubes are frozen.
- Store single portions of frozen food in a zipped sandwich bag, and keep these together in a heavy-duty bag or larger storage container.
- Freeze whole berries or fruit chunks spread out (not touching) on a small sheet pan. Once the fruit is frozen, you can transfer it to a heavy-duty storage bag or larger storage container.
- Freeze yellow fruit, which tends to discolor when exposed to oxygen, in orange juice instead of water.
- Very small plastic containers are perfect for baby-sized portions.

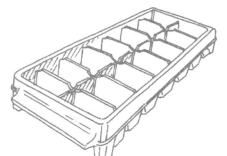

First and Foremost: Choking

As your baby begins eating solid foods, you'll want to make sure you're aware of what to do if he starts choking. The American Red Cross offers life-saving first aid classes for parents and caregivers of infants. Each local chapter of the Red Cross is listed in the phone book, and class schedules are available on request. I highly recommend that all parents take an infant CPR/first aid class so that you can be prepared if the unthinkable should happen. Choking in particular is a very serious concern, accounting for many preventable deaths and injuries in babies and small children each year.

It can be easy to mistake choking for gagging, which is much more common, especially as a young baby first becomes accustomed to swallowing solid food. Gagging is caused by food, liquids, or even teething toys that fall to the back of the tongue and trigger a gagging reflex without obstructing the windpipe. Choking is much more serious and is signaled by extreme difficulty breathing, perhaps accompanied by a high-pitched crowing sound, the inability to cough an object out of the throat, or, worse, the inability to breath at all, resulting in the baby turning blue, starting at the lips. Babies will frequently display the "classic" signs of a choking victim (hands to the throat or limbs flailing), or they may simply begin to cry without sound. Time is the most important factor in saving the life of a choking victim, so it is very important that babies and children be closely supervised while they are eating. Also, allowing a child to roam around the house or playground while they are eating is more likely to invite a choking incident than if your child is seated. Of course, eliminating foods such as popcorn, jelly beans, nuts, etcetera will also reduce the risk of choking.

In any case of choking, it is important to call for emergency medical help immediately. Have someone else make the call, or bring the baby to the phone after the first attempt to dislodge the obstructing object. Even after a choking incident has passed, it is important to observe the child carefully for unusual behavior or difficulty breathing and be prepared to seek medical help because it is possible that an object may be lodged in the lower respiratory tract.

CPR for Babies Under a Year Old

If your baby is younger than one year old, the first step is to hold him face down along your forearm, with his chin cradled in your hand. His head should be lower than his body at about a 60-

---

Defrosting Baby Food in the Microwave

Each microwave oven is slightly different, but for most models, one-half cup of pureed food will defrost completely after two minutes on the medium setting. Use defrosted food the same day, or store in the refrigerator immediately for use the next day.

SEPTEMBER

Grocery List

degree angle. Brace your arm against your thigh for support. Or, if the baby is too large to hold in this manner, lay him across your lap with his head lower than his trunk. With the heel of your free hand, administer five quick and forceful blows between the baby's shoulder blades. Hopefully, the object will be dislodged and the baby will begin to cough and/or cry and breathe freely. If not, roll him over to lie face up on your other arm, cradling his head in your hand, and administer five consecutive chest thrusts. Position two or three fingers half way between, and one finger width below, an imaginary line connecting his nipples, being careful not to press below the end of the baby's sternum. Each chest thrust should compress the sternum to a depth of ½ to one inch. If the object is still not dislodged repeat this procedure again, beginning with five back blows followed by five chest thrusts.

If the baby goes limp or loses consciousness, or if several series of back blows and chest thrusts have not dislodged the object, place the baby face up on the floor or, better, on a table. Look in his mouth, holding his tongue with your thumb. If you can see the object, carefully attempt to sweep it out using your pinkie. Do not use a pincer grasp to try and remove the object as this may force it further back in the throat. If you cannot see an obstruction, and if the baby is not conscious or breathing, tilt his head back and lift his chin to clear the airway. Place your mouth over the baby's mouth and nose and, making a tight seal with your lips, give a puff of air from your mouth (not with the force of your lungs as you would with an adult). If the breath goes in or if you can see the baby's chest rise, continue to give one breath every three seconds until the baby is breathing on his own or until emergency help arrives. If the breath does not go in, repeat the sequence, beginning with five back blows, followed by five chest thrusts, followed by a check in the mouth for an obstruction, followed by mouth-to-mouth breathing. Do not give up, because the baby's muscles will relax as time passes, making it more likely that you will be able to dislodge the object.

CPR for Babies One Year and Older

If your baby is older than one year and able to stand, it is safe to administer the Heimlich maneuver. If she is conscious, kneel behind her and wrap your arms around her waist. Place your fist against her stomach just above her navel, but well below her ribcage and sternum. Grasp your fist with the other hand and administer six to ten inward and upward thrusts. If the child is unconscious, place her face up on the floor and kneel at her side (do not straddle the baby). Place the heel of one hand midway between her navel and sternum, and place the other hand on top of it, administering six to ten quick inward upward thrusts. The smaller the child, the gentler this maneuver should be. If, after a few attempts, the child does not begin to cough, cry, or spit the object out, proceed with a check in the mouth for the object as above. If you are not able to see the object and sweep it out, administer mouth to mouth breathing as above, pinching her nose closed between two fingers and forming a tight seal around her mouth with your lips. Repeat this entire procedure until the baby is breathing on her own or until emergency help arrives.

How to Prepare Some Basic Foods

Some of us grow up cooking and feel as comfortable in the kitchen as in the living room. Many people, including myself, have had to simply figure out basic cooking techniques as we go along. Others have never learned how to cook many basic foods and feel completely lost unless cooking involves picking up the phone to order pizza or taking the dinner out of the box and popping it in the microwave. If you fall into this last category, or if you still feel as if you are trying to figure things out, don't worry. Every good (or even adequate) cook has to start somewhere, and having a baby to feed is as good a reason to start as any.

Firm Fruits and Vegetables

Boiling firm fruits and vegetables produces the quickest result. However, many nutrients are then lost in the cooking water. If you can steam firmer fruits and vegetables, it is better, but it may take some time before the food is soft enough (fork tender) for pureeing. A good compromise is to boil the fruit or vegetable in as little water as possible and then hold the water aside when you drain out the food. You can incorporate some or all of this water, and its nutrients into the pureed food by stirring it in after the food is milled or adding it while the food is being pureed in the food processor. Add the water carefully so that you don't end up with a mixture that is too soupy. Always boil or steam over medium heat in a covered saucepan, and check about halfway through the cooking to make sure the water has not been boiled away, which will scorch your pan and burn the food. Carrots and beets should be peeled before cooking. Potatoes can be baked or boiled.

Not-So-Firm Vegetables

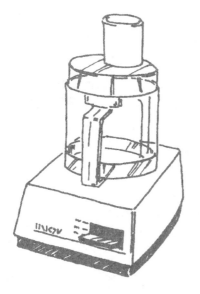

These vegetables can almost always be steamed in a very short period of time. Use a tightly covered saucepan with an insert for steaming. You can also buy special plastic cooking dishes that will enable you to steam food in the microwave oven, which some people find very convenient for making baby food. Again, the food should be fork tender before you puree or grind it for baby food. When cooking tomatoes you may want to skin them and remove the seeds. This is accomplished by first boiling a medium pot of water. With a small knife, make a shallow score in the shape of a small X in the skin of the tomato on both the stem end and at the bottom. Using tongs, place the tomatoes in the boiling water and remove the pan from the heat. Leave the tomatoes in the water for 30 seconds and then remove them. With a small paring knife, you should be able to easily remove the skin. To remove the seeds, cut the tomato in half horizontally, and squeeze out the seeds. You may have to dig a few seeds out with your fingers. Tomatoes prepared in this way are ready to be pureed as is.

Dried Fruits

You may want to soak dried fruit for 30 minutes or an hour (longer is fine also) before you cook it; this will cut down on the time it takes to cook. Simmer the fruit in a small amount of water or in its soaking water for 5 to 20 minutes. The drier the fruit, the longer it will take to cook. Smaller pieces of fruit will cook faster than larger pieces. Again, check partway through cooking to make sure the water has not boiled away. The fruit will be ready for milling or pureeing when it is swollen and plump.

Root Vegetables

Preheat the oven to 425 degrees. Scrub the vegetables under cold running water to remove any excess dirt. With a thin-bladed knife, carving fork, or ice pick, punch several deep holes in the vegetables. Put the vegetables directly on the oven rack and place the rack in the center of the oven. For yams and sweet potatoes, you may want to put a sheet pan on the rack below to catch any drippings. The vegetables will require different cooking times, depending on how large they are, but will usually be done within an hour to an hour and a half, sometimes a little longer. They are done when you can easily slip a pointy knife deep into the interior. When choosing root vegetables at the market, pick ones that are approximately the same size so they will cook in the same amount of time.

Winter Squash

Preheat the oven to 350 degrees. Scrub the squash and cut it in half lengthwise with a heavy chef's knife or butcher knife (be careful). Scoop out the seeds and the pulp.

Put about a tablespoon of butter in the hollow of each half of the squash. You can also add a little dried herb seasoning like oregano or ground rosemary. Bake on a sheet pan in the center of the oven for about one hour, or until tender. A larger squash will take longer to cook than a smaller one. To puree, cut the squash in chunks and remove the skin.

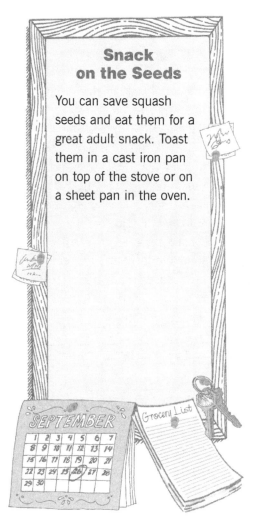

Snack on the Seeds

You can save squash seeds and eat them for a great adult snack. Toast them in a cast iron pan on top of the stove or on a sheet pan in the oven.

Rice

Most varieties of rice will cook well with a ratio of about twice as much water to rice in a small to medium covered saucepan. Use cold water, and put the rice over a high heat at first, watching it closely until the water begins to boil. As soon as the water is boiling, turn the heat down fairly low, so that the water is just simmering. Don't remove the lid. Let the rice steam until all of the water is absorbed. This takes 15 to 20 minutes for white rice, but may take as long as 45 minutes or an hour for brown rice. When you think the rice is almost done, tilt the pan to see if any water is remaining. If it is gone, you can turn off the heat and serve the rice immediately, although it is better to let the rice sit covered for a few more minutes to continue steaming. Wild rice can be boiled in a larger amount of water until the grains burst open to reveal the white inside. You can then drain the rice and serve.

Pasta

To cook pasta properly, you will need to bring a medium or large pot of water to a rolling boil. When the water is boiling, add a small amount of salt. Do not add olive oil to your pasta water. Pour in the dried pasta and cook it in the boiling water for seven to fifteen minutes. Larger cuts of pasta like penne or linguine will cook more slowly than small cuts like orzo or spaghettini. To test if the pasta is done, remove a piece and taste it. Remember that the pasta will continue to cook for a few minutes even after the water is drained off. When cooking dried pasta for a baby, you should make sure that it is cooked very thoroughly so that it is soft (most adults would think this is overdone). When cooking fresh pasta or filled pasta like raviolis, bring the water to a boil, but turn the heat down to medium just before you put the pasta in. Fresh pasta will cook much more quickly than dried pasta (about four to seven minutes). Pasta cooking water has a great deal of starch in it. If you will be making a simple sauce like olive oil with grated cheese

Comparing Brown and White Rice

Although brown rice takes longer to cook, it's worth it for the nutritional benefits. White rice is processed to remove the outer hull, which contains many of the most nutritious portions of the grain. Brown rice has much more protein, fiber, calcium, zinc, and vitamins B and E than white rice. Although most Americans are not accustomed to its chewy texture and nutty flavor, many people prefer brown rice, especially children who grew up with it.

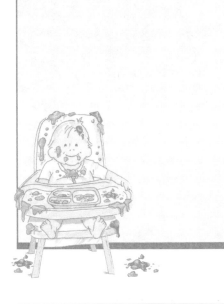

or sautéed greens, you can use a little of the pasta water to give the finished dish body and flavor.

Oatmeal

Buy rolled oats instead of steel cut oats for making oatmeal for your baby. Rolled oats will cook more quickly, are less chewy, and can be eaten easily by small babies. Mill the oatmeal for a baby who is still eating mostly pureed food. Use three-quarters cup of cold water to a half-cup of oats with a dash of salt and bring to a boil over medium heat in a small saucepan on top of the stove. Stir, remove from the heat, and cover with a tight lid; wait about five minutes for the oatmeal to steam before serving. You can also cook oatmeal in the microwave for about two and a half minutes on high. Instant oatmeal is slightly easier to prepare (just add boiling water), but it may include ingredients that are not good for babies, like preservatives or sugar.

You can serve oatmeal with milk, soy or rice beverage, molasses, applesauce, wheat germ, bananas, yogurt, sweet cream, butter, or many other tasty additions. I always like to pour in a little maple syrup. Oatmeal is a fabulous breakfast for a toddler, because it is warm and nutritious and very, very easy to prepare.

Dried Beans

You can cook dried beans simply in a large pot of boiling water, which takes longer, but can be accomplished in one step. Bring six cups of water to a boil in a heavy kettle and add one cup of beans. Cook for two to three hours at a low boil until tender, stirring occasionally and watching to make sure the water does not boil away.

Another method involves adding one cup of beans to four cups of boiling water. Once the water has returned to a boil, let it cook for two minutes and remove from the heat. Let stand for one hour and then drain. Bring four cups of fresh water to a boil and add the soaked beans. Cook for one to two hours at a low boil until

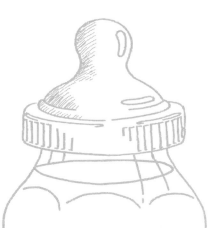

Whole Wheat or Enriched Pasta?

Although enriched pasta has added folic acid and some vitamins and minerals, this is merely an incomplete attempt to replace nutrients that have been stripped from the pasta flour in processing. Whole wheat pasta, on the other hand, has more protein, fiber, folic acid, and minerals such as zinc, iron, and chromium. In general, babies love pasta. If they always have whole wheat, they will be given an important nutritional boost.

tender, stirring occasionally and watching to make sure the water does not boil away.

The most common method for cooking beans involves soaking them overnight in cold water. Start with one cup of beans and cover them in water. There should be two to three inches between the beans and the surface of the water to allow for expansion. The next day, drain the beans and add them to four cups of rapidly boiling water. The beans should cook in about a half an hour. Stir occasionally.

Always wash beans in cold water before soaking or cooking, and sort through them carefully to remove any small stones that may be mixed with them. Presoaked beans tend to be more tender and flavorful than beans cooked in one batch. They also cause less gas and are more easily digestible. One cup of dried beans will make about three cups of cooked beans.

Dried Lentils

Lentils do not need to be soaked before cooking. Add one cup of lentils to three cups of rapidly boiling water. Let the water return to a boil before reducing the heat to a simmer. Cover and cook for 40 minutes to an hour, stirring occasionally and watching to make sure the water does not boil away. Cooked lentils will be tender, but separate. They will begin to break down and meld together if you cook them longer, as you would for lentil soup. One cup dried lentils makes about two cups cooked.

Eggs

In truth, there are literally thousands of ways to prepare eggs, but I will just cover the three simplest: hard-boiled, soft-boiled, and plain scrambled eggs, which are all great food for babies. However, because egg whites are a common allergen, you should serve only the egg yolks until your baby is over a year old. Cooking times given for hard- and soft-boiled eggs assume that you have just taken the eggs out of the refrigerator. If the eggs are at room temperature, you should cook them about two minutes less. For hard- and soft-boiled eggs bring a saucepan filled with water to a boil over medium heat. Before adding the eggs, reduce the heat to a simmer. For hard-boiled eggs, cook at a simmer for about 17 minutes. Put the eggs in cold water when they're done to stop the cooking and keep the yolks from discoloring. You can serve them as soon as they are cool enough to peel, or keep them in the refrigerator as a handy snack. For soft-boiled eggs, cook for five to six minutes at a simmer. Everyone likes the yolk cooked to a different consistency, so you may need to experiment with different cooking times before you get it just right. When making scrambled eggs for my baby, I kept things as simple as possible. I would scramble the egg thoroughly in a small bowl (no milk or any other seasoning), and would pour the egg out onto a hot, dry nonstick skillet (medium heat). When the egg had cooked on one side, I flipped it like a pancake or a fried egg to cook the other side. I would then cut the cooked egg in bite-size pieces and toss it in the freezer for a minute to cool down. Simple.

Great Combos for Homemade Baby Food (Six Months to One Year)

You can cook and puree these foods ahead of time and mix a few small portions together at mealtime. Or, you can cook some items at mealtime, and mix with cold leftovers and defrosted food cubes. Bananas and avocado and egg yolk can be mashed with a fork when they are needed. Not only are these combinations proven baby pleasers, they will provide your little one with a variety of foods for great nutrition: *grains* for protein, fiber, folic acid, iron, zinc and B vitamins; *fruits* for fiber, vitamins C, A, and E and potassium; *legumes* for protein, fiber, folic acid, and iron; *veggies* for a wide variety of vitamins and minerals; and *eggs* and *poultry* for protein, vitamin A, B vitamins, and minerals.

- Cooked oats with prunes and bananas
- Sweet potatoes and peas
- Corn and winter squash

- Beets and cottage cheese
- Peaches and banana
- Yogurt with carrots and peas
- Brown rice with yogurt and sweet potatoes
- Zucchini and lentils with carrots
- Avocado with brussels sprouts and chicken
- Kiwi with banana and yogurt
- Cooked egg yolk with broccoli and yogurt
- Applesauce with beets
- Chick peas with yogurt and summer squash
- Asparagus with cottage cheese and carrots

Easy Foods for Babies Older than One Year

Considering that many babies begin to refuse food as a matter of course as they get older, it doesn't pay to spend a lot of time on preparation. Focus instead on providing healthy foods your toddler is likely to enjoy, slipping in more variety whenever possible. Some babies mostly prefer finger foods, and others will take the greatest pleasure from spoonable entrees. When serving finger foods, make sure they do not present a choking hazard. If the dish is best eaten with a spoon, try to make the consistency sticky. Slurpy items make great "dippy" sauces.

- Hummus and other bean-based purees
- Muffins and quick breads
- Oatmeal and whole grain hot cereals
- Yogurt and cottage cheese with fresh fruit or avocado
- Fruit smoothies
- Taboule
- Mashed potatoes
- Scrambled eggs
- Avocado in chunks or mashed
- Meat loaf or meatballs
- Couscous cooked in chicken stock with pureed beans

Food Safety Tips: Preventing Food-Borne Illness

- Most food-borne illness is spread by people's hands. Wash your and your baby's hands with soap and warm water before handling food and frequently during meal preparations, especially when handling raw meat.
- Thoroughly clean all countertops and cutting boards before use. Regularly disinfect kitchen surfaces (including the sink and faucets) with a dilute mixture of chlorine bleach and water (one-quarter capful to two quarts of cold water).
- Harmful bacteria multiply at temperatures between 40 and 140 degrees Fahrenheit. Don't allow prepared foods to sit at room temperature for longer than a few minutes. Warm and serve your baby's food immediately. Before storing hot cooked food, place it uncovered in a shallow dish or container in the refrigerator to cool as quickly as possible. By the same token, use the quickest method possible to thaw baby food, or thaw in the refrigerator overnight.
- Don't heat baby food more than once after it has been refrigerated or frozen.
- If you feed your baby directly from the jar, throw away any unused portion, because germs on the spoon can spoil the food. Don't store opened jarred baby food for longer than two or three days before serving. Keep a marker in the kitchen to label and date open baby food jars, homemade portions, and frozen batches.
- Be especially careful when handling raw poultry, meat, or fish. Wash your hands with soap and hot water, and thoroughly clean any kitchen surfaces that have come into contact with raw poultry, meat, or fish.
- Raw fruits and vegetables can also be a source of harmful bacteria (and contaminants if not organic). Soak fresh produce for 5 to 10 seconds in a dilute solution of water and dish detergent (1 teaspoon per gallon), and then rinse with lukewarm water. Firmer produce can be scrubbed while soaking with a vegetable brush, and then rinsed. Peeling or shucking most other fruits and vegetables (like corn, cucumbers, bananas, and the like) is sufficient for removing most residues.

- Pasta with pureed squash and zucchini
- Brown rice with tomato sauce cooked with tiny chunks of vegetables
- Chunks of turkey or chicken breast
- Chunks of tofu
- Macaroni and cheese
- Whole grain pancakes and waffles
- Peanut butter and mashed sweet potato sandwiches
- Cubes of mild cheese
- Tuna fish salad
- Small pieces of fruit: kiwi, banana, peaches, melon, citrus, apple, pear, pineapple, or peeled or quartered seedless grapes.

Kitchen Safety Tips for Babies and Toddlers

- Never let your toddler or young child operate the stove. Give your child another task to do like shucking corn, snapping string beans, stirring mixtures, or tearing lettuce while you do what's necessary at the stove.
- Never hold your baby while trying to juggle hot pans, hot coffee or tea, or sharp knives.
- Turn handles to face the back of the stove and use the back burners to prevent scalding accidents.
- Hot food can easily scald the inside of your baby's mouth. Baby food and formula or milk should always be warmed only slightly above room temperature. Babies' mouths are much more sensitive to heat than those of adults. If you heat in a microwave, mix the food thoroughly and test it carefully. Although commonly practiced, heating your baby's bottle in a microwave is not recommended. If you do this, be sure to mix the contents thoroughly to dissipate scalding hot spots. Terrible internal burns can occur from microwave-heated bottles.

- Don't allow electrical cords to dangle from countertop appliances. Toddlers can use them to pull the appliance down on their heads.
- Don't use tablecloths and placemats until your child is older. Toddlers can pull them down, along with any objects on the table.
- Keep a fire extinguisher in the kitchen (and in two or three other locations in the house). Know what to do in case of a grease fire.
- Keep all sharp objects out of your baby's reach, including wax paper, cling wrap, or foil boxes with a cutting blade built into the box.
- Don't allow too many distractions in the kitchen. Keep the dog and cat outside and eliminate toys on the floor, especially in a small kitchen. You'll need a clear pathway to carry boiling pots, hot pans, and sharp knives.
- Remember it's OK if things get messy. If having your child in the kitchen while you cook will distract you too much, consider another option. Accidents are more likely to happen when you are under stress.
- Never store kitchen chemicals or cleaning products within reach of your baby. Never, ever store chemicals in recycled food containers.
- Install latches on the kitchen cabinets and drawers that contain sharp objects and poisonous chemicals. Keep several cabinets and drawers accessible to your baby, especially those that contain fun, safe objects like pots and pans, plastic containers, and wooden utensils. Your baby will have a ball exploring these cabinets, pulling the objects out and putting them back in, over and over again.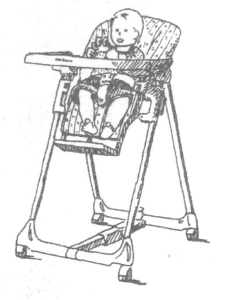
- Keep the phone number for the local poison control center by each telephone in your house. Have a bottle of syrup of ipecac available in case you are instructed to use it by a health professional. Note that the most common cause of childhood poisoning in the United States is iron poisoning, usually from vitamin tablets.
- As your baby grows, keep in mind that her reach with grow along with her. She will also quickly learn how to move and use a stepstool (or anything else she can move and step on) to

gain access to counters and tables that were previously out of reach. Keep knives, hot pans, and heavy items far back on counters and in the middle of tables so that she can't reach them. I had a lot of trouble remembering to do this, with knives especially, so I used a piece of masking tape to mark the place beyond which my son could not reach. I used this for only a few days, but it helped me to remember from then on.

- Always observe your child carefully while he is eating for signs of choking, and take action immediately if choking occurs. Take a first aid class through your local chapter of the American Red Cross. Never leave your child unattended while he is eating.

- Teach your child about safety from an early age. "Be careful!" "Hot!" "Sharp!" and "Not for eating!" should be a regular part of your conversations with your young child. Unfortunately, a few minor boo-boos are usually a part of the learning process, but your baby will learn quickly with consistent guidance.

Nutrition Boosters

- **Yogurt.** Natural full-fat plain yogurt with live cultures of Lactobacillus bulgaricus, Streptococcus thermophilus, and/or Lactobacillus acidophilus is one of the healthiest foods for babies. Check the package for the words "live and active cultures," to ensure you are getting the most nutrition. Yogurt can be introduced to most babies at about nine months, before they are able to tolerate fluid cow's milk because most of the intestinally irritating lactose is already broken down into lactase during culturing. Besides providing beneficial bacterial cultures that are good for the digestive system, yogurt is an excellent source of protein and calcium. Yogurt is not only a nutrition booster when mixed with other foods, but it can be a vehicle for other nutritious foods that might otherwise be refused. Even picky eaters often gobble up yogurt plain or mixed with applesauce, hummus, mashed sweet potatoes, artichoke hearts, almost anything. Steamed broccoli florets and carrot sticks may suddenly become acceptable when drizzled with a yogurt sauce or presented with a yogurt-based dippy sauce.

- **Wheat germ.** This is the most nutrient-rich portion of the whole wheat berry and is an excellent source of insoluble fiber, unsaturated fat, protein, B vitamins, vitamin E, and iron as well as a host of other vitamins, minerals, and antioxidants. You can purchase raw wheat germ, which should be stored in the refrigerator to be toasted as you need it (a cast iron pan on the stove is best), or buy it already toasted and store it in an airtight container. Wheat germ is incredibly versatile, sprinkled over cereal; mixed into oatmeal, yogurt, or smoothies; and stirred into hundreds of different dishes. You can give your baby small amounts of wheat germ beginning at eight months. If your baby is prone to wheat allergy, avoid introduction until after at least one year.

- **Nutritional yeast.** Also called brewer's or torula yeast, this is available at most health food stores and is power-packed with protein, B vitamins, and many micronutrients. It has a flaky texture that easily combines with a variety of foods without adding much flavor. Your baby probably won't reject a food that has a small sprinkling of nutritional yeast, because it's relatively innocuous. A little is all you need.

- **Tahini or ground sesame seeds.** Tahini is the nut butter made from sesame seeds, just like almond or peanut butter. You can also grind your own sesame seeds in a mortar and pestle to get a similar nutrition boost. Sesame seeds are a great source of protein, unsaturated fats, fiber, calcium, niacin, folic acid, zinc, iron, vitamin E, and selenium. Tahini is traditionally used in Middle Eastern cuisine and is an important ingredient in hummus. You can also add it to yogurt, oatmeal, or homemade baby food. Dishes with added sesame may not thrill your baby if you use too much because they have a distinctive, almost bitter flavor, so go lightly. A little will be plenty to add a bit of nutrition.

The same is true of all natural nut butters, but sesame is by far the most nutritious.

- **Finely grated vegetables.** If you can't get your baby to eat vegetables, try to sneak them in in other ways. Grated zucchini in waffle or pancake batter; carrots in muffins and quick breads. Don't give up on veggies.

- **Pureed squash, yams, and sweet potatoes.** Because of their sweet flavor and smooth consistency, vegetables in the squash and yam families are usually a hit with babies. You can also cook them ahead and keep some pureed in your freezer to use as you need them. Vegetables in this category have lots of beta carotene (vitamin A), folic acid, and fiber. You can easily mix these vegetables into yogurt, stews, soups, and even baked goods.

- **Tofu.** Lots of babies love tofu. In fact I've had more than a few moms tell me that tofu was their fallback food, which they knew they could bring out when the baby would eat nothing else. I suppose it's because of the bland flavor and chewable texture, but some babies love nothing more than noshing on cubes of raw tofu. However, if your baby is not that sort, tofu is easy to add ground up to many foods, including scrambled eggs and smoothies. The soybeans in tofu give it a high calcium content as well as being one of the richest vegetable sources for iron.

Tips for Making Healthy Homemade "Convenience" Foods

- Cook on the weekends. Make a point of making at least one large batch of yummy soup, stew, macaroni and cheese, spaghetti sauce, dippy sauces, and so on every weekend. Freeze batches in small containers or heavy-duty freezer bags. After a few months, you'll always have several choices of convenience foods to defrost and serve on weeknights.

- Always cook extra vegetables, legumes, potatoes, rice, pasta, couscous, or beans when preparing meals for the adults in your family. Set small amounts aside in the refrigerator, or freeze larger batches to use later in quick meals for your baby.

- Include your toddler in preparing his own meals or meals for the family. If you don't have time to play together and to prepare dinner, why not do both at the same time?
- Grow a garden. If you have to spend time working on the yard, why not plant a small vegetable patch or put in some herbs? Your child will be thrilled to eat foods he has seen growing in the garden, and you'll save on money and trips to the supermarket.
- Some nights, don't cook at all. Once your baby has some of his molars for chewing, he's ready for thinly sliced raw vegetables like carrots, green peppers, blanched broccoli, cherry tomatoes, cucumbers, and celery served with a yummy dippy sauce.

Packaged Foods for Older Babies

In the past few years, so-called transitional baby foods have been making their way to grocery store shelves and freezer sections. The companies that make these products would like you to believe that toddlers have nutritional needs parents may not be able to fill with food they prepare themselves. The reality is that the baby food business is a significant part of the food industry, and manufacturers are seeking to increase sales by following national eating trends, namely the emerging category called "Home Meal Replacement." Unfortunately, more time at work and less time for household duties makes for an easy sale of these convenience foods. However, you only have to examine the labels of these foods to know that most "transitional" foods are not the best choice for feeding your older baby. Indeed, some of these foods (especially fully prepared canned meals) have ingredient lists as long as your arm that include some obvious no-no's like sugar, high-fructose corn syrup, hydrogenated oils, preservatives, and sodium. These ingredients are included only because they are cheap and/or increase shelf life, not because they have any nutritional value.

Great Cookbooks for Baby- and Toddler-Friendly Recipes

It might seem crazy now, but as your baby begins to have three meals a day every day, you will run out of ideas for meals. You may be surprised to learn how many baby food cookbooks there are to choose from, but the books I have chosen here are a small cross section that represents just a sampling of what's available.

Mommy Made and Daddy Too: Home Cooking for a Healthy Baby and Toddler, by Martha and David Kimmel

Into the Mouths of Babes: A Natural Foods and Nutrition Guide for Infants and Toddlers, by Susan Tate Firkaly

The Whole Family Cookbook: Two-Tiered Meals to Please Both Parents and Kids, by Kristene Fortier

Super Baby Food, by Ruth Yaron

Of course, many of the popular toddler foods are OK. Meat and chicken sticks and cooked water-packed diced vegetables and fruits do not have any "bad" ingredients. Sometimes you may want to give them to your child, which will not make you a terrible parent. I want to make the case, however, that serving fresh food is often no less convenient (and is always less expensive) than popping open a jar or can. There are also many benefits to serving your child home-made, not manufactured, "convenience" foods. Experts are concerned that a child who regularly eats prepacked foods will be encouraged to eat the entire portion regardless of her appetite, potentially leading to obesity. It is also widely acknowledged by child psychologists that early food experiences are directly related to the incidence of eating disorders later in life. Teaching your child about the joys of healthful eating, and the important part it plays in family life, can be only a positive influence on later eating habits. Also, learning where food comes from (the produce aisle and not the freezer) is part of your child's understanding of the world around her and where she fits in the natural order of life. One more thing: Homemade food just tastes better!

Where Should I Shop?

In many communities across the country "health food" is still a foreign concept. I understand that I am fortunate to live in a fairly large city, San Francisco, which has dozens of natural food stores to choose from, with one right in my neighborhood. I realized how spoiled I am recently when I visited my mother in rural North Carolina and found it a little difficult to shop for food. The nearby grocery store was large, modern, and quite busy, but I couldn't find many ingredients I had come to rely upon, for example, plain, unsweetened, whole milk yogurt. I felt as if I was in a different world when I walked through an entire large aisle in the store that was stocked exclusively with different kinds of soft drinks and sugared "fruit" drinks. Still, I was pleasantly surprised to find many items I assumed would not be available, such as tofu, quite a few varieties of dried fruit, and a good selection of seasonal fruit and vegetables (some organic). With the advent of more sophisticated distribution systems and a growing interest in food among the American public, even foods that were once thought to be esoteric are becoming available nationally.

If you are lucky enough to have a good local natural foods store or co-op, it can be very worthwhile to shop there. Some stores promote their buying philosophies to customers, such as supporting local organic farmers or buying packaged foods that do not contain ingredients harmful to the environment. This is true of a few growing national natural food grocery chains and many local independent stores as well. Often, people assume that natural food stores will be more expensive, which is sometimes true, sometimes not. I think the most important thing natural food stores offer their customers is choice. Supermarkets are locked into buying national brands because the buying public expects to find products they've seen advertised on television. Also, mass-market producers will frequently pay a "slotting fee" to the larger supermarket chains to ensure that their products are displayed prominently.

Healthy Shopping at the Supermarket

Even with natural food chains growing at a rapid pace, most people shop at supermarkets, where there are plenty of healthy options. To find the best foods for your family, mainly shop on the perimeter, where fresh produce, dairy products, eggs, meat, fish, and poultry are stocked. When shopping at the salad bar, ask if the dishes are prepared on site. If they are, the ingredients are usually straightforward (you can usually obtain a list of ingredients for each dish if you ask). Beware prepared foods that are purchased from an outside company, because they will often have preservatives. Read ingredient labels for packaged and canned foods and frozen entrees. Do you know what's in there? Buy simple foods for your kids whenever possible: graham crackers, fresh bread, pasta, plain crackers, rice cakes, fresh fruit and vegetables.

Price Comparison: Healthy Food vs. Junk Food

While it is true that you sometimes pay a premium for healthy foods, this is certainly not always the case. I came across one example recently at my local natural foods store, where I picked up a 12-ounce box of breakfast cereal that cost $2.79. I bought the cereal for my son because it featured koala bears (which he loves) on the front and advertised itself as being made from a variety of whole, organic grains grown without the use of genetically modified organisms (GMOs). Afterward, I went over to the regular grocery store across the street to get a newspaper, and I couldn't help noticing a huge display of a new cereal for kids that was supposed to be just like a popular brand of cookies (for breakfast?). A 14-ounce box of this sugar, artificial flavor/color, hydrogenated oil–laden junk food cost $4.79!

The Facts on Junk Foods

While *junk food* is not a widely accepted technical term, most people understand it to mean food that does not provide nutritious calories and that frequently contains too much sodium, saturated fat, and other ultrarefined ingredients.

- Fast food hamburgers contain not only saturated animal fat from the beef but added grease for frying, and they are usually dressed with mayonnaise and sauces made with shelf-stable hydrogenated oils (the worst kind of fat). Add to this lots of sodium and a nonnutritious refined-white-flour bun, and all you have are a bunch of empty calories. We're not even talking about adding bacon and cheese at this point.
  A plain kid's hamburger at one popular fast food chain has 360 calories and 460 milligrams of sodium (the AAP recommends a minimum of 500 milligrams of sodium a day). Hamburgers for adults have between 320 and 730 calories and 700 to 1500 milligrams of sodium.
- French fries are at least made from a vegetable, and many restaurants claim to fry in more healthful oils such as corn or vegetable oils. What they don't tell you is that these oils have

Foods to Look for at a Natural Food Store

- Bulk foods: fresh whole grain flour, brown rice, dried beans, fruit bars, dried fruit, rolled oats

- Nutrition boosters: wheat germ, nutritional yeast, unsweetened whole milk yogurt with live active cultures, tahini, tofu

- A large selection of juices that do not contain additional sweeteners

- Tasty whole grain crackers and snack foods that are not made with hydrogenated oils and that are often lower in sodium

- Bulk and packaged dry mixes for foods like taboule, hummus, stews, and soups that may provide an easy midweek meal option

- Fruit juice–sweetened treats and cookies

- Frozen entrees made with simple ingredients and fewer or no preservatives

- Hot and cold breakfast cereals that are healthful but appealing to children

- Organic produce, juices, and packaged goods

usually been hydrogenated or partially hydrogenated to promote stability during repeated use, and that a large order of fries has between 200 and 300 milligrams of sodium. Needless to say, potato chips are just as bad.

- Soft drinks are the worst form of empty calories, providing approximately 10 teaspoons of sugar along with a host of artificial flavors, colors, and, frequently, caffeine in each typical 12-ounce can. Not far behind are fruit drinks or cocktails, which often contain very little juice and lots of corn syrup and artificial flavors and colors. Gelatin desserts and hard candies also fall into this category.

- Commercial baked goods of many stripes (cookies, snack cakes, donuts) should be approached with caution. They are usually made from refined white flour, sugar, and frequently hydrogenated or partially hydrogenated shortening.

- Sugar-coated cereals, which are designed primarily for children despite the fact that they are most nutritionally damaging to them, provide very little beyond the milk that is poured on them, and frequently a profusion of other undesirable ingredients such as hydrogenated oils and artificial colors and flavors. Don't be fooled by statements such as "fortified with 9 essential vitamins and minerals." By and large, sugar-coated cereals are not healthy foods for children (or adults, for that matter).

- Hot dogs and cured meat snacks (jerky) are not suitable foods for babies and don't have much to recommend them to children or adults either. Not only do they have a high proportion of saturated fat, but they also have nitrates and nitrites, which should be consumed in strict moderation if at all, and much too much sodium. A hot dog has an average of 500 milligrams of sodium.

Should I Buy Organic?

The debate over commercial versus organic agriculture is currently raging, with passionate arguments on every side. Americans are all too often out of touch with information about the practices promoted by multinational agriculture corporations. However, many people who wouldn't normally give organic fruits and vegetables a second glance, pause to consider them when deciding what to feed their babies. The decisions you make about what to feed your baby are your own, and the more information you have, the better you can feel about those decisions.

Whether or not you choose to use organic products or ingredients, remember that there are many other components to a healthy diet. Fresh fruits and vegetables, whole grains, and minimally processed ingredients are more important to overall health than any other factor. On the other hand, there is still much we do not know about the long-term effects of commercial farming practices on the health of adults, much less growing children. If you are concerned, educate yourself and make wise choices. Avoid buying commercial produce that is known to contain large amounts of contaminants, and wash all produce carefully, even if it is organic.

Organic Facts

- Sixty percent of herbicides, 90 percent of fungicides, and 30 percent of insecticides used in commercial agriculture are known to cause cancer.
- Babies and children consume, on average, more than 60 times the amount of fruit as adults, per pound of body weight. This increases their risk of exposure to agricultural residues, which are tested for safe levels using statistics relevant to a 160-pound man.
- Organic produce generally costs about 20 percent more than commercial produce. Organic grains, dairy products, and meats cost even more. Proponents of organic agriculture point out that cleaning up environmental pollution caused by commercial agriculture represents a cost to society that does not appear in the per pound price of commercial produce.
- Soaking, rinsing, and peeling produce carefully is known to reduce contaminants in commercial produce by 30 to 100 percent.
- Recently, several brands of frozen organic fruits and vegetables have come onto the market and are available at larger health food grocery stores. If you are not too concerned about the cost, these veggies can be a very convenient option (I used them constantly to prepare those smaller portions before my

baby ate with the rest of the family). Also, contrary to popular belief, frozen vegetables often have more nutrients than fresh, because the nutrient value has not been degraded through distribution and handling.

Current National Organic Regulations

At this writing, there are no national standards by which agricultural products may be labeled "organic," a situation which federal authorities are working hard to remedy. Using several state-determined definitions as a guide (such as the California Organic Foods Act of 1990), the USDA has submitted a 663-page proposal for national standards, which may go into effect as early as the beginning of the year 2002. This proposal reflects revisions to the original guidelines submitted by the USDA in 1998, which generated enormous public controversy and an unprecedented 24,000 consumer comments sent directly to the USDA. The controversy centered primarily on organic status being granted to foods produced using practices associated with "big agriculture," such as genetically modified seed, irradiation of food, and the use of sewage sludge as a fertilizer. The new proposal no longer allows for foods grown using these practices as well as other methods considered unacceptable by organic farmers, but which are common to conventional agriculture. These new regulations will go a long way towards eliminating consumer confusion over the source and healthfulness of the foods they eat. Highlights of the new proposed regulations include the following:

- Toxic pesticides or toxic "inert ingredients" may not be used in production.
- Antibiotics, growth hormones, or rendered animal protein may not be fed or administered to animals slaughtered for meat or used for egg or milk production.
- Animals may not be subjected to intensive confinement.
- Synthetics or chemicals may not be used in organic production unless approved by the National Organics Standards Board.

- Preexisting private and state organics certifiers may also uphold standards higher than national standards.

Genetically Modified Organisms

Genetically Modified Organisms (GMOs) are just beginning to get the attention of the American public and have become a hot topic quite recently. A GMO is a plant grown from seed that has been genetically modified in the laboratory to make it less expensive to grow or distribute. A GMO may be genetically altered so that it will be resistant to larger doses of herbicides used to kill weeds, or it may include genetic information that acts as a pesticide. Other GMOs are modified to decrease the likelihood of spoilage during the distribution process. Critics of these practices say that we do not understand the implications of widespread use of biotechnology in our food supply and warn that bypassing the process of evolution may have dire consequences. GMOs are already widely distributed and used in packaged foods, and critics point to this as an experiment that the public has not agreed to be a part of. Indeed, polls indicate that 80 to 90 percent of Americans would not buy foods containing GMOs if they were labeled as such, and most other industrialized nations have either imposed bans or severe restrictions on the importation of GMOs. On the other hand, proponents of GMOs point to advances in biotechnology as a way to provide the world with a more reliable food supply.

Many baby food producers have already stated they will not use GMOs in their products, and new FDA standards prohibit the use of GMOs in organic agriculture. Unfortunately, one of the consequences of modifying the genetic structure of a plant is the phenomenon known as "genetic drift." Genetic information from a modified plant can travel as far as eight miles to pollinate conventionally or organically grown crops. In the year 2000, approximately 71 million acres of farmland were planted with genetically modified crops. Much more will be learned about GMOs in the coming months and years.

CHAPTER SIX

Baby's Evolving Diet from 6 to 24 Months

Infant Development and Eating Behaviors

Babies are marvelous creatures. In the womb, they get all the nourishment they need through the umbilical cord, and in the first few months of life their tastes remain simple. A diet of breastmilk or formula will provide your baby with all of the nutrition he needs to grow and develop at a rate that will never be equaled at any other time in his life. For example, if you weighed 150 pounds and were to grow at the same rate as a newborn infant, you would weigh 450 pounds at the end of 12 months. It's incredible to imagine.

Once your baby gets her first taste of slurpy cereal, however, she will embark on a journey of tastes and sensations that will enhance her whole life. These months are important for helping your child to discover the joy in eating. Her ability to digest new foods will barely keep pace with her desire to try tasty new things and the development of new skills that will assist her in learning to feed herself. For you, it will also be a time of discovery. However, as with most transitions, anxiety can play a role, and you may find yourself reexamining your attitudes about food. Or, you may suddenly discover that you and your partner have different opinions about the healthfulness of certain foods and whether or not they are appropriate to feed to your baby. You may also feel impatient with your baby's unwillingness to try new foods. Overall, though, most parents find these months exciting as they guide their baby through the transition to solid foods.

Your baby's growth will probably slow tremendously sometime shortly after his first birthday, and his appetite may take a sudden downturn. For parents who are accustomed to the challenge of shoveling spoonfuls of baby food as quickly as possible, this sometimes dramatic change can be distressing. By all means, discuss any concerns you may have with your child's doctor, but be aware that this phenomenon is not uncommon. Unfortunately for worried parents, this change often coincides with your baby's growing need to express himself and to exert some control over his situation, which is often manifested in habitual food refusal. Also, your baby may be eating less pureed baby food at the same time, so your measure for your baby's consumption (a whole jar, three defrosted frozen food cubes, a half-full small bowl) is suddenly erased. This may lead worried parents to discount or forget about a hearty mid-afternoon snack that precedes a dinner that is hardly touched. However, most parents weather this sometimes trying period and feel somewhat in control in time for the next set of dramatic changes, which typically happen between 18 and 24 months.

Child Development and Eating Habits

In the last six months before your child turns two, she is quickly growing from babyhood to childhood, and her desire to use her newfound coordination and mental ability will astound you. More than ever, she wants to mimic how you do things and to "do it myself." This can be a harrowing experience as you begin to let her experiment with drinking from an open cup, and when she insists on climbing into and out of the high chair or booster seat on her own. During these months your child is overwhelmingly dis-tracted by the task of learning to communicate and to manipulate the world around her (including the manipulation of her parents). However, allowing her to follow her desires may also be a powerful new bargaining chip when you encourage her to try healthy new foods and increase the variety in her diet. In the parental balancing act of setting limits while allowing for growth and experimentation, it can be easy to lose sight of your child's nutritional needs. If you have not started this process already, it is time to eat together more regularly as a family. Not only will your child learn good eating habits from you, but she will learn invaluable social skills as well.

You will learn a lot about your child's personality through his eating habits—not all of it to your liking. It's important to remain relaxed and to keep an open mind. Remember that your child's tastes and abilities are changing on a daily basis and that you can only continue to experiment. Throughout this chapter you will notice many quick suggestions for feeding the reluctant eater. I call

Food Fads

Young children are particularly prone to faddy eating, meaning that they will select one or only a few preferred foods to eat for a remarkably long (by adult standards) period of time. This is why it is so important to pro-vide only healthy foods for your child. The parent of a child in the middle of a food fad based around tuna fish, yogurt, and bread will sleep much better at night than the parent whose child will eat only hot dogs and french fries. Also, be aware that at the end of the food fad, your child may suddenly decide he never wants the once-favorite food again (and who could blame her?).

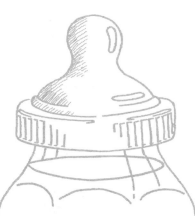

Tricks of the Trade: The Puppet Trick

Here is a trick that took me by surprise. Use a hand puppet to grasp the spoon for feeding your baby. This is so funny to some babies that it actually distracts from eating, but others are fascinated and happily accept food from their new friend. If you have a hand puppet that is meant to be used as a bath toy, this will work particularly well as it will be easier to clean when it gets covered in food.

these the "tricks of the trade," and have collected them from other experienced parents who have probably tried them all. Unless your baby is one of the rarest sorts that happily accepts everything you offer, I encourage you to try them also. Some will work, others won't. Then you can try them all over again.

When Should I Introduce New Foods?

4–6 Months

It pays to be conservative when introducing new foods to babies this young. In fact, many pediatricians see no problem in waiting until six months or even longer to introduce any solid food at all if your child seems satisfied with more frequent or longer breast- or formula-feedings. The reason is that not all children are mature enough at this age to properly metabolize solid food, which can lead to problems with digestion and with later allergies. However, some children do quite well with a small number of solid foods introduced during this time, particularly iron-fortified cereals and a few other strained or finely pureed foods. If your baby is eating solid food before six months, try to let feedings be a time of experimentation and learning rather than a replacement for more than one or two breast- or bottle-feedings. Also, be aware that the usual diet of rice cereal and bananas is often a recipe for constipation. If this happens, try giving prunes or prune juice and/or another variety of infant cereal like oat or barley (but not wheat).

6–9 Months

Most babies are ready to begin eating solid food in earnest at this age and will gradually develop a pattern of eating about three solid meals each day, with continued breast- or formula-feedings in the morning, between meals, and at night. Introduction of new foods should be spaced three to four days apart so that adverse reactions can be easily traced. Once each new food has passed muster, it can be combined with previously introduced foods. At about seven or eight months (sometimes earlier), some babies will have the manual dexterity and desire necessary to try some early finger foods like soft pieces of cooked fruits or vegetables, whole wheat bread, or O-shaped cereal. However, most of your baby's food will continue to be pureed or finely fork mashed. Most experts recommend waiting to cautiously introduce wheat products, hard-boiled egg yolks (not whites), and cultured dairy products like yogurt or cottage cheese (not fluid cow's milk) until eight or nine months to avoid allergic reactions. If you choose to feed your baby meat, poultry, or fish (not shellfish), it is OK to begin introducing these according to the Food Introduction Timeline in Chapter 4, although serving these foods is not nutritionally necessary.

9–12 Months

As your baby's diet continually expands, her ability to eat more textured foods will increase as will her desire to become more involved in the feeding process. Many babies learn to hold their own cup or bottle sometime during these months, and it is common for most babies to enjoy eating finger foods like elbow macaroni, pieces of steamed zucchini, or chunks of banana. A few babies will be able to attempt self-feeding with a spoon, but most won't be able to master this skill until sometime after the first year. Often, willingness to eat many different foods will peak during this time, and it is important to take advantage of this by encouraging a varied diet that includes several types of whole grains and a variety of fruits, vegetables, and legumes. As your baby nears her first birthday, more of her nutrition will be supplied by solid food as opposed to breastmilk or formula, and as a result you should begin to pay more attention to the amount of protein, fat, iron, and calcium she is getting in her diet. Most forms of dairy products, except fluid cow's milk, are OK to feed your baby at this age.

12–18 Months

At 12 months, most pediatricians give the green light to whole cow's milk, whole eggs, honey, nut butters, berries, and possibly shellfish if your child does not seem to be susceptible to allergies.

Tricks of the Trade: The Container-Switch Trick

Many instances of food refusal have more to do with your baby's need to experiment with control than her actual likes and dislikes. Try dumping the same food into a different container (you may even want to do this right in front of her). You might be shocked that she will now happily eat food she staunchly refused just seconds ago.

Many important transitions that impact eating behaviors occur during these months—walking, talking, growing molars, and the development of dexterity skills that assist in self-feeding. All of this means that your baby will be eating more "table foods" (foods you eat yourself) and less baby food. Unfortunately, the advent of fussy eating is also not uncommon at this age, which may be a preview of other less charming toddler behaviors. It is also common for your child's growth to taper off as compared to the first year, which will diminish her appetite. On the other hand, you will probably settle firmly into a routine of three small main meals with substantial snacks between meals at some time during these months. Don't be fooled that your baby is fully ready for more adult foods, however, and don't be too concerned if he is still eating many foods you would describe as baby foods. As with many transitions, there will be a lot of backsliding with each step forward. There is no particular rush in any case.

18–24 Months

Your baby is now a full-fledged toddler, and the "terrible (or terrific) twos" are just around the corner. Now is the time to include your baby's meals with those for the rest of the family. Many parents fall easily into the trap of preparing separate meals for each of their children, depending on each child's peculiarities. This often coincides with an overreliance on less healthful convenience foods. While your baby is not ready for foods that adults commonly eat, like spicy or greasy dishes, there are ways to prepare two-tiered meals that will please both parents and children. Your baby may already be the dreaded picky eater. Try not to let this become a source of tension within your family. It may help to remember that it is your job as the parent to provide a healthful variety of foods appropriate for your child's age, to make sure that too much snacking doesn't spoil mealtimes, and to allow your child to eat according to her appetite. It is not uncommon for a child's appetite to decline as the day goes on and to vary widely from day to day. Knowing that these are a child's natural tendencies, it does not help to be either too permissive or too strict

Tricks of the Trade: The Chopstick Trick

My friend Andrea swears by this trick. When her son Sam refuses to eat his meal, she simply offers him the same food with chopsticks. This different mode of food transport is interesting enough to him to make him forget that he didn't like his lunch and happily eat every last bite. One word of caution: Don't try this trick too frequently or the novelty will wear off and it won't work anymore for a long time.

about your child's eating habits. Allowing your child to eat any food at any time according to her desires is just as detrimental as attempting to force her to eat according to your expectations by use of threat or bribery.

Changes and Progress

At first, your baby will have rice, barley, or oatmeal cereals and simple fruits and vegetables like strained bananas, apples, pears, or sweet potatoes. These early feedings, though, are actually more important as practice for later meals. Very gradually, predictable mealtimes will emerge, as your baby becomes more accustomed to solid food as part of her diet. Usually by 9 to 12 months, your baby will be ready for more textured food, fork-mashed or coarsely chopped, but still soft and mushy. With the development of fine motor coordination, she'll begin to eat with her fingers. She'll delight in eating O-shaped cereal or chunks of banana. As the menu continually expands to include more and more finger foods (usually around her first birthday), she'll begin to show an interest in using her own spoon. Don't worry if your child doesn't follow this same pattern. Some children go at their own pace and will not be rushed. Others can't be bothered to wait for you to offer them their first taste of macaroni and cheese before they've snatched it off your plate and shoveled a handful down.

As the second year progresses, it is likely that your baby, now a toddler sporting brand-new molars for chewing, will start eating more of the foods you eat yourself. This is the time to examine whether the food in your home is healthful for both you and your child and to learn about the different nutritional needs of toddlers. This is a critical period of exploration for your toddler, and many lasting attitudes about the world around him (especially about food) will be formed during this time. It is also a time when he will begin to test his limits (and your patience), and mealtimes and food choices will suddenly be fraught with potential conflict. You can weather this somewhat trying period by staying as relaxed as possible while providing consistent guidance and making absolutely

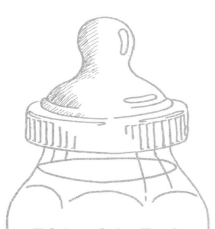

Tricks of the Trade: The Tinkling Wind Chime Trick

Recently, I met a father at the playground, and we commiserated about our babies' quirky eating behaviors. He confessed to me that he and his wife often use the "tinkling wind chime trick." This sounded intriguing, and he explained that they had hung a sparkling glass wind chime in a sunny window right by their son's high chair. Whenever it seemed they would have trouble feeding him, they would call his attention to the wind chime and set it to swaying. Amazingly, he would sit mesmerized by its flashing and chiming while he dutifully opened his mouth for bite after bite.

sure that all of the food choices available to your child are healthy ones. For more information about infant nutrition, see Chapter 8. Also keep in mind that your child grows much more slowly in the second year, and it's not uncommon for his appetite to decrease dramatically from just a few months before. Unless your child seems ill in another way, you shouldn't be too concerned.

Sippy Cups

Drinking from a cup is a skill that varies widely from one baby to another. Some babies are taking sips of water directly from a parent's glass at five or six months of age and quickly learn to use a sippy cup. More commonly, parents will offer baby drinks in a sippy cup for weeks before she gets the hang of it because the action is very different from drinking from a bottle, not to mention the breast. If your baby already knows how to hold a bottle, she will quickly adjust to drinking from a sippy cup in the same way. On the other hand, she may want you to hold the cup for her, which is fine for a while. She'll quickly learn about holding the cup herself, though, if you make a game of pretending to drink from an empty cup. She'll think your noisy drinking of the pretend beverage in the empty cup is hilarious and when you hand the cup to her, she will probably model your behavior. Soon, she'll make the connection between the toy cup and her own cup, and overnight she'll be drinking out of her cup like a pro.

Teaching Your Baby to Use His Own Spoon and Fork

There's no way around it, this is going to get messy, and there's no other way for your baby to learn about eating with his own utensils than by practicing. Some babies will suddenly insist on using their own spoon at about 10 or 11 months as part of a blossoming sense of independence and competence. Others, perhaps dismayed by all the other changes that come with growing, crawling, teething,

---

Don't Serve Juice in a Bottle

Many doctors recommend, and I agree, that the bottle be used exclusively for milk or formula, and the cup for juice, water, and milk or formula. Giving juice to your baby in a bottle may extend the bottle habit beyond what is necessary and make weaning from the bottle more difficult later.

and so on, are quite content to continue the comforting ritual of being fed by Mommy or Daddy. If your baby is not using a spoon by her first birthday, it's probably time to start practicing.

A special spoon with a short curved handle is extremely helpful in helping your baby learn how to get the food near (and then in!) her mouth. It also helps to give her food that sticks on the spoon well. Starchy foods, such as potatoes, sweet potatoes, oatmeal, or mushy rice are especially good for this purpose. She won't be able to master dipping the spoon in the bowl to retrieve the food for a while yet, so it's best to do that part for her and set the spoon on the high chair tray for her to grasp. She might like to copy you and put the spoon in the bowl of food, but usually to no avail. There will be some food throwing, spoon dropping, and finger smearing, so be prepared. You may want to use a machine washable drop cloth if things get really messy (we used an old shower curtain). Soon enough she'll get the hang of it. Remember that her feeding herself will not mean that she doesn't need supervision while she's eating—choking accidents are always a concern.

The Wonders of Dipping

Some children are very eager to master spoon use but become quite frustrated if fine motor skill development has not yet caught up with their desire to self-feed. If spoon use practice is resulting in a dramatic meltdown, try something easier that is just as satisfying— dipping. Give your baby a bowl full of something a little slurpy like yogurt mixed with hummus or mashed avocado, and give him something to dip in it like bread, rice cake, or crackers. Dipping his bread in the tasty (and nutritious) sauce is a surprisingly simple way to eat, and once the initial frustration wears off, he may be ready for more spoon practice.

Great Ideas for Yummy Dippy Sauces

Babies and toddlers love to dip their food. Whether you are serving crackers, bread, vegetables, or fresh fruit, these sauces are sure winners.

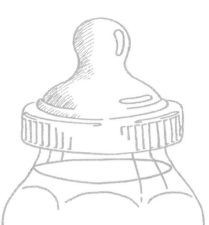

Tricks of the Trade: The Two-Spoon Trick

Some babies are so anxious to use a spoon, they want to play with it from the very first feedings. Obviously, this will not work for a five-month-old baby, but the frustration of Mommy or Daddy withholding the spoon-toy may be too much for your little one to bear. Give her another spoon to hold while you feed her with the original spoon. You might have to do some trading to get through the meal, but this will usually work reasonably well.

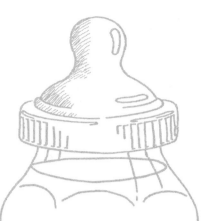

- Whole milk yogurt mixed with mashed avocado
- Hummus (a spread made with pureed, cooked garbanzo beans, olive oil, fresh garlic, and lemon juice), served plain or mixed with yogurt
- Cottage cheese mixed with pureed fresh fruit such as bananas or peaches (a great breakfast dip with French toast or toasted challah bread)
- Ketchup or creamy salad dressing (one without a lot of salt, sugar, or preservatives)

Tricks of the Trade: The Double-Dip Trick

I received this tip from Christina, the e-mail maven in our local new mother's group. She swears her son Christopher fell for this trick every time. Dip your baby's spoon into the less-favored food first, then dip it into a food he finds more appealing. Many pounds of peas have been consumed in this way, camouflaged by peaches. It sounds unappealing to an adult, but Christopher never complained.

How Many Meals Each Day?

At first, your four- to seven-month-old baby will have only one or two solid food meals each day, with nursings or bottle-feedings still meeting almost all of his nutritional needs. Gradually, he will transition to having three or four small meals each day, with nursings or bottle-feedings between meals, in the morning, and at bedtime. For some babies this may take some time, and you may still be coaxing him to have more solid food around his first birthday. Try to be patient. By 12 to 16 months, most babies will be having three small meals and two substantial snacks every day, supplemented with milk. If your baby is still nursing, this will provide a welcome nutritional boost to his regular diet.

Teaching Your Baby to Drink from an Open Cup

Most parents dread the prospect of a sudden obsession with drinking from an open cup. Depending on your child's age and proclivities, you may or may not want to encourage this activity. However, usually somewhere between the ages of 18 and 24 months (sometimes much older), babies develop the fine motor coordination and patience skills necessary to hold their own open cup and drink without spilling. As frequently happens, a baby's desire to do it himself may outpace his ability to do it without spilling milk, water, or juice all over the kitchen or living room, and his and your clothes for good measure. Still, if your baby is determined and you have the patience, he may not be as far off as you think. Like any of the other skills he has honed over the previous months, such as crawling, walking, and talking, he will need to try and fail, perhaps many times before he eventually succeeds. However, knowing the extreme potential for messes may make it difficult for some parents to go forward with the process until they absolutely have to.

Once you decide the time is right, make sure you have the proper equipment. A light, unbreakable cup is best, and filling it with as little liquid as possible is wise. The bottom half of a sippy cup would seem obvious, but many babies become extremely distressed when they are given their "drinking cup" with a sippy cup lid again later. Better to choose a special new cup. Your child may derive special excitement from using a variety of unbreakable drinking cups, from little colorful teacups to wide-mouth thermos cups. Offer her a choice of cups to appease her sense of independence right off the bat. Although she is anxious to try this new skill, she may be more sensitive to the potential for failure than you realize. Find ways to help her feel confident. You may want to dress her in a special waterproof artist's smock or long-sleeved bib for the occasion, just in case.

As your baby practices his new skill, stay involved as much as possible. Most babies will *not* let you help them to hold the cup, so you will need to find other ways of helping. I know a woman who actually coached her daughter through the entire process until she eventually got the hang of it. She would sit right with her and encourage her each step of the way, saying, "OK now, sip. Good! Now, swallow. Good! Now, put the cup down. Very good!!" This might sound extreme, but believe me, if it saves on aggravation, spilled drinks, and inconsolable tears, it's worth it. Remember that this isn't easy for your child, and success is extremely important to his sense of accomplishment.

Most babies do not abandon the sippy cup once they've mastered drinking from an open cup, which is fortunate. Having beverages in a sippy cup is extremely handy for when you are away

Tricks of the Trade: The Squeeze-Bottle Trick

Try serving food to your baby garnished with a squirt of tomato sauce (or some other liquid food your baby loves, such as yogurt mixed with hummus) from a squeeze bottle like the kind used for condiments at a restaurant. You can squeeze a dab on each spoonful.

• • •

Tricks of the Trade: The Old Airplane-in-the-Hangar Trick

I didn't even try this trick with my son for months because I thought it was just an old cliché, but "Here comes the airplane! Open the hangar doors!" really does work. Especially if you make all the accompanying airplane noises and open your own mouth at the right moment to show him how it's done. This is definitely one you'll want to avoid using if you have company over.

from home or if you want to allow your child a beverage in the living room. Often a child will continue to use a sippy cup occasionally or frequently well into the preschool years.

Soup and Other Messier Fare

As your baby gets closer to her second birthday, you'll be anxious to expand her repertoire of food choices. One of the best new foods at this age is soup. Many babies love the novelty of food with bits of other food floating in it (alphabet soup isn't a favorite for no reason, you know). And soup is an outstanding way to get your toddler to eat vegetables. Still, soup is a challenge in the same way that drinking from an open cup is. Coping with a spoonful of liquid food requires a great deal of dexterity. Fortunately, the spillage from a spoonful of soup doesn't compare with what can be spilled from a cup. My best suggestion is to use a long-sleeved bib, available at many baby supply stores (try to find one with a pocket) or an artist's smock and to lay a thirsty towel in your child's lap. This will greatly assist in cleanup later.

Picky Eaters

Almost all children go through a period when they seem to refuse any food you want them to eat and chow down on foods you would rather not see them eating at all. Can a 10-month-old really thrive on only applesauce and dry cereal? How do toddlers keep going at all when they seem to eat practically nothing? Fortunately, no children starve to death because they refuse to eat, and yours won't either. Also, chances are she eats a lot more than you realize. If you're really concerned, contact your pediatrician and have your child examined. Otherwise, relax and follow a few simple guidelines. The good news is that your child has inherent instincts you can use to your advantage to encourage healthy eating.

Tricks of the Trade: The "Space" Trick

This is definitely not the right trick for every baby, but after my son Max had mastered using his own spoon, I discovered that he frequently ate better when I gave him "space." If I hovered around after I gave him a bowl of food, he would frequently just play with it, and then, worse, throw the whole bowl on the floor. Instead, I would casually drop off his dinner and make myself busy with something else in the kitchen. Of course, I would surreptitiously watch him to guard against choking or food throwing, but he usually ate better with minimal interference from me.

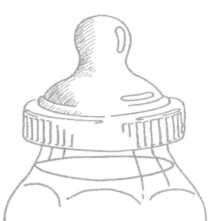

1. *Everything goes in the mouth.* Much to the dismay of many parents, most babies have a tendency to put *everything* in their mouths, especially between the ages of 6 and 18 months. When introducing new foods in the early months, this can be a benefit. Babies are much more likely to become fussy eaters after 12 months, when the tendency to explore the world with their mouths subsides. If you take advantage of the time when she is more adventurous, you will have provided your baby with a solid foundation of healthful foods that will certainly benefit her during these critical months and will likely result in better eating habits when she is older. Don't assume that your child won't enjoy a certain food because of your own preconceptions, and *never* tell her that she won't like healthy food offered to her. She might just surprise you.

2. *Monkey see, monkey do.* Children instinctively want to do what you do. From the time your baby takes his first bite, he is trying to copy the eating behaviors he's been observing in adults for months. Parents have taken advantage of this phenomenon for ages. You take a bite, exclaim "Yummy, yummy!" and then baby's mouth pops open to do the same. As your baby gets closer to his first birthday, this doesn't seem to work as well. Sitting in a high chair when he would rather be crawling or toddling around might just be the problem. He might be bored with what you've been feeding him, or he might just not be hungry right at noon (but he probably will be by 12:15!). Go ahead and fix your own lunch. Heat up some lentil soup, or make a nice egg salad sandwich. He'll probably be pretty interested in what you're doing, and by the time you sit down with him on your lap, he'll be ready to share a good portion of your lunch with you. Remember, babies are growing and changing every day. Feeding patterns that worked yesterday will not work forever, and your baby might be ready for a break in the routine.

Eating Streaks

It is perfectly normal for a baby's appetite to vary from time to time as his need for calories fluctuates. Sometimes appetite will be decreased when your baby is fighting an infection or has a temporary problem with diarrhea or constipation. Other times, your baby will simply not be as hungry as usual. Maybe he isn't growing very much right now. In this case, you will notice a return in appetite within a week or so. You may also notice that your baby suddenly has a voracious appetite, which may continue for a week or more. This usually indicates a growth spurt.

3. *A growing need for independence.* Around their first birthdays, babies usually begin the lifelong process of wanting to "do it myself." This might be the time to let your baby try to use her own spoon. Get her a spoon she can easily hold herself, with a curved handle that makes zeroing in on her mouth easier. Some babies are so excited to feed themselves that they will eat practically anything (including food they refused two seconds ago) when they are given the opportunity to feed themselves.

4. *Employ reverse psychology.* Teenagers are famous for doing the opposite of what their parents want them to do, but babies can be vulnerable to this trait as well. This does not mean that you should say a food is yucky in an attempt to get your baby to eat a new food. Instead, try not to provide overt negative attention for food refusals. At this age, a strong negative reaction to your son throwing his oatmeal on the floor is fairly likely to make him want to repeat this action over and over to see again the dramatic color change in your face.

5. *Provide a relaxing atmosphere for dining.* Mealtimes should be as relaxing as possible for your child. Let her set the pace. If she refuses the glorious stew you've just spent half an hour preparing, don't fret. Maybe she's just too hungry to want to please you right now and will respond more positively to something more familiar. Give her a few bits of dry cereal or a crust of bread, and try again in a few minutes. Always have a healthy backup plan, and offer the original meal again, without becoming too stressed about it.

6. *Food refusal isn't forever.* It can be easy to misinterpret a child's refusal of a certain food. If your baby turns up his nose at broccoli several days in a row, it might be tempting to come to the conclusion that he doesn't like vegetables anymore. This is hardly ever the case. Babies' preferences tend to periodically return to a small number of favorite foods (usually sweet ones like bananas or applesauce), especially during a time of illness or

transition. An illness can affect a child's appetite for days or even a week after other symptoms have disappeared. This can seem like an eternity to an anxious parent, but you should trust that your baby will know when he is ready to reintroduce old favorites into his diet. In the meantime, don't give up, and don't assume that today's preferences are here to stay.

7. *Small stomachs make for smaller appetites.* Babies and toddlers have very small stomachs and therefore need to eat smaller amounts of food more frequently than do adults. Most parents respond to this by providing three small meals a day with a mid-morning and mid-afternoon snack between meals. The truth is that most toddlers will eat heartily at only two or three of these meal-snack times each day. Also, toddler appetites frequently wane at the end of the day.

8. *Understanding picky behaviors.* Toddlers are notoriously picky eaters. This may be partly due to instincts that helped children to survive in more primitive conditions. If a walking baby is free to roam about in the outdoors, he is wise to be suspicious of new foods that may very well be poisonous. Remember that fussy eating behaviors have nothing to do with the quality of the food you prepare for your child.

9. *Babies are accustomed to a liquid diet.* Remember that your baby's transition from getting all of his calories from formula or breastmilk to getting the majority of his calories from solid food takes a very long time. Many babies cling to liquid calories as a form of comfort. If your baby isn't eating well at mealtimes, ask yourself if he might be drinking too much milk or juice. Babies should still be getting about half of their calories from formula, breastmilk, or cow's milk (if they are ready for it) at 12 months, and by the end of the second year, this proportion is considerably less. Each baby progresses through the stages from a liquid to a solid diet at his or her own pace; however, you may determine that your baby is simply not eating enough

Don't Give Up!

Some experts recommend that you attempt to introduce new foods to your baby as many as 15 times before giving up. Space your attempts several days or a week apart, and don't make a fuss if the food is refused. If you want, try again in a few months. Variety is the important factor, not any individual food.

solid food. If you think he might be making up for this by drinking too much, try to limit his liquid intake by offering less milk or diluting juice with more water. His solid food intake should then begin to climb.

10. *Curiosity fills the tummy.* Children are naturally inquisitive and love to learn about the world around them, especially when it comes to food. As your baby becomes a toddler, help her learn where the food she is eating comes from. Involve her as much as possible in the preparation of the family meal. There are many tasks she can actually help with, such as peeling bananas or tearing lettuce. Let her become involved in the selection of fresh fruit and vegetables at the market. If you have a yard, consider planting a vegetable garden. Understanding how food grows is a wonderful way to make healthy eating a part of your child's everyday life. As your child grows, her experiences around food and eating will enhance her social, intellectual, and emotional development in innumerable ways. Take advantage of this and make sure to have fun.

Toddler Table Manners

As your baby becomes more independent, she will naturally begin to test the limits you have already set, or which you are trying to institute. As she realizes that she doesn't always have to cooperate with your wishes, she is paradoxically influenced by a powerful desire to please you. Because meals and snacks happen on a daily basis, and because you as the parent have undeniable expectations for your child's behavior during meals, the stage is set for a few dramatic interludes. If you are like me, the whole scenario will be compounded if you yourself are hungry and/or tired. If you begin to find yourself getting a little steamed up, take a step back and think about the situation at hand. Your toddler is learning about what you consider to be acceptable behavior in the same way she is learning about climbing on the jungle gym. There are bound to be a few slips and boo-boos. Just as you might help her to safely climb in the playground, you must find creative ways of reinforcing good behavior at the table.

The first rule of behavior modification is to realize that the more attention you pay to a behavior, the more likely your child will be to repeat it. Amazingly, it doesn't matter so much to your child if the attention is positive or negative. This doesn't mean you should serenely clean up a messy bowl full of chili that has been hurled from the high chair. However, you will probably not be able to stop the behavior simply by shouting, "NO! Do NOT throw your food!" Instead, you'd be wise to suggest an alternative behavior and provide lots of attention for this conduct instead of the undesired behavior. In our case, Max's high chair was next to the table, and each time he would throw his food down, I would tell him this wasn't good and put the food on the table, explaining that if he didn't want his food, he should put it on the table. It took a little while, and I'll admit that I wanted to scream if I had to clean up another splattered mess, but when he finally started putting the food on the table next to him, I literally lavished him with praise. It really worked.

When you are dealing with a behavior problem, you are faced with two choices. Either you go through the process of finding an alternative that will meet your desires while allowing your baby to test out his newfound autonomy, or you may simply decide that a particular issue is really not that important right now and just let it slide. As often as not, this is just as effective an approach, and your toddler will tire of having his feet on the table quickly enough on his own. Each parent will draw the line at a different place, which is just fine. The most important thing is that once you decide which route to take, you should stick with it. Your toddler will not understand if it's OK to put his feet on the table on Tuesday, it's suddenly not OK on Wednesday, and it's OK again on Thursday. If, on the other hand, you've consistently tried to change a behavior to no avail and you decide it's just not worth the battle anymore, it's all right to just give up. The key is to not resume the battle again a few days later.

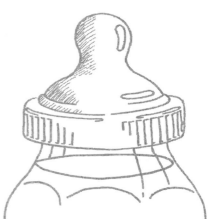

Toddler Appetites

Unlike young babies, who frequently "stock up" on their food supply at the end of the day in order to make it through a long night, older babies often eat the least amount in the evening. If someone else is caring for your baby during the day, it becomes especially important to ask the caregiver whether or not your baby has eaten well so you can interpret the quantity consumed at dinner accordingly.

Serious Feeding Difficulties

Some health experts in Britain estimate that as many as 1 in 20 children under the age of five go through a phase marked by serious feeding difficulties at some point in their development. In some cases, this can result in a phenomenon known as failure to thrive, in which a baby's growth tapers off or stops and does not keep pace with pediatric growth charts. However, it may take weeks or months before failure to thrive can be identified and addressed. In the meantime, anxious parents may become increasingly desperate to get their child to eat, which often compounds the problem. If you answer yes to several of the following questions, and the behaviors described are persistent, continuing for several weeks or more, your child may have a serious feeding difficulty.

- Does your child refuse to eat at many mealtimes?
- Does your child eat only very small amounts?
- Does your child regularly become upset or misbehave at meals?
- Is your child often irritable or listless?
- Are meals frequently a battle or drawn out for long periods?
- Do meals cause you a considerable amount of frustration, stress, or worry?

Strategies for Coping with Feeding Difficulties

- Choose the food offered with care, making sure that it contains as many calories and protein as possible to help make up for the small amount of food consumed. Good choices are cheese, eggs, whole milk yogurt or cottage cheese, custard, and peanut butter.
- Evaluate whether or not your child's eating habits are appropriate to his current age and abilities. For example, maybe your child is feeding himself with a spoon when he may not have mastered this skill yet.

Mealtime Misbehavior and Solutions

The following is a list of a few common toddler table manner issues and some suggestions for solutions.

Misbehavior	Alternative
Throwing food on the floor	Provide an alternative place to put unwanted food.
Doesn't want to wear a bib	Let baby choose which bib she wants to wear. Find a bib she can put on herself (with a little surreptitious help from you as you pull her hair out of the way). Abandon the bib, and let her wear a dishtowel around her neck, fastened with a clothespin. This is much more grown up, and you can easily bring a clothespin out with you.
Doesn't want to sit in the high chair	Let him fasten the safety strap himself (watch out for pinched fingers!). Let him climb into the high chair himself if that's safely possible. Give him an alternative place to sit; his own little table and chairs, a booster seat at the big table.
Won't stay in chair or booster seat	This one is tough. Even bribery with a favorite food is sometimes not enough to quell a restless spirit. In general, though, it's best to try and keep her involved in the meal with the rest of the family. Ask her to identify what's for dinner. Ask her what color each of the foods is or to count the number of peas on her plate if she is learning her colors and numbers.
Putting feet on the table	Another tough one. If you simply can't live with feet on the table for a few weeks until the novelty wears off, try finding a compelling reason for the feet to stay under the table. Maybe the family dog simply won't be able to know that the baby is home unless his feet are under the table.
Pouching: holding food in her mouth for long periods	This behavior is usually caused by the baby putting something in her mouth that she doesn't really want. If the food stays in there for a long time, she could possibly choke, and it's not very good for her teeth, either. You can usually ask her to spit the food out, swipe it out with your finger, or, if all else fails, hold her nose until she spits it out herself. If the problem persists, ask her why she is pouching. Maybe she needs help in deciding whether or not she wants something before it goes into her mouth.

- Evaluate your child's mealtime situation. Does your baby eat with the rest of the family? Are there any distractions during mealtimes, such as the television or an unruly older sibling? Is your baby comfortable with his current high chair, chair, or booster seat?

- Evaluate your current mealtime routine. Do mealtimes happen at predictable intervals? When, if ever, is your child hungry? Are meals too early or too late? Are there cues that help your child know that mealtime is approaching? How long do meals typically last?

- Be careful not to provide too much attention for not eating. This is a very easy mistake to make. Instead, offer praise for any interest in eating, and withdraw without comment when food is refused.

- Be sure to offer at least two courses at each meal so that your child has several opportunities to eat. Do not withhold a healthy end-of-the-meal treat because other foods were refused. In the case of severe feeding difficulties, calories are of paramount importance.

- Set a good example by eating well yourself at meals. Try to help mealtimes become a more enjoyable experience for the whole family.

- If both parents are at home, make sure you are both willing to stick with the same strategies for coping with a feeding difficulty. Once you have agreed to a plan, stick with it.

- Keep a record of your experiences, including your ideas for improvement, any small successes, and your impressions of whether or not your strategies are working.

Ruling Out Underlying Medical Problems

If you suspect your child may be experiencing a serious feeding difficulty, it is extremely important to consult her doctor. If your child does not seem to be growing properly, the doctor may wish to conduct tests to rule out any possible physical conditions that may be to blame. These include anemia, chronic infection or illness, enlarged tonsils or adenoids, allergies or asthma, and

Emotional Stress and Appetite

There is every indication that babies feel stress as keenly as adults—perhaps more so since they haven't been able to develop any coping mechanisms for stress and are unable to communicate to others the cause of their anxiety. As in adults, anxiety can often have an adverse effect on a baby's appetite. Babies may experience stress for many reasons, including an unstable living situation, a nonexistent or erratic routine, or the loss or absence of a loved one. If there is nothing you can do to eliminate the source of your baby's anxiety, try to help him to cope with it as best as you can.

Perhaps you can arrange to have him spend more time with you or another close family member or loved one. If he is old enough to understand and if you feel it won't increase his distress, talk with him about what you suspect is the cause of his anxiety. Let him know that he is not alone in feeling sad or angry, and that you will be there to help him. Resist the temptation to take the family on a trip or offer other distractions, such as the addition of a family pet. Frequently, these "compensations" only further disrupt a young child's sense of stability.

gastrointestinal problems such as parasitic infections or constipation. Less common medical causes for loss of appetite are endocrine imbalance, heart disease, or neurologic conditions such as cerebral palsy or mental retardation. It is important to note that most serious or chronic illnesses almost always have other symptoms besides loss of appetite.

- *Anemia.* Iron deficiency is one of the most common reasons for decreased appetite in small children and can be easily detected by a simple hematocrit or hemoglobin test that can often be conducted right in the doctor's office and assessed immediately. Iron deficiency anemia can be treated in the short term with a liquid iron supplement (use only as prescribed by your child's doctor). Once your child's appetite returns, you will need to be especially careful to make sure his diet contains sufficient iron.
- *Constipation.* If your child is constipated, she may have very little appetite, which is unfortunate, because filling, high-fiber foods are the best cure. Constipation can be easy to overlook as a contributing factor in decreased appetite, so be sure to mention it to your child's doctor when she is trying to make an assessment. Managing constipation requires making dietary changes in addition to other treatments your child's doctor may recommend.
- *Food allergies and intolerance.* In particular, celiac disease, more commonly known as gluten intolerance. This condition is fairly rare, affecting about 1 in 250 adults and children. People who are diagnosed with celiac disease are unable to tolerate gluten, a protein found in wheat, barley, rye, buckwheat, and alfalfa. Babies suffering from celiac disease will frequently experience diarrhea, malnutrition, and failure to thrive. However, once celiac disease is diagnosed, it can be completely cured by the elimination of gluten from the diet.

CHAPTER SEVEN

Understanding and Using Growth Charts

E ven the most laid-back parent is likely to worry about their child's growth at one time or another. The mother of a breastfeeding newborn may wonder if her baby is getting enough milk to gain weight as quickly as he should. A dad who has just learned to keep up with the voracious appetite of an 11-month-old girl may be taken aback by a sudden slowing of both growth and appetite right around her first birthday. These concerns are natural. After all, everyone wants his or her child to grow and thrive.

What Are Growth and Percentile Charts?

Pediatric growth charts have been in use since 1977 when they were developed by the National Center for Health Statistics (NCHS). These versions of the charts have been used by pediatricians, pediatric nurses, lactation professionals, dieticians, and parents ever since. There are other charts known as Body Mass Index (BMI) charts in use for older children and adults, but the charts discussed in this chapter reference weight for age, length for age, and head circumference for age, with separate charts for both boys and girls between birth and 36 months of age. Weight, length, and head circumference are all considered important measurements in the evaluation of an infant's growth. These charts plot the growth of a statistically significant number of infants over time, which appears on the graph as a series of curves, called percentiles. The smallest babies in the study are represented on the lowest curve on the chart as the 3rd percentile. The largest babies are shown on the highest curve, called the 97th percentile. The percentiles refer to the fact that within this large group of babies, 50 percent were below the median size or weight (the 50th percentile), and 50 percent were above the median. The babies analyzed for these studies were in good overall health and were considered in the "normal" range for weight, length, and head circumference. Of

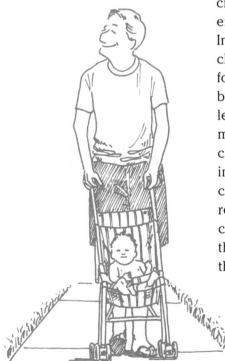

course, each child does not follow the same growth pattern. For this reason, the chart's developers have averaged the statistical information on all of the babies' growth so that each percentile appears as a smooth curve. The NCHS pediatric growth charts have also been adopted by the World Health Organization (WHO) for international use.

New Growth Charts Released in 2000

This book includes the latest revised growth charts from the NCHS and the Centers for Disease Control (CDC) released on May 30, 2000. How are they different from the charts first developed by the NCHS in 1977? The data used for the revised charts, covering birth to 36 months, was collected from five national health examination surveys conducted between 1963 and 1994 and five supplementary data sources. The previous charts used data collected primarily from Caucasian formula-fed babies in southwestern Ohio, which did not accurately reflect diverse ethnicities and breastfed infants in the United States. The new charts also extend the percentiles shown from the 95th to the 97th percentile and the 5th to the 3rd percentile. Improved data and statistical curve smoothing procedures have also made the charts more valuable for clinical use.

How Charts Are Used to Evaluate Your Baby's Growth

Health professionals use growth charts in two very important ways. First, the charts are an invaluable tool for the evaluation of a child's development. In some cases, a deviation from normal growth patterns may even be the only indication a pediatrician has of an underlying medical problem. Second, doctors and nurses use growth charts to educate parents about their child's growth patterns. Many parents do not understand how to use the charts to interpret their child's developmental progress, so this consultation with the doctor is essential.

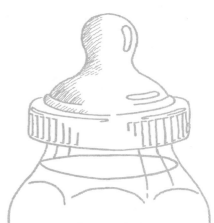

Guessing Your Child's Full-Grown Height

Although there is no perfectly predictable way to gauge what your baby's height will be when she is fully grown, you can use the following formula to make a pretty strong guess. Add together the height of both parents, and divide by two. Girls will usually be about two and a half inches shorter than this figure. Boys will be about two and a half inches taller.

Body Mass Index Charts for Children Aged 2 to 20

While the revised growth charts for infants is significant, the introduction of Body Mass Index (BMI) charts for older children is probably the most important outcome of the CDC's new charts. The BMI is cross-referenced with a child's weight for stature (height) measurements and gives pediatricians and health care providers a more accurate means to asses a child's growth and development for his age. With the increased prevalence of overweight and eating disorders among young people, this tool can be invaluable in spotting a trend early and correcting it before it becomes a problem.

Beginning at birth, and continuing at regular checkups, your child's pediatrician will measure her weight, head circumference, and length and will plot these measurements on each graph at the line representing her age. Where she falls in relation to other babies will determine her percentile. If she falls at the 50th percentile for weight, for example, she is currently right in the middle of normal babies. If she falls at the 20th percentile, 80 out of 100 normal babies of her gender and age would be larger than her; 20 out of 100 of these babies would be smaller than her. If she falls at the 75th percentile, 25 babies would be larger than her and 75 smaller. It is not uncommon for parents (and especially grandparents) to place too much emphasis on these figures. All of the babies who fall within the range of the graph are considered normal. The doctor, on the other hand, is more concerned with looking at the measurements in relation to one another and the pattern of growth over time.

For example, a doctor who sees that a baby's weight was at the 45th percentile at birth and progressed more or less normally until 6 months will be concerned if this baby's weight suddenly dips below the normal range at 9 months. A sudden unexplained change of this nature may signal a serious problem, and the doctor will probably conduct a thorough examination to determine the cause.

In another case, the baby's weight may have increased from the 60th to the 95th percentile between 24 and 30 months, with a lower but steady 35th percentile for length. If one or both parents suffer from obesity, this may be an early sign of the same problem in the child. The doctor will probably discuss with the parents ways for preventing obesity as the child continues to grow, so that his height can catch up with his weight.

Other Factors Affecting Growth

Pediatricians know that babies' growth patterns are frequently erratic, with weight and length gain usually occurring in bursts several weeks or months apart. This can be worrisome to parents who expect their child's progress to conform to the smooth curves depicted in the charts. In reality, very few children, if any, grow in this manner. Often, however, if a baby's growth seems to have slowed down more than is expected during the second half of the first year, it may be the result of a series of minor illnesses common at this age. Some babies even lose weight after a prolonged gastrointestinal illness. In this case, the doctor may ask the parents to bring their baby back in two weeks or a month to confirm that his growth will catch up and continue normally. In the intervening time, most babies will have a growth spurt that makes up for lost time. If you are concerned that your baby is not growing properly, most pediatricians will take more frequent measurements to allay your fears, so don't hesitate to ask.

Genetics

Genetics also plays a large role in a baby's growth pattern. Most people and babies fall into one of three categories of body type. An *ectomorph* is tall and thin and would become apparent in the higher percentiles for length, and a comparatively low percentile for weight. A *mesomorph* usually has nearly equivalent percentile measurements for length and weight. And a baby who falls into a higher percentile for weight than length tends toward the *endomorph* (pear-shaped) body type. A baby's body type is strongly linked to that of his parents, so pediatricians will frequently evaluate whether or not a child's growth pattern is normal by observing the parents.

Breastfed vs. Formula-Fed Infants

A breastfed infant will typically show a slowing in weight gain at around six months of age. Sometimes, their weight percentile may even cross over from above to below the median for their age. The same babies will usually continue to gain in length at the same rate as before. This adjustment is expected and rarely causes any concern for pediatricians, although parents may find it unsettling.

Higher-Birth-Weight Infants

Babies who are 9 to 10 pounds (or heavier) at birth, but whose parents are of average weight and height, will usually gain weight more slowly starting at 4 to 6 months. This trend is usually completed by 18 months, during which time the babies settle into their true place in the percentile charts.

Low-Birth-Weight Infants

Babies who are born small because of premature birth will usually catch up with their peers by their second birthday, but some preemies remain somewhat small throughout their lives. This pattern should then be considered normal for this child. When evaluating the growth of a low-birth-weight infant who was born prematurely, it may be useful to plot his measurements at the point he would be at were he born at his due date. Often, this shows that a baby falls well within the normal range with his peers for their gestational age. Some pediatricians may choose to use growth charts specifically established for premature infants.

Babies who are born small because of fetal alcohol syndrome, exposure to drugs or infection in the womb, a decreased supply of blood to the placenta, or a chromosomal disorder may never catch up with other babies. Even though our society places a lot of importance on stature, parents would do well to forget about their child's difference in height. As long as your baby is healthy and growing steadily, her pediatrician will be satisfied with her progress and you should be also.

CDC Growth Charts: United States

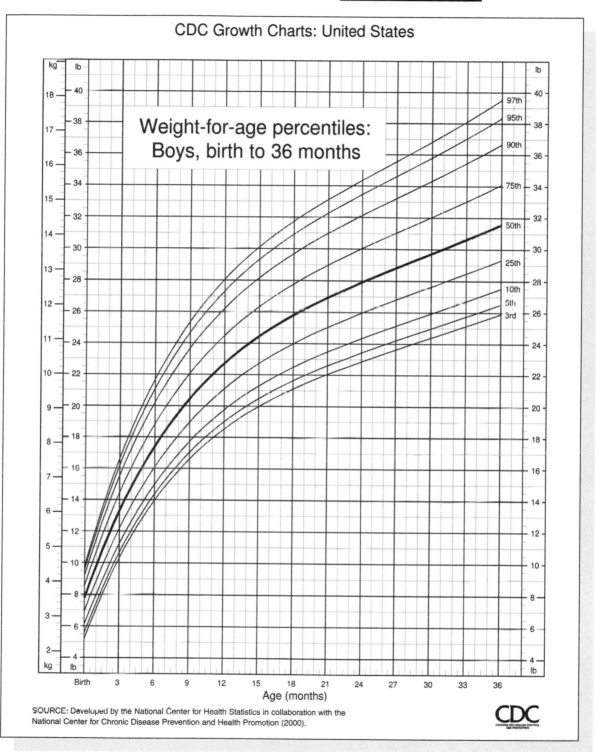

Weight-for-age percentiles:
Boys, birth to 36 months

Age (months)

SOURCE: Developed by the National Center for Health Statistics in collaboration with the National Center for Chronic Disease Prevention and Health Promotion (2000).

CDC
CENTERS FOR DISEASE CONTROL AND PREVENTION

CDC Growth Charts: United States

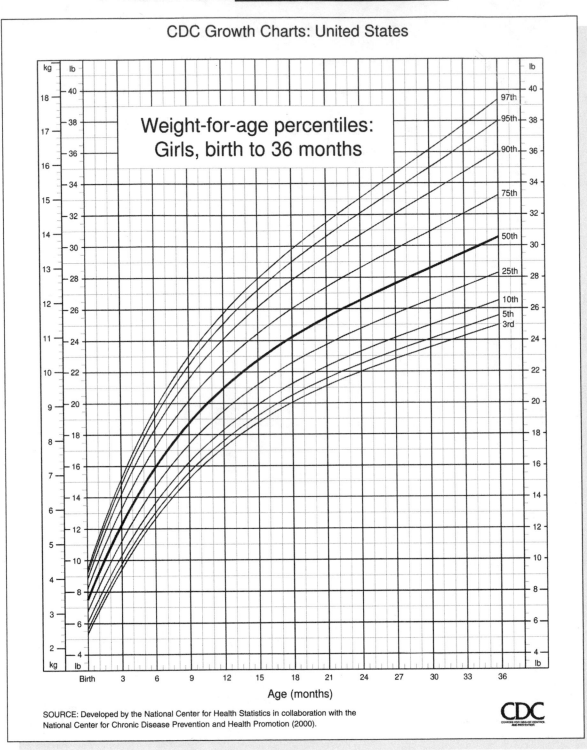

Weight-for-age percentiles:
Girls, birth to 36 months

Age (months)

SOURCE: Developed by the National Center for Health Statistics in collaboration with the
National Center for Chronic Disease Prevention and Health Promotion (2000).

CDC

CDC Growth Charts: United States

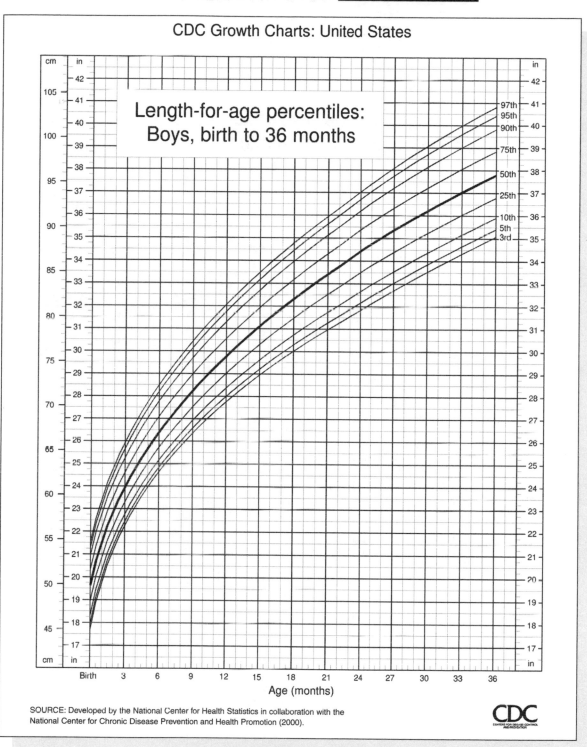

Length-for-age percentiles:
Boys, birth to 36 months

SOURCE: Developed by the National Center for Health Statistics in collaboration with the
National Center for Chronic Disease Prevention and Health Promotion (2000).

CDC
CENTERS FOR DISEASE CONTROL
AND PREVENTION

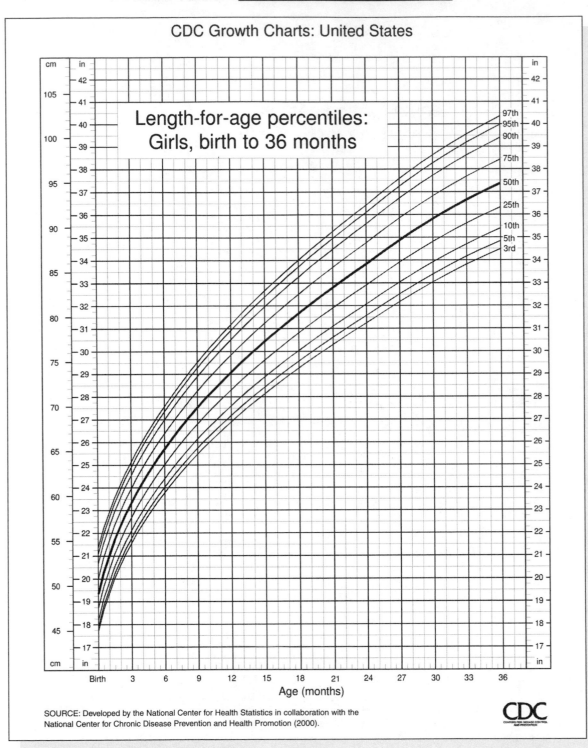

CDC Growth Charts: United States

Length-for-age percentiles:
Girls, birth to 36 months

SOURCE: Developed by the National Center for Health Statistics in collaboration with the
National Center for Chronic Disease Prevention and Health Promotion (2000).

CDC
CENTERS FOR DISEASE CONTROL
AND PREVENTION

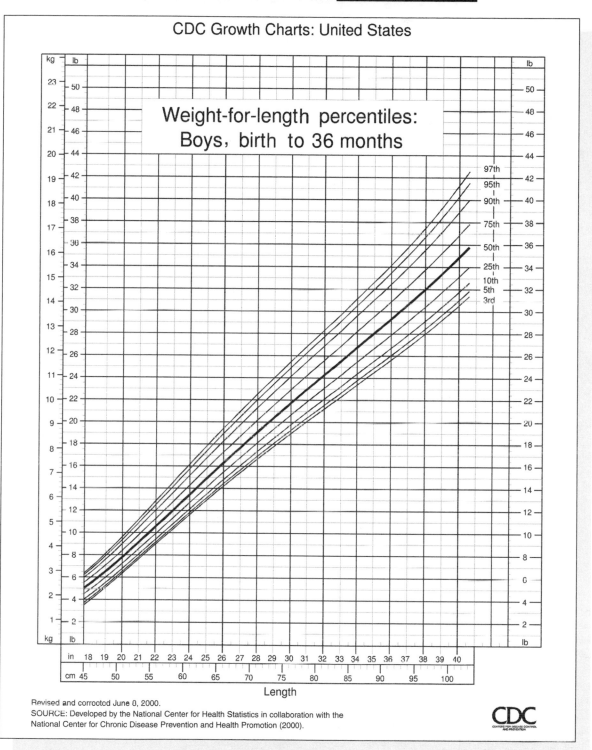

CDC Growth Charts: United States

Weight-for-length percentiles:
Boys, birth to 36 months

Length

Revised and corrected June 0, 2000.
SOURCE: Developed by the National Center for Health Statistics in collaboration with the
National Center for Chronic Disease Prevention and Health Promotion (2000).

CDC
CENTERS FOR DISEASE CONTROL
AND PREVENTION

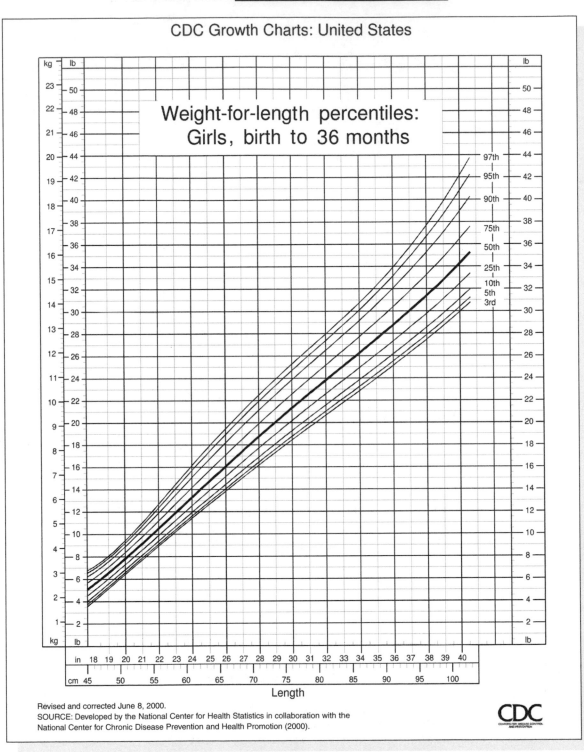

CDC Growth Charts: United States

Weight-for-length percentiles:
Girls, birth to 36 months

Length

Revised and corrected June 8, 2000.
SOURCE: Developed by the National Center for Health Statistics in collaboration with the
National Center for Chronic Disease Prevention and Health Promotion (2000).

CDC
CENTERS FOR DISEASE CONTROL
AND PREVENTION

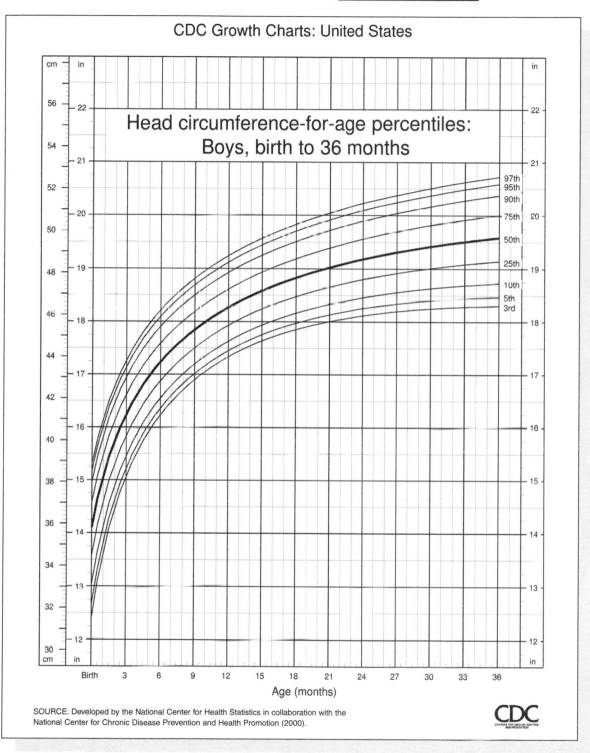

CDC Growth Charts: United States

Head circumference-for-age percentiles:
Boys, birth to 36 months

SOURCE: Developed by the National Center for Health Statistics in collaboration with the
National Center for Chronic Disease Prevention and Health Promotion (2000).

CDC
CENTERS FOR DISEASE CONTROL
AND PREVENTION

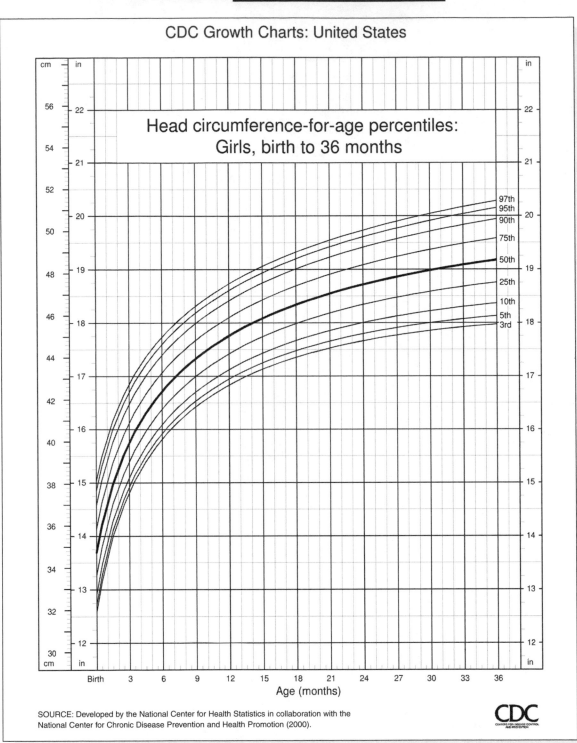

CDC Growth Charts: United States

Head circumference-for-age percentiles:
Girls, birth to 36 months

SOURCE: Developed by the National Center for Health Statistics in collaboration with the
National Center for Chronic Disease Prevention and Health Promotion (2000).

CHAPTER EIGHT

Every Bite Counts: Infant Nutrition 101

Nutrition Basics

Unfortunately, American children are likely to suffer from poor nutrition now more than ever before. Only 20 percent of children get the recommended five or more daily servings of fruits and vegetables, and believe it or not, french fries comprise a quarter of the vegetables! It's no wonder that the percentage of overweight children has doubled since the 1960s. Parents complain that they can't get their children to eat healthy foods, and hectic school and work schedules only make the situation worse. However, starting early and reinforcing healthy eating habits at home later have been shown to make a dramatic difference in childhood nutrition. Becoming familiar with the information in this chapter is wonderful, but more important is your overall approach to healthy eating as a family.

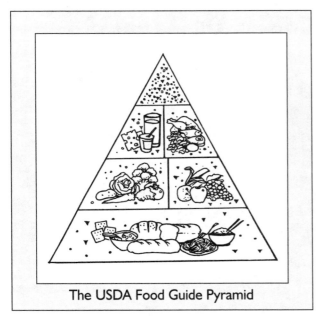

The USDA Food Guide Pyramid

The Food Guide Pyramid

The Food Guide Pyramid was developed in 1992 by the USDA to replace the old "four basic food groups" we learned about in school. The new pyramid places a larger emphasis on grains as the mainstay of a healthy diet and gives more guidance to consumers as to the proportion of different foods to eat each day. The Food Guide Pyramid was modeled to a certain extent on the "Mediterranean Diet," which is a diet that has been practiced for centuries throughout Italy, Spain, Greece, and other Mediterranean cultures. In these cultures, grains in pasta, bread, rice, and other baked goods and cereals are the staple foods of the diet, while fresh fruits and vegetables are consumed several times each day, with a smaller amount of beans, legumes, and animal products providing the balance of nutrition. This diet represents the reverse of the traditional American diet, which places a heavy emphasis on animal products, with fewer fiber-containing foods and fresh fruits and vegetables. The robust well-being of Mediterranean people is a testament to the healthfulness of their traditional diet.

Understanding Serving Sizes

The most common mistake people make when attempting to follow the guidelines put forward in the Food Guide Pyramid involves a misunderstanding of serving sizes. You may feel daunted by the challenge of eating three to five servings of vegetables a day, until you realize that you can complete your entire daily consumption of vegetables in one stir-fried vegetable supper. In actual fact, the serving sizes for each level of the pyramid are much smaller than we realize. The AAP recommends the following serving sizes in each category for children one to three years of age:

Food Group	Serving Size
Grains	Bread, $\frac{1}{2}$ slice
6–11 servings/day	Cereal, rice, pasta, cooked, $\frac{1}{4}$ cup
	Cereal, dry, $\frac{1}{3}$ cup
	Crackers, 2–3
Vegetables	Vegetables, cooked, $\frac{1}{4}$ cup
2–3 servings/day	
Fruits	Fruit, cooked or canned, $\frac{1}{4}$ cup
2–3 servings/day	Fruit, fresh, $\frac{1}{2}$ piece
	Juice, $\frac{1}{4}$ cup
Dairy	Milk, $\frac{1}{2}$ cup
2–3 servings/day	Cheese, $\frac{1}{2}$ ounce
	Yogurt, $\frac{1}{3}$ cup
Meats and other proteins	Meat, fish, poultry, tofu, 1 ounce
2 servings/day	(two 1-inch cubes)
	Beans, dried, cooked, $\frac{1}{4}$ cup
	Egg, $\frac{1}{2}$

From *American Academy of Pediatrics: Guide to Your Child's Nutrition* by W.H. Dietz and L. Stern, copyright ©1999 by W.H. Dietz and L. Stern. Used by permission of Villard Books, a division of Random House, Inc.

Grains: The Base of the Food Guide Pyramid

Grains are by far the most abundant food source on the planet, and almost all cultures cultivate them as a staple food. About two-thirds of the calories in grains come from complex carbohydrates, which are absorbed slowly by the body to provide sustained energy. Nutritionists therefore recognize grains as the most important staple

food in a healthy diet. Grains are almost always the seed of a plant, which means that they are packed with all of the nutrition a plant will need to regenerate, which is why they are so good for you. Grains are also naturally low in fat. When you think about it, grains naturally satisfy your body, and many so-called comfort foods are made primarily of grains, such as bread, pancakes, pasta, rice pudding, risotto, and oatmeal.

Grains (6–11 servings per day)

Grains like whole wheat, brown rice, oats, corn, barley, wild rice, and rye are an important source of complex carbohydrates, fiber, folic acid, B vitamins, and minerals like zinc and iron. They are also a great source of complete proteins when mixed with dairy products or legumes. Wheat in bread, pasta, and rice are probably the most common sources of grain nutrition in the American diet. You can boost the nutritional content of these foods tremendously by choosing whole wheat and brown rice. White flour and rice have been stripped of the nutrient-rich bran and germ in the grain, leaving only the largest part of the grain, called the endosperm.

Wheat is unfortunately also a common allergenic food, especially in children. If your child is sensitive to wheat, meeting the grain requirement in the food pyramid will be challenging. Fortunately, there are many other grains that may not be as well known but that make delicious baked goods and cereals. Buckwheat, rye, amaranth, quinoa, and millet are all becoming more commonly used in healthy baked goods along with corn and rice. In fact, even if your child is not allergic to wheat, it's a good idea to look for these grains in the foods you give him, because variety provides for more balanced nutrition.

The great news is that babies and children (and adults) love grains. We all have favorites in this category: rice pilaf, grits, polenta, oatmeal, fresh crusty bread, Spanish paella, pasta of all stripes, waffles, tortillas, barley soup, risotto, savory crackers, hearty muffins—the list could go on forever.

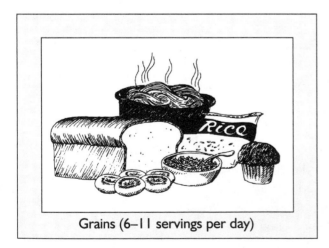

Grains (6–11 servings per day)

Fresh Produce: For Vitamins, Minerals, and Fiber

Fresh fruit and vegetables are almost as important to a healthy diet as grains, but for different reasons. First of all, they provide a natural counterpart to grains and make them more palatable in many cases. Why else would spaghetti seem naked without tomato sauce? Where would your pancakes be without a glass of orange juice alongside them? Also, fresh produce provides many important nutrients that are lacking in grains, such as vitamin C and calcium. According to the Food Guide Pyramid, we should be having five to nine servings of fresh fruits and vegetables every day, which may be a challenge for some.

Fruits and Vegetables (5-9 servings per day)

Vegetables (3–5 servings per day)

Vegetables provide the most variety of any food source. Often the whole plant—seeds, roots, stems, and leaves— is edible and nutritious. Vegetables provide complex carbohydrates, fiber, folic acid, calcium (as in dark greens and soybeans), and vitamins C, E, and A. No one vegetable provides all of these nutrients, however, which is why eating a variety is important. Later in this chapter you will find a list of nutrient sources found in foods. You may wish to study it, but eating a variety of foods is really the best hedge against compromised nutrition. The good news is that your body can combine different nutrients that have been eaten over several days to balance your diet.

Getting Value from Your Veggies

- Choose a variety of colors in your vegetables. Orange, red, and yellow vegetables are an important source of beta-carotene (vitamin A); dark leafy greens and soybeans contain significant amounts of calcium.
- Steaming rather than boiling will preserve a greater amount of nutrients in your vegetables. Raw vegetables are the most nutritious of all.

- In season, locally produced or vine-ripened vegetables usually retain the most nutrients, because they have been less degraded during the distribution process.
- Store your vegetables in a plastic bag in the refrigerator to prevent decay and water loss.

Fruits (2–4 servings per day)

Fruits are as important to a balanced diet as vegetables, but for different reasons. First, fruits are a delicious way to get more fiber, vitamin C, calcium, and folic acid. Perhaps equally important, though, is that kids really love fruit, and introducing them to the incredible variety and seasonality of fruit can provide a gateway to pleasurable eating experiences that will benefit them their whole lives. Sure, you can get strawberries grown in hothouses year round these days, but somehow the experience of eating fresh in-season organic strawberries cannot be matched. One of my most cherished childhood memories is of sitting in our strawberry patch in summer, eating dozens of ripe, sweet berries (and our family was definitely *not* the grow-it-yourself type). As with vegetables, providing a variety is the most important component to balanced nutrition, which should be no trouble with fruit. One thing to consider, however, is that the list of nonorganic produce items containing the most pesticides and chemical residues in Chapter 5, includes some of the most popular fruits (only one vegetable appears on the list). The average baby or child consumes about 60 times the amount of fruit per pound of body weight than does an adult. When buying fruits, especially, consider organic or be sure to wash the fruit carefully.

Fruit Juice

Babies and kids love juice, which is a good thing in moderation. Juice does have some nutrients, and it can be the easiest way to get fluids into your child. However, juice is never as nutritious as the whole fruit or vegetable, and it has almost none of the fiber you need from these sources, along with plenty of fructose (fruit sugar). How much juice is too much? Experts disagree slightly on guidelines for juice consumption, but my pediatrician put it best, "Just

---

Feeding Your Baby in the Real World

"I think that people give their children way too much fruit juice. It's full of sugar (even if it is natural sugar), which can lead to sugar cravings, cavities, and even obesity . . . kids can get full on it and then won't eat food that is good for them. So I started both my kids on water (or milk) in their sippy cups so that it would be 'normal' for them to drink water. Sometimes Sophia (my three-year-old) asks for juice because she's been introduced to it elsewhere, so I give her a cup that is 10 percent juice and the rest is water. As long as she sees a little color in the water, she's satisfied that she is drinking 'juice.'"

—Christina, mother of Sophia and Christopher

make sure he doesn't become a juice-a-holic!" Some babies have a higher tolerance for juice, but you'll know she's getting too much juice and other fruits as part of her diet if she gets a bright red, painful rash around her anus because of the high acidity in these foods. Another problem that can occur, producing gas, intestinal pain, and diarrhea, happens when a child is unable to properly digest the sugars in the juice. Generally, you should always dilute juice for babies ($\frac{1}{3}$ juice to $\frac{2}{3}$ water, or even weaker if your baby will accept it), and make sure she doesn't get more than six to eight ounces of undiluted juice per day. Also, be sure to buy 100 percent juice, not the stuff sweetened with high fructose corn syrup.

Protein Powerhouses

While this portion of the Food Guide Pyramid is smaller in comparison to its grain and fresh produce counterparts, it provides some of the most appealing and certainly the widest variety of foods. It is this section of the pyramid that makes our diets varied and interesting and that answers that burning question, "What's for dinner?" These foods also provide the critical missing protein link that is begun by eating grains. If you examine this section of the Food Guide Pyramid carefully, you will understand that in this section you have the most powerful tool for creating a diet that fits the needs of your family, your tastes, and your lifestyle. The pyramid recommends four to six servings from the entire category daily. When using this guideline to feed a baby over one year who does not have any significant food allergies, I would make the following recommendations: About two to three of the daily servings in this category should come from dairy products such as milk, yogurt, and cottage cheese. There should be at least one serving each day comprised of legumes, nut butters, or soy products, such as soy milk and tofu. The rest of the requirement may then be met with servings of eggs, meat, poultry, and fish, which can be served a few times a week. If

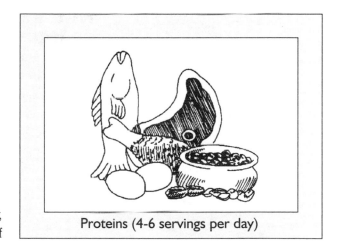

Proteins (4-6 servings per day)

you wish to follow a lacto/ovo vegetarian lifestyle, simply keep eggs and increase the number of daily servings of legumes, nuts and seeds, and soy products.

Legumes (2–3 servings per day—or nuts or meat)

Legumes or beans are a commonly overlooked source of protein, fiber, calcium, folic acid, zinc, and iron. Choosing foods made from soybeans is an easy way to increase your and your baby's consumption of legumes. Cultured soy bean curd (or tofu) alone is amazingly versatile. You can drop firm tofu cubes in soups or stews, sauté it with vegetables in a stir-fry, or blend it into a fruit smoothie or dippy sauce. Soy drinks, which are great poured over cereal (making a complete protein source), and tempeh or plain steamed soybeans are also wonderful ways to serve soy. All of this said, you may not have to do much coaxing to include soy in your baby's diet, since small cubes of cold plain tofu are a favorite finger food for many babies. Other popular legumes are lentils, garbanzo beans, and kidney or black beans. If you buy any of these beans canned, be sure to wash them thoroughly to rinse away some of the sodium they are usually packed with.

Nuts and Seeds (2–3 servings per day— or legumes or meat)

Nuts and seeds are actually similar in function to grains and legumes in that they contain all of the genetic material and nutrients for regeneration of the plant. Nuts and seeds are a powerhouse source of essential fatty acids, protein, fiber, folic acid, B and E vitamins, and minerals like calcium, zinc, and iron. Some children may be allergic to nuts (particularly peanuts), so proceed with caution. Sesame seeds are the best first introduction for babies who have shown no sign of, and have no family history of, food allergies. You can try tahini (sesame butter) mixed with yogurt, oatmeal, or any number of other dishes sometime after 10 months. If your baby has no adverse reaction to sesame, try almond butter or

High Protein Food Combinations

Animal foods (meat, poultry, fish, eggs, or milk) are the only source for complete proteins, which contain all of the amino acids essential for good health. However, eating large quantities of animal foods is not necessary because different plant foods may be combined to provide complete proteins. Also, dairy products may be added to dishes composed primarily of plant foods to provide a good source of complete protein. Most of these healthy food choices are made without us even realizing them. Who would want a bowl of granola without milk, yogurt, or soy beverage poured over it? Similarly, most traditional cuisines provide complete protein meals as a matter of course. Rice and beans, hummus and pita bread—even the old peanut butter sandwich is an example. It isn't even necessary to eat two foods together that contain complementary proteins, because your body can store and combine amino acids consumed at different times. For more about protein, see the "Nutritionary" later in this chapter.

High Protein Food Combinations	Examples
Whole Grains and Legumes	Brown rice and beans or lentils, soy "veggie" burger on whole wheat bread, tofu stir fry with brown rice, whole grain breakfast cereal with soy beverage, bulgur taboule with hummus, nut butter on whole wheat bread, whole wheat pasta e fagioli.
Whole Grains and Dairy Products	Whole grain breakfast cereal and milk or yogurt, crackers and cheese or cottage cheese, whole wheat pasta with a sprinkling of parmesan, home-made pizza with cheese, oatmeal and milk, polenta with milk and cheese.
Vegetables and Dairy Products	Broccoli and cheese sauce, baked potatoes and sour cream, scalloped potatoes.
Seeds and Dairy Products	Tahini or nut butter and yogurt.

flaxseed oil next. Remember that your baby will not be able to eat whole nuts until his molars come in (most pediatricians recommend waiting until three years of age to reduce risk of choking), so butters or finely ground nuts and seeds are the best option. When buying nut butter, be sure to choose the natural kind even though you will have to mix the oil back in. Conventional, processed

peanut butter has unhealthy hydrogenated oils blended into it to keep it from separating and to increase shelf life (check the label).

Tips for Buying and Using Nuts and Seeds

- To get the most nutrition and shelf life from nuts and seeds, buy them raw, but hulled, and store them in an airtight container in a cool place or in the refrigerator. Buy nuts with freshness in mind. Many health food stores sell large quantities of nuts and are, therefore, more likely to have fresh stock.
- When it comes to nuts and seeds, organic is best because the seed portion of any plant is most likely to store pesticide residues, and it is not possible to wash them.
- Roast nuts or seeds for flavor, if you wish, by simply heating them in a cast iron pan on the stove for five minutes or so over medium heat, turning with a wooden spoon occasionally. You can also roast on a sheet pan in the oven or in the toaster oven. You won't need to add any oil because there's plenty already in the nuts. Some people like to sprinkle them with a little soy sauce or tamari, but I think there's nothing better than a warm, freshly toasted plain walnut.

Meat, Poultry, Fish and Eggs (2–3 servings per day—or legumes or nuts)

Some parents choose to wait until their baby is a little older before introducing meat or poultry into his diet, and some never introduce them at all. This is fine. Although meat is a good source of complete proteins, this requirement is easily met through other sources in a diet that includes whole grains, legumes, eggs, and nuts and seeds. In fact, most Americans get more protein than they need without even trying. Not only that, animal fats are higher in percentage of saturated to unsaturated fat, and low in fiber. It's not that meat and poultry don't have nutritional components; they do. Beef and animal livers are a good source of iron, for example, and meats also supply B vitamins. Some parents object to feeding meat to their children because of the unknown effect of hormones, antibiotics, tranquilizers, and other drugs commonly used to treat livestock. Fortunately, free-range and organic meat and poultry are becoming available in more parts of the country.

Although not essential, meat and/or poultry can have a healthy place in a child's diet, but it is best to serve them sparingly. Serving meat and poultry to your baby two to four times a week is about right. You can also use them more frequently as accents to a dish that is composed primarily of vegetables and grains or legumes. Black bean chili with beef is a favorite served with rice and a dollop of sour cream. Parents should remember that meat is grouped with legumes, nuts and seeds, fish, and eggs because all of these foods meet the requirement outlined by the USDA.

Fish is a better source of nutrients than meat and poultry. Fish, for example, has the same amount of protein as meat as well as lots of healthy unsaturated fat (namely omega-3, which is very important for brain development) and iron and vitamin B-12. There is an unbelievable variety of seafood, however, and not all of it is good to feed your baby.

Fish Selections: Best Bets for Feeding Your Baby

- Shellfish is a commonly allergenic food and it is best to wait until after your baby's first birthday to cautiously introduce it. If your baby is susceptible to food allergy, wait until she is two or three before cautiously introducing shellfish.
- Cold-water fish like salmon and tuna are highest in healthy unsaturated fats.
- Grilled or broiled fish is preferable to fried, and packaged fish sticks are the least healthy of all.
- Freshwater fishes, such as trout and bass, and bottom-feeders, such as flounder and catfish, are the most likely to contain pollutant residues unless they are farm-raised.
- Babies and children should never eat raw fish or shellfish, i.e., sushi, sashimi, or raw oysters.

Eggs make great baby food, and most babies readily eat them with gusto. They are an important source of high-quality protein, as well as several vitamins and minerals like calcium, zinc, and iron. Recently, eggs have become available that come from chickens given a diet high in omega-3 fatty acids. While these eggs are not yet widely available, consuming them can have a positive influence on healthy brain development for growing children. Hard cooked egg yolk is easily mashed up and incorporated into homemade baby food, and scrambled eggs make great finger food for your older baby. Egg white is a possible allergen in younger babies, so you should stick with only yolks until your baby is about a year old.

Eating eggs has been discouraged in recent years due to their high cholesterol content. However, recent research indicates that because eggs also have low amounts of saturated fat, they are in fact a healthy food when consumed in moderation (two or three eggs a week is good). There are literally thousands of ways to prepare eggs: egg salad, egg fritatta with potatoes and peppers, omelets with myriad fillings, egg bread, egg custard, French toast, and so on. Eggs can unfortunately be an unwanted source of salmonella food poisoning, so make sure to check that eggs are not cracked, and to wash your hands after handling raw eggs. Babies should never be given raw eggs.

Dairy Products (2–3 servings per day)

Fluid cow's milk is the most obvious form of dairy nutrition (other than breastmilk) for a baby over the age of one year. It provides almost all of the basic nutrients a child needs, including protein, calcium, vitamin A, riboflavin, folic acid, and vitamin D (but not iron). These nutrients can be replaced from other sources, but milk is so readily consumed by most babies and children, that its convenience cannot be matched. There has been a lot of buzz in recent years about lactose intolerance and milk allergy. If your child is lactose intolerant or has an allergy to milk, your first line of defense should actually be other dairy products. Yogurt, cottage cheese, and other cheeses are often well accepted by allergic or intolerant children. This is because the allergenic proteins in milk are often broken down during culturing and fermentation. Similarly, lactose is largely

Dairy Products (2-3 servings per day)

broken down to become digestible lactase, in cheese and the more aged a cheese, the less lactose it will contain.

It's important to understand the difference between lactose intolerance and milk allergy, because the two are commonly confused. Lactose intolerance is your body's compromised ability to digest the lactose (milk sugar) found in cow's milk products. Lactose intolerance can cause bloating; diarrhea; abdominal pain; and a red, painful rash around the anus in infants. The intolerance may be mild or severe and is usually an inherited trait. Adults are more likely to experience lactose intolerance than babies and children. Children and adults may also experience temporary intolerance following a stomach upset. Some dairy products have more lactose than others do. Nonfat milk has more lactose than low-fat or whole milk, and yogurt has more lactose than cheese.

Milk allergy, on the other hand, is the body's reaction to the proteins found in cow's milk, and can cause a runny nose, an eczema-like rash (especially on the cheeks), asthma, or recurrent bronchitis. Milk allergy is rare in children and adults, but affects approximately 75 percent of infants under the age of one year. This is why doctors recommend waiting until your baby is a year old before giving her milk. Yogurt is OK at nine months because the proteins are partially digested and more easily tolerated, and the same is true of cheese. A few infants may even have allergic reactions to their mother's breastmilk after she eats dairy products. Children older than one year who continue to experience milk allergy usually outgrow it by the age of two or three. If you suspect your baby has lactose intolerance or milk allergy, be sure to discuss this with her pediatrician. The nutrients found in dairy products are important and must be replaced through other sources.

Milk Rationing

It is a good idea to limit the amount of milk your child drinks to less than 24 ounces a day when he is between the ages of 12 and 24 months. If he still drinks 18 ounces or more of milk a day when he is two years old, you might consider switching to low-fat milk a little earlier than you normally would. To keep track of the

Skim Milk vs. Whole-Milk

Is low-fat (or skim milk) more healthy for babies? The answer is an unreserved no. As mentioned earlier, cow's milk should not be introduced before your baby is one year old. After a year and until two years old, whole milk is preferred to provide the fat necessary for the child's rapidly growing brain. Low-fat milk products may be used after two years.

amount of milk your child is drinking and eating with cereal, measure his daily "allotment," and keep it separately in a clean jar in the refrigerator.

The Tip of the Pyramid: Fats and Sweets

In an attempt to steer Americans away from less healthful eating habits that include far too many foods containing saturated fat and much too much sugar, the USDA has overstated its point somewhat, in my opinion. Yes, dessert every night is not a good idea, but if more frequent desserts also contain healthful elements such as whole grains or fresh fruit, less caution may be in order. Similarly, while saturated fat has been shown to have a detrimental effect on health, oils that contain healthy unsaturated and polyunsaturated fats are actually healthful to use in moderation.

Fats, Oils, and Sweets (Use Sparingly)

Contrary to popular belief, fats and oils *are* necessary for good health, especially for growing children, but they should be the right kinds and should always be consumed in moderation. For more information regarding essential fatty acids and saturated, unsaturated, and hydrogenated fats and oils, refer to the "Nutritionary" later in this chapter. Sweets (meaning candy, cookies, ice cream, cake, and so on), on the other hand, are not nutritionally necessary, and many parents choose to limit them in varying degrees for their children. If you do allow sweets, be moderate and make sure the ingredients they include besides sugar are as healthful as possible.

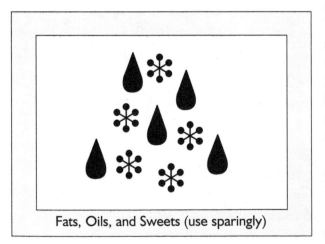

Fats, Oils, and Sweets (use sparingly)

Good Fat vs. Bad Fat: Health Choices for Your Baby

Choosing the right kinds of fats to help your baby grow is as important as making sure she has enough fat in her diet overall. In general, you should try to limit saturated fats as part of the overall fat content of her diet. However, a few foods containing saturated fat, like eggs, whole-milk dairy products, or avocados have so many other nutritional benefits that babies can eat them more freely than can adults. Hydrogenated fats are not good for anyone's health.

Sugar: Good or Bad?

Many people who are fond of sugary treats like to point out that all carbohydrates are eventually broken down by the body into simple sugar or glucose. By this logic, they conclude that the eventual result is the same for whole wheat bread as it is for Twinkies. Not exactly. While it is true that all carbohydrates eventually become glucose, complex carbohydrates, like those found in whole grains, fresh fruits, and vegetables, come with myriad other nutrients and fiber built into their molecular structure, which provide the body with sustained energy. Simple carbohydrates such as those found in high-sugar foods like candy, soda, and commercial baked goods, are quickly absorbed into the bloodstream, causing a roller coaster effect with a rapid increase in blood sugar levels followed by a steep crash as the body quickly runs out of energy. It's not really the sugar that's bad for you, but the lack of other nutrients in foods containing large amounts of sugar.

Understanding how simple and complex carbohydrates differ becomes even more critical when you are feeding a growing child with a variable appetite. If your child is in refusal mode, don't fall into the trap of offering sweets because you're afraid she won't eat anything at all. Sugary foods do not provide anything that will help your child grow, and the energy she does obtain from sweets will not last very long. Better to wait and offer her real "grow food" when she is truly hungry. This does not mean that you must banish all sweet foods from your child's life (although some parents do choose this route). Any number of other sweet treats like fresh or dried fruit or whole grain muffins and cookies delight most children if they are considered normal options in your household. Don't expect your baby or toddler to be happy with his healthy

Fat Calorie Needs: Babies and Children vs. Adults

While many adults are concerned about limiting the amount of fat in their diets, it is a mistake to try to use the same measures when examining the fat content in the diet of a baby or child. Fat for both children and adults should be as healthy as possible, meaning a lower proportion of saturated to unsaturated fats. The percentage of calories from fat for babies, children, and adults are as follows:

0–12 months	50 percent
1–3 years	40 percent
3–5 years	30–35 percent
adult	less than 30 percent

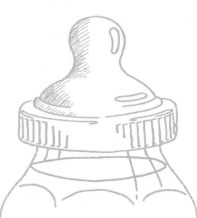

How Much Sugar Do You Eat?

In the late 1800s the average American consumed approximately 12 pounds of sugar annually. By 1975, this figure had increased to an astounding 118 pounds, and by 1990, the average American was consuming 137.5 pounds of sugar each year. That's about a third of a pound every day.

treat, though, if you are munching away on a candy bar at the same time. Kids are much smarter than that!

Does Too Much Sugar Cause Behavioral Problems?

Excess sugar intake has been blamed for an assortment of behavioral problems from simple crankiness to Attention Deficit Disorder (ADD). Research into possible links between sugar and behavior is ongoing, and results still vary drastically. We do know that for all people a drop in blood sugar levels corresponds with an increase in adrenaline levels. If the balance of blood sugar to adrenaline becomes too far apart, hypoglycemia results, which is usually experienced as shakiness, sweating, and altered thinking and behavior. Studies have found that children are more sensitive to rapid decreases in blood sugar levels caused by eating sweets, with hypoglycemia occurring at blood sugar levels much higher than it does in adults. Further, hypoglycemia is greatly exaggerated in children, with adrenaline levels remaining up to 10 times higher than that of adults up to five hours after the initial "sugar rush."

Malnutrition

Surprisingly, malnutrition is not limited to poor families in the United States. Malnutrition can be caused by several factors that may affect a family regardless of its economic status, such as chronic illness, extreme feeding difficulties, eating disorders, the imposition of a nonfat diet on a child, or simply poor diet. Your child's doctor will most likely alert you if she believes he is not growing properly, but there are other signs you can look for as well.

- Dull or bloodshot eyes
- Easily bruised skin
- Skin that is loose on the body
- Circles under the eyes
- Hair that is falling out, brittle, or wiry
- Tender muscles
- Prominent ribs

Good versus Bad Fats

Good Fats

Cooking fats: olive, canola, pumpkin seed, safflower, sunflower, corn and peanut oils

Animal fats: dairy products, eggs, fish, lean poultry, or meat

Snack fats: nut butters, cheese, avocados, hummus, corn chips made with healthy oils

Sweet fats: ice cream, fruit yogurt, whole grain baked goods

Bad Fats

Cooking fats: margarine, vegetable shortening, cottonseed, palm kernel, coconut, and hydrogenated vegetable oils

Animal fats: lard, butter, bacon, sausage, fatty cuts of red meat

Snack fats: potato chips, snack foods made with hydrogenated oils

Sweet fats: baked goods made with hydrogenated oils, candy bars

- Bleeding gums
- Pale tongue
- Poor teeth
- Thin, brittle nails
- Pale, cracked, swollen lips
- Bowed legs

If you are concerned that your child might be suffering from malnutrition, keep a careful record of her diet and make an appointment to see her pediatrician.

Nutritionary: A Glossary of Terms

Antioxidants. Antioxidants are micronutrients that carry a positive molecular charge. They bond with other molecules called free radicals in the bloodstream, which carry a negative charge and result from the body's absorption of oxygen during digestion. Free radicals are linked to damage to the body's cells that may lead to many health problems, including colorectal cancer. When a free radical bonds with an antioxidant, it is unable to cause damage. Beta-carotene, vitamin C, and vitamin E are known to be particularly effective antioxidants.

Calorie. A calorie is a unit of measure expressing the energy value of foods. Our bodies draw this energy from three primary sources: carbohydrates, protein, and fat. When metabolizing fat calories, the body burns less energy than when digesting calories from other sources, and the body is more likely to store fat calories than to burn them for immediate use. This is why it is important to pay attention to the proportion of fat calories in the foods you eat if you are overweight. Note that growing babies need a higher percentage of fat in their diets than do children and adults.

Carbohydrate. A carbohydrate is an energy-producing organic compound composed of carbon, hydrogen, and oxygen and appears in food as starch, sugar, and fiber. Carbohydrates are the main source of energy in the human diet and are broken down during digestion into simple sugar, or glucose. Complex carbohydrates, commonly known as starches, contain long strings of different kinds of sugar molecules that also contain a variety of other nutrients, which make them a preferred energy source. Simple carbohydrates are found in milk, fruits, and a variety of sweeteners (honey, maple syrup, table sugar, and so on) and are more quickly metabolized by the body. Fiber is a complex carbohydrate, but our bodies lack the proper enzyme for its digestion, so fiber alone is not an energy source.

Cholesterol. Cholesterol is a combination of steroids and alcohol present in the human body and animal food sources. It is an important component in the cellular structure of the brain and nervous system and in other cells throughout the body. It is chemically part of the hormones that control the adrenal system and sexual functioning. It is important in the digestion process because the body uses it to produce bile in the stomach, and it is instrumental in the production of vitamin D. Cholesterol enters the body through food containing cholesterol, and the amount of cholesterol in the bloodstream can also be elevated when fat is consumed. Your body can produce all the cholesterol it needs, however, without any dietary source of cholesterol.

There are two kinds of cholesterol. LDL cholesterol is transported throughout the body in the bloodstream to cells that need it. However, excess LDL cholesterol is deposited in the artery walls and is a leading cause of heart disease. HDL cholesterol, on the other hand, removes excess LDL cholesterol from the bloodstream and delivers it to the liver, where it is converted into bile. In most people, the body can regulate its own cholesterol production to compensate for varying quantities of cholesterol in the diet. Some people's bodies lack this ability, usually due to heredity, and they are therefore more prone to heart disease. However, anyone whose diet is too high in fat or cholesterol (especially LDL cholesterol) is at risk for heart disease.

Enzyme. An enzyme is an organic catalyst created by the cells in your body to act on ingested proteins in order to break them down for digestion. There are hundreds of varieties of enzymes, each designed to break down different protein compounds. They are generally named for the compound that they digest. For example, lactase digests lactose. Enzymes are also present in the foods you eat, and some people take them as supplements to their diets in order to aid digestion.

Essential fatty acid. Fatty acids are the main structural component of fats and form a necessary part of every cell in the body. Fatty acids are also vital to the well-being of your nervous system, hormonal functioning, and many other bodily functions. Additionally, ingested fats and stored fats are the most efficient source of energy for your body. Of the 20 or so fatty acids necessary for your health, your body can produce all but two, called essential fatty acids: linoleic acid (omega-6), and linolenic acid (omega-3). This means that you must have a dietary source for omega-6 (corn, sunflower, and safflower oils are good sources for omega-6) and omega-3 (seafood, canola oil, flaxseed, soybeans, and some nuts are good sources for omega-3). Most Americans have plenty of omega-6 in their diets and lack omega-3. Inadequate levels of omega-3 fatty acid have been linked with many health problems such as heart disease, poor brain function and development, arthritis, and deficiencies in immunity.

Fiber. Fiber, which is always derived from plant sources, is not digested by the body and provides no energy, but it still performs a vital function. There are two kinds of fiber in the human diet: soluble fiber and insoluble fiber. Soluble fiber soaks up water and mixes with the other foods in your digestive tract, helping to control the rate at which sugar enters your bloodstream. Insoluble fiber also absorbs water and carries waste through the digestive tract, promoting softer stools. Insoluble fiber also helps to adjust pH levels in the intestines, nurturing healthy bacteria and yeasts. Soluble fiber is found in dried beans, oat and rice bran, and barley. Wheat bran is one of the best sources of insoluble fiber. Insoluble fiber is also present in fruit and vegetable skins and peels, and leafy plants.

Hydrogenated oil. Hydrogenation is the chemical process whereby healthy unsaturated and polyunsaturated oil is made more saturated. This industrial process forces hydrogen atoms into the fat molecules in the oil, causing it to solidify at room temperature and become more stable. Hydrogenation is used by the food industry to increase the shelf life of food products. A byproduct of this process

is the creation of transfatty acids in the oils, which have never appeared in the human diet before. Transfatty acids have been shown to increase levels of LDL cholesterol and decrease levels of HDL cholesterol in the blood, leading to heart disease. Transfatty acids are also suspected carcinogens. Hydrogenated and partially hydrogenated oils are a common ingredient in mass-market snack foods and baked items and margarine. Also, fast food restaurants often use them for frying foods. Avoiding hydrogenated oils in restaurants can be particularly difficult, since the restaurant will often claim to use an otherwise healthy oil, like corn oil, and neglect to state that the oil is hydrogenated.

Mineral. Minerals and trace minerals are inorganic insoluble chemical compounds that cannot be manufactured by the body and must be consumed in food, water, or supplements. While many minerals are toxic when consumed in excess, they are nevertheless important to health and nutrition. Unfortunately, many minerals are stripped from whole foods when they are processed and/or refined. Minerals may act in concert or antagonistically in the body. For example, potassium and sodium work together to maintain water balance in the cells of the body. On the other hand, excess phosphorus can inhibit the body's absorption of calcium, which is critical to healthy bones.

Generally, Americans should be concerned about limiting the amount of sodium and phosphorous in their diets. Excess consumption of sodium has been linked with high blood pressure and heart disease, and is found in table salt, fast foods, packaged and prepared foods, and many cured or pickled foods. Infants who are breastfed longer usually consume less sodium than babies older than one year drinking primarily cow's milk, because cow's milk has three times the amount of sodium as breastmilk. Also stay away from added salt; it is common sense that children who develop a taste for salty foods early in life will have a more difficult time reducing the intake of sodium later. Phosphorous is found primarily in soft drinks, meat, and fast foods. Excess phosphorous inhibits calcium absorption.

Several studies indicate that as many as 50 percent of children in the United States consume inadequate amounts of one or more

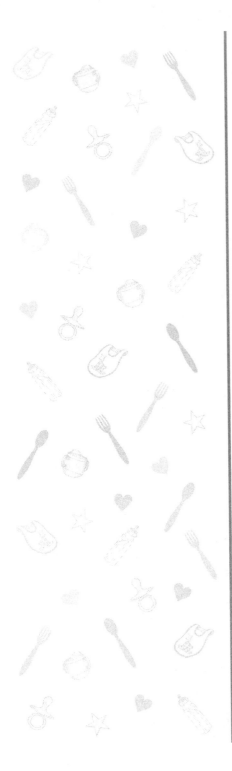

of the three essential minerals. The three essential minerals are as follows (for good sources, see the RDA chart later in this chapter):

Calcium, a critical component in healthy nerve and muscle functioning, is needed by growing children and pregnant and lactating women. Calcium also serves as the basic building block for your bones and helps in the absorption of iron.

Iron is another particularly important nutrient for babies, children, and women who are pregnant or lactating. Iron carries oxygen in the bloodstream to all of the cells in the body. Iron is also critical to the formation of delicate nerve cells in the brain and throughout the body. When a baby is born, he has enough stored iron in his body from his mother to last for several months. Additionally, there is a small quantity of highly absorbable iron in breastmilk, and all brands of formula are supplemented with iron, so there is little concern about iron deficiency in the early months of life. However, the body's original iron stores are usually depleted at eight or nine months of age, and pediatricians will often test for possible anemia (iron deficiency) at this point. You should never give an infant an adult vitamin or iron supplement, because they contain too much iron for a child. Iron toxicity is a leading cause of poisoning in babies and children, so keep vitamin tablets and all other medicine out of your child's reach.

Zinc deficiency is not routinely tested for at the pediatrician's office, but it is nevertheless a concern. Zinc not only strengthens the immune system, but it is a critical component to enzyme functioning, which regulates metabolism. It is also important to processes of cell division, growth, and protein synthesis, some of which occur only in childhood. Chronic zinc deficiency in children can cause permanent stunted growth. Zinc deficiency is rarely a concern before six months, because both breastmilk and formula contain adequate amounts.

Protein. Proteins are composed of any combination of 22 known amino acid molecules and are used in the development and periodic regeneration of every single cell in your body. Because babies and children are growing new cells as well as maintaining existing cells, their protein needs are proportionally greater than those of adults, and their needs increase during periodic growth spurts. Of the 22 amino acids, 9 are "essential," meaning that the body cannot manufacture them, and there must be a dietary source. These nine essential amino acids are present in many foods, especially grains, legumes, and nuts and seeds, and they complement one another to form the complete proteins necessary for the body's functions. Most people get enough protein without even trying, and too much protein is almost never a problem. Animal food sources, like breastmilk, dairy products, eggs, meat, fish, and poultry comprise all nine essential amino acids at once. Additionally, protein obtained from animal sources is more easily digested, so people who choose a vegan diet and eat no animal products, including dairy and eggs (not a diet recommended for babies and children), need to increase their protein consumption from plant sources by 25 percent.

Saturated fat and oil. Saturated fat is found primarily in food obtained from animal sources such as meat, poultry, lard, butter, and eggs. It is also in some tropical plant oils: coconut oil, palm oil, and cocoa butter. A fat molecule is saturated when each available space of its carbon strand structure is filled with a hydrogen atom. When a fat molecule is saturated with hydrogen atoms, it will attract other saturated fat molecules, and they will lump together. This is why saturated fats and oils will solidify at room temperature (like butter) and why excess saturated fats in the bloodstream will collect in your arteries.

Sugar. Simply stated, sugar is a simple carbohydrate and is therefore an energy source for the body. It differs from a complex carbohydrate in that the simple carbohydrate contains only one or two sugar molecules, rather than a long strand of sugar molecules combined with other nutrients. Almost all sugar acts the same way in the body, as it is broken down more quickly than other carbohydrates and stored for immediate use as glycogen or for long-term use as fat. Different kinds of carbohydrates are rated for the time they take to enter the bloodstream, using the glycemic index. A carbohydrate with a high glycemic index tends to be very sweet and raises blood sugar levels quickly, leading to rapid mood shifts. When

What about Olestra?

Olestra is a chemical ingredient in snack foods that tastes like fat but has been modified in such a way that the body cannot digest and store it as body fat. To the diet-conscious, this sounds like the perfect solution, but unfortunately Olestra also strips fat-soluble vitamins A, D, E, and K from your body and has been shown to cause myriad digestive problems. The long-term health impact of consuming this kind of ingredient has yet to be shown, but why take the risk, especially when it comes to feeding children.

simple carbohydrates are consumed at the same time as complex carbohydrates, this rapid blood sugar swing is less dramatic. Sweet simple carbohydrates come in many forms: as table sugar refined from sugarcane or sugar beets, as fructose, as honey, as molasses, and so on.

Unsaturated fat and oil. There are two kinds of unsaturated fats: monounsaturated and polyunsaturated. The carbon strand that makes a monounsaturated fatty acid has one available space that does not contain a hydrogen atom. A polyunsaturated fatty acid has more than one available hydrogen space on its carbon strand. As a general rule, monounsaturated fats are found in nut oils, olive oil, and canola oil, and polyunsaturated fats are found in vegetable oils and seafood (both omega-3 and omega-6 essential fatty acids are polyunsaturated). Both kinds of unsaturated fats are better for your health than excess quantities of saturated fats, because the fat molecules do not bond with one another to collect in the artery walls. And while the body needs saturated fatty acids, it can make these from unsaturated fats.

Vitamin. A vitamin is an active compound present in foods that interacts with other vitamins, enzymes, and hormones and that is essential to good health. With the exception of vitamin D, which is activated in your skin through exposure to sunlight, vitamins cannot be produced by the body and must be consumed in food or supplements. There are two kinds of vitamins: fat soluble and water soluble. Fat-soluble vitamins (A, D, E, and K) need fat in order to be metabolized and are stored in the fat cells of the body, reducing the likelihood of short-term deficiency. Water-soluble vitamins, on the other hand, are needed on a more frequent basis because they are quickly flushed through the body. A balanced diet with a variety of foods, especially adequate fruits and vegetables, will generally supply a person with all of the vitamins needed for good health, and absorption of vitamins is usually better in food sources than in supplements.

Vitamins that are especially important for proper nutrition are as follows (for good sources, see the following RDA chart):

Vitamins A (beta-carotene), C and E. These are all antioxidants, which means that they may play a critical role in disease prevention later in life. Beta carotene, which is converted to vitamin A in the body, promotes healthy vision, skin, and teeth and bolsters the immune system.

Nutrient Sources and Recommended Daily Allowances for Babies and Young Children

Nutrient	US RDA (6–12 Months)	US RDA (1–3 Years)	Food Sources
Protein	14 grams	23 grams	Grains, legumes, nuts, seeds, eggs, seafood, poultry, meat
Vitamin A	375 micrograms	400 micrograms	Liver, green and yellow vegetables, yellow-orange fruits, seafood
Vitamin D	10 micrograms	13.3 micrograms	Egg yolk, vitamin D–fortified milk, direct exposure to sunlight at least 15 minutes per day
Vitamin E	4 milligrams	6 milligrams	Vegetable oils, seeds, nuts, whole grains, tomatoes, avocados, peaches
Vitamin K	*	*	Green leafy vegetables, cauliflower, onions
Vitamin C	35 milligrams	40 milligrams	Citrus fruit, berries, melon, green vegetables, tomatoes, potatoes
Thiamin (B-1)	.4 milligrams	.7 milligrams	Whole grains, seeds, nuts, legumes, seafood, meat, avocados, artichokes
Riboflavin (B-2)	.5 milligrams	.8 milligrams	Dairy products, organ meats, seafood, eggs, green vegetables, legumes, meat
Niacin	6 milligrams	9 milligrams	Legumes, whole grains, green vegetables, seafood, dairy products, seeds
Vitamin B-6	.6 milligrams	1 milligram	Seafood, whole grains, legumes, carrots, eggs, bananas, meat, prunes, potatoes

(continued on page 186)

Nutrient Sources and Recommended Daily Allowances for Babies and Young Children (continued)

Nutrient	US RDA (6–12 Months)	US RDA (1–3 Years)	Food Sources
Folic acid	35 micrograms	50 micrograms	Dark green vegetables, legumes, nuts, whole wheat, avocado, papaya, fortified cereals
Vitamin B-12	.5 micrograms	.7 micrograms	Seafood, meat, dairy products, eggs
Calcium	600 milligrams	800 milligrams	Dairy products, dark leafy greens, soy products, molasses, fortified orange juice, fortified cereals
Phosphorus	500 milligrams	800 milligrams	Milk, cheese, nuts, cereals, legumes, carbonated beverages
Magnesium	60 milligrams	200 milligrams	Nuts, legumes, whole grains, dark leafy greens, milk
Iron	10 milligrams	10 milligrams	Meat, poultry, seafood, legumes, eggs, dried fruit, molasses, fortified formula, breads, cereals
Zinc	5 milligrams	8 milligrams	Wheat germ, seeds, nuts, cereals, eggs
Iodine	50 micrograms	70 micrograms	Seaweed, many vegetables (particularly those grown in iodine-rich soil), iodized table salt
Selenium	*	*	Nuts, whole grains, dairy products, legumes

* No supplements recommended.

Vitamin C increases iron absorption, promotes wound healing and immune system functioning, and helps to build strong muscles and bones. Vitamin E helps to prevent anemia and is important for brain functioning.

B vitamins and folic acid. Vitamin B-6 is important in helping the body to metabolize proteins. It also boosts immune system functioning and helps to build the neurotransmitters in the brain. Vitamin B-12 is a necessary component in healthy red blood cells and helps to build the myelin sheath insulators around each nerve in the body. Folic acid is critical in the spinal formation of a developing fetus. It also aids in the production of DNA and red blood cells.

Daily Vitamins and Mineral Supplements

Before the introduction of solid food, breastmilk or formula will supply all of the vitamins and minerals your baby needs. After this time, a balanced diet that includes a wide variety of foods should supply these needs just as well. However, in reality, children often do not get quite the variety of foods we would like, either due to general fussy eating habits or a week-long obsession with a particular food. Add to this are periodic illnesses that affect your baby's appetite, and you may be concerned that she isn't getting all of the vitamins and minerals she needs.

This said, the AAP does not recommend the use of a daily vitamin-and-mineral supplement for a healthy child eating a varied diet roughly corresponding to the Food Guide Pyramid. The AAP does not recommend the use of supplements unless advised by your child's pediatrician. You may want to check with your child's doctor about the possiblity of fluoride supplements. If you live in an area where the local water supply is unfluoridated, your pediatrician may prescribe supplements for your baby at six months. If you have a well, it is recommended that you check the fluoride content of the water and notify your pediatrician or dentist so the appropriate supplement can be prescribed.

One thing is certain: Supplements designed for adults should never be given to children or babies unless prescribed by a doctor.

Resources for Veggie Babies

For more information about raising a healthy vegetarian, consult two classic books written by Sharon Yntema and published by McBooks Press: *Vegetarian Baby* and *Vegetarian Children*.

Feeding Baby in a Vegetarian Household

The AAP and most dieticians agree that a lacto/ovo vegetarian diet (lacto/ovo includes eggs and dairy products) is safe and healthy for infants and growing children. Some pediatricians also recommend occasional servings of fish to supply DHA and omega-3 fatty acids. In fact, land-based meat, while nutritious, is not necessary for children or adults, because there are many other sources for the nutrients found in meat such as protein, vitamin B-12, iron, and zinc. If your child is sensitive or allergic to eggs and/or dairy products, I recommend you consult a dietician in order to ensure that your child's nutritional needs are adequately filled.

Alternative Diets for Infants and Families

Of course, the entire world does not feed its children according to recommendations laid out by the USDA. Many traditional cultures nurture active, healthy children using staple foods that may or may not include meat, poultry, fish, dairy, or eggs. In addition, a growing number of adults who practice alternative diets for health or philosophical reasons are learning to raise healthy children without compromising their beliefs. While it is not my intention to neglect the subject of alternative diets for infant nutrition, I recognize that these diets take thousands of forms and are the result of a complicated interchange of culture and climate. People who choose an alternative diet as adults would be wise to educate themselves about nutrition, or even consult a registered dietician familiar with their chosen diet, before attempting to raise a child according to their beliefs. In many cases, the nutritional needs of children are different from those of adults, and it is therefore a mistake to impose an adult diet on a child. That said, much can be learned from other cultures and beliefs about foods that are healthy for and palatable to infants. What follows is a brief description of several prevalent alternative diets.

The Macrobiotic Diet

The macrobiotic diet originated in Japan and is best described as a philosophy that emphasizes eating whole, natural foods containing the properties of yin (the quiet principle/female) and yang (the moving principle/male). According to this theory, all foods are classified as yin or yang, and adherents strive to combine ingredients so that a balance is achieved between the two. Traditionally, the macrobiotic diet does not include the milk of other animals, because it is believed that we should consume only the milk that nature intended for humans to consume as babies. Mothers are therefore encouraged to breastfeed for at least one year while the child is slowly weaned, starting at six months. Foods that are fed to macrobiotic infants include, but are not limited to, brown rice and other whole grains, nuts and seeds, soy beverages, tofu, legumes, calcium-rich leafy greens, sea vegetables, and fruits. Clearly, while many people find the macrobiotic diet exceedingly healthy, it is not to be undertaken lightly and requires study and training.

The Vegan Diet

A vegan eats no animal products, including eggs and dairy products. This poses several challenges for parents raising children, and most pediatricians and dieticians recommend against a vegan diet for infants and children. In particular, parents must be aware of the different plant sources that when combined will comprise the complete, high-quality proteins necessary for health and development. They should also make sure that children are getting enough vitamin B-12, which is available only from animal sources, supplements, or enriched foods. Vitamin D can be obtained through exposure to sunlight unless the child is living in a northern climate. While calcium can be obtained from plant sources, the plant foods that contain the largest quantities of calcium are not always palatable to children, such as kale and collard greens. Fortunately, there are many foods that are now available enriched with calcium, such as orange juice and soy and rice beverages. Extending breastfeeding to beyond one year is also helpful. One big challenge presented by an all-plant diet is getting enough calories to meet a child's needs when his stomach capacity is not large enough to hold very much food at one time. These children should be encouraged to eat very frequently as a result.

Finding a Registered Dietician

To find a registered dietician in your area, you can contact the American Dietetic Association at *www.eatright.org* or phone them at (800) 877-1600.

CHAPTER NINE

Encouraging Healthy Family Eating Habits

Everyone's eating habits are different. They are suited to our tastes and personality, are a product of our background and culture, and are governed by available ingredients and our economic status. When two adults live together, changes invariably occur and the seeds for a family eating style are planted. Once a new baby joins the group, the opportunity arises to examine this eating style and to make decisions that will forever affect the health and well-being of your little one(s). Your eating habits and attitudes toward food will have a profound effect on your child(ren) in the years to come. This is true whether you are a fast-food junkie or are obsessed with counting calories and eliminating fat. Finding a balance that will allow your child to grow into a confidant and healthy adult is not always easy in the modern world of junk food and crash diets.

Why should you be concerned with these issues when your child is still a baby? Common sense would tell you that the best way to solve a problem is to prevent its happening in the first place. This absolutely does not mean that you should be counting calories and choosing nonfat or low-fat foods for your 18-month-old because you're concerned he might be getting a little chubby. Rather, this should be a time when you are shaping his tastes and providing him with foods that will help him grow, not just fill his tummy. Once your child becomes accustomed to particular foods, it becomes very difficult to change his habits, and as time goes by, the concern for health problems will increase. While an overweight five-year-old has a less than 20 percent chance of being overweight as an adult, an overweight teen has a greater than 75 percent chance of struggling with weight issues as an adult.

Health Concerns Linked to Poor Diet

Soon, obesity-related illnesses will match smoking as a cause of preventable death in the United States. Statistics show that the percentage of overweight children increased from 5 to 13 percent between 1964 and 1994. If this trend continues, these children are at risk of a host of serious health problems that may affect them throughout their lives. At the same time, eating disorders such as anorexia and bulimia, once thought to be a problem only for adolescent girls and young women, are now affecting girls as young as seven and even boys and young men. Clearly, an increased focus on being skinny (which has relatively little to do with being healthy) is not the answer either.

Promoting Good Family Eating

Familiarizing yourself with the basics of infant nutrition can be very helpful, but as everyone knows, it's not so much what you say as what you do that really counts with a child. The following pointers are meant to serve as guidelines for parents.

Eat Healthy Foods Yourself

"Do as I say, and not as I do," doesn't work for eating habits or for anything else. Your children will model their behavior on your own. If you are concerned that your baby might grow up struggling with poor eating habits because you suffer from them yourself, the time to address the problem is now. If you allow your baby to learn to eat unhealthy foods that are available in your home now, it will be much more difficult to break her of those habits later. Also, it may take some time to adjust to a lifestyle change relating to your diet. It is best to give yourself some time to learn which foods will satisfy your needs so that when the time comes for family dining, you will feel comfortable. Start eating healthier foods now, while your baby is still young.

Provide Healthy Foods for Your Family

If the only food choices in your home are healthy ones, guess what your kids will eat. Stock the pantry and refrigerator with whole grain breads, crackers, and snacks and fresh fruits and vegetables.

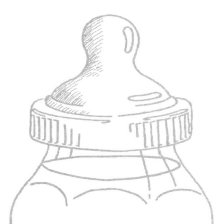

The American Diet: Bad and Getting Worse

The American diet is typically high in fat, especially saturated fat, and sodium; low in fiber from fruits, vegetables and whole grains; and low in calcium. This diet is cited as a significant contributor to coronary heart disease, stroke, and some forms of cancer, which are the three leading causes of death in the United States. Diet also plays a major role in the development of high blood pressure, osteoporosis, and diabetes. In fact, according to the USDA, poor diet usually combined with a sedentary lifestyle is responsible for 14 percent of all deaths in the United States.

Whole Grains Really Are Better

Choose whole grains whenever possible. White flour and rice have a fraction of the nutrients found in whole wheat flour and brown rice. For example, refined white flour is stripped of the nutritious bran and germ during processing and subsequently "enriched" with B vitamins and iron and sometimes vitamin D, folic acid, and calcium. These additions do not come close to replacing the 22 vitamins and minerals that are depleted as a result of the original processing. If your child is introduced to whole grains early, she will be less likely to refuse them later on.

Provide fresh foods like yogurt, cheese, eggs, and fish. Buy tofu, nut butters, and dried fruit. Get into the habit of preparing simple dishes like rice with stir-fried vegetables or pasta several times a week. Cook simple but healthy soups and stews and freeze containers for quick, easy meals later. Healthy foods are not tasteless, contrary to what your father-in-law may claim.

Provide Variety

Anyone would get bored with apples and bananas week after week. More varieties of produce are becoming available every year (who heard of kiwi fruit 10 years ago?). Enjoy the seasonality of produce and make regular visits with your child to the local farmers' market. New brands of healthy snack foods with a wide variety of ingredients are appearing on store shelves every day, and people are rediscovering different varieties of grains (quinoa, spelt, bulgur, barley, amaranth, wild rice, and so on). I even found a new snack food recently that includes a significant portion of concentrated kale and spinach as an ingredient, and my baby really loves it. Remember that a wide variety of foods is more likely to meet all of a growing child's nutritional needs.

Never Restrict the Amount of Healthy Food Your Child Eats

A child should never be put on a diet without the guidance of a doctor. If foods that provide empty calories, meaning foods that are loaded with sugar and/or saturated fat, are not available to your child on a regular basis, you will be well on your way to avoiding health problems related to diet. Unless a child has a rare glandular disorder, weight problems are often the result of regular consumption of junk foods combined with too little exercise. Also, when one or both parents is overweight or obese, the child is at greater risk for being overweight. Usually a doctor will suggest an intervention in a child's weight gain pattern after the age of two years only with persistent, climbing disparities in weight-to-stature percentiles, measured by the BMI chart (see Chapter 7). Even then, the doctor will rarely recommend a limit in the amount of healthy foods a child should eat. Rather, a reduction in the amount of junk food consumed, combined with regular physical activity, will be recommended so that her growth will have a chance to catch up to her weight.

Make a Policy about Sugar

Many families struggle with the sugar issue. Kids love sweet stuff from the beginning, preferring applesauce to strained peas. Even breastmilk and formula are sweet. With outside influences ranging from advertising and product placements, designed to attract children, to indulgent grandparents and babysitters, sticking to a policy can be difficult. Some parents follow an outright ban on all varieties of added sugar, with varying degrees of success. If this is not the route you plan to take, decide on a middle road that is practical for your family. There are many ways to satisfy a sweet tooth without breaking out the candy. If you shop wisely, you may even be able to satisfy some of your child's nutritional needs while doling out a special treat. Fresh fruits, fruit-juice-sweetened cookies or cake made with whole grains, fruit sorbet, or a slice of whole grain bread with honey may all be acceptable to your child as sweet treats, if he has not come to expect junk food sweets. Remember that it is often not simply the sugar that is the nutritional saboteur, but the fact that many sugary treats come with no other wholesome ingredients to feed a growing child. Remember, every bite counts.

Read the Label

Packaged foods often include highly processed grains ("enriched" usually indicates that a grain has been stripped of its original nutritional content), ultrarefined sugars like high fructose corn syrup, or hydrogenated/partially hydrogenated oils, along with a host of other additives that you may or may not want your child eating. Make informed decisions when purchasing products for your family by reading ingredient and nutritional labels.

Self-Regulating Food Intake

Researchers at Penn State University studied the eating habits of preschoolers, three to five years of age. They discovered that while most three-year-olds would stop eating when their appetite was satisfied, five-year-olds were far more likely to continue eating until the entire portion was consumed, regardless of its size. You can diminish your child's tendency to overeat when he is older by trusting him to regulate his intake now. The child who learns early to eat for the satisfaction of others is possibly more likely to respond to outside cues, such as overly large portions, rather than his own inner sense of "hungry" and "full."

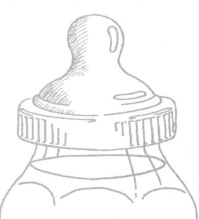

Sugar-Free Kids

A few parents are brave enough to try eliminating sugar from their kids' diets completely. This can be a difficult task. Because sugar is a hidden ingredient in so many packaged foods, parents who have imposed a ban on sugar have limited choices. Still, there are lots of recipes for treats to give your kids that do not include sugar. Many of these are included in the book *Sugar-Free Toddlers*, by Susan Watson, published in 1991 by Williamson Publishing Co. This book is also great for parents who simply want to limit sugar.

Provide Alternatives

Many tasty and nutritious foods are alternatives to sugary cereals and fatty, salty snack foods popular with young children. You may be surprised to learn that there are many brands of healthy, appealing cereals and snack foods that have become available since you went through your "tofu and granola" phase in college. Experiment with many different kinds of healthy foods, such as dried fruit, whole grain crackers, and yogurt, until you learn which are your child's favorites. Never become locked in a defeatist attitude about what you offer, assuming that because it's healthy, your child is guaranteed to dislike it.

Boost Nutrition in Foods You Know Your Kids Will Eat

Find ways to boost the nutritional value of the foods your child already loves eating. Blend wheat germ and/or tofu into a fruit smoothie, or mix cooked pureed vegetables or beans in with the macaroni and cheese. Grate carrots or zucchini into pancake batter. Mix nut butter into yogurt. It doesn't need to take a lot of time; just having these ingredients on hand helps to get the creative juices flowing.

Be Moderate

"Everything in moderation." This dictum applies to life in general and food especially. It seems that every time you turn around, someone is telling you that you'd be healthier if only you would eat cabbage at every meal or some other nonsense. This type of mentality breeds what are know as fad diets, which, besides taking all of the pleasure out of eating, are not beneficial to adults and are downright dangerous for children. Similarly, a family eating style that is too restrictive puts a child at risk for bingeing on forbidden foods simply out of rebellion. On the other hand, ice cream for dessert after every meal is too much pleasure to be enjoyed properly. Being very permissive in this way sends the message that the child makes the decisions about what the family should be eating, which is all wrong.

Reading and Understanding Labels

As parents, we owe it to our children to make informed decisions about the foods we give them. However, food choice is one of the most controversial aspects of modern culture. Advocates of every stripe urge us to buy foods or not buy foods for reasons of health, economy, the preservation of the environment or, not to forget, simple pleasure. A literal alphabet soup of governmental regulators made up of the FDA, the USDA, the WHO, the FAO, and the EPA all oversee the safety and healthfulness of the foods we eat. It is no coincidence that all this controversy stems directly from a trillion-dollar-plus industry. In the meantime, parents struggle to make good decisions when their 21-month-old daughter will eat nothing but peanut butter and jelly.

When confronted with these issues, many people tend to react in one of two ways. Either they shut down when challenged with so much conflicting information, or they latch on to a few understandable nuggets, building a food philosophy around, for example, a nonfat diet. While understandable, neither approach is particularly productive. I hope that some of the information in this chapter will help in the process of demystifying some of the issues surrounding food choices for you and your family.

Reading Ingredient Labels on Packaged Foods

The ingredient label and Nutrition Facts panel are the most important tools for anyone concerned with the healthfulness of the packaged foods they eat. Nutritional claims on the front of the package are designed solely to sell the product and, as a result, are often misleading. Understanding how to read ingredient labels and Nutrition Facts can be enormously helpful to parents when deciding which foods to buy for their kids.

Ingredient labels are required on all packaged foods, and they list every ingredient in descending order from the highest weight-by-volume ingredient to the lowest. Sounds simple, but reading

Popular Snack Foods and Healthful Alternatives

Snack

- Potato chips
- Soda, juice-flavored drinks
- Cookies
- Ice cream
- Popsicles
- Candy
- Cake

Alternatives

- Whole grain crackers, puffed rice or corn cereal, baked snack chips
- 100-percent fruit juice with sparkling or still water added
- Fruit juice sweetened cookies, fig bars, graham crackers
- Yogurt with fresh fruit, sorbet, fruit smoothies
- Homemade or store-bought fruit-juice ice pops
- Raisins, dried apricots, plums, or pineapple
- Homemade or store-bought whole grain muffins or quick breads

an ingredient label can be anything but easy; you often feel as if you need a Ph.D. in chemistry to understand it. To cut down on the confusion, I recommend buying foods that primarily have ingredients you would use in your own home: whole grains, minimally processed oils and sweeteners, and as few additives and preservatives as possible. Personally, the shorter the list of ingredients, the more likely I am to want to buy the product. I am especially wary of food dyes, artificial flavors, and hydrogenated or partially hydrogenated oils, and I usually reject products that contain them.

Additives: The Good, The Bad, and the Unknown

There are about 3,000 additives currently in use in the U.S. food supply. Of these, about 2,000 are specifically used for flavoring, often replacing or enhancing flavors that have been denuded as a part of the manufacturing process. Many additives are consumed without a person's knowledge because they are used to treat fresh produce, as with fungicides that are applied to grapes to retard spoilage. We also unwittingly consume indirect food additives such as hormones, antibiotics or tranquilizers that are used to treat cattle, pigs, poultry, or farmed fish. However, food additives are nothing new, and their use has continued and evolved from the time, thousands of years ago, when early humans discovered the curing properties of salt.

The FDA and the USDA are responsible for monitoring use of food additives, and manufacturers must limit their use of them according to regulations known as Good Manufacturing Practices (GMP). New additives must be approved before being used and are subjected to a number of tests that assess potential toxicity. Many more additives are approved for use because they are Generally Recognized as Safe (GRAS). These are products, ranging from oregano to nitrates, that have been used for long enough that it is reasoned they must be safe. The GRAS list has been under constant review since the Nixon administration, but many people feel

Dried Fruit and Dental Hygiene

If your baby is old enough to safely enjoy dried fruit, be aware that it will stick to his teeth, and be careful to brush his teeth very thoroughly to avoid tooth decay.

that much more work should be done to ensure the safety of all of these ingredients.

Additives are also used to increase consumer acceptability, as with dyes that are used to make the skins of oranges appear more orange or texturizers that keep cocoa particles from settling on the bottom of a container of chocolate milk. Preservatives enable foods that were traditionally sold fresh within a few days or weeks to be more widely distributed and stocked in supermarkets for longer periods. Frequently, additives are used to facilitate in food preparation, as with emulsifiers that assure evenness of texture and efficient mixing in bakery preparations and ice cream. Additives are also used to enhance a product's nutritional properties or to replace some (but usually not all) nutrients lost in processing.

The AAP argues that the use of additives is not harmful when GMPs are followed, allowing us to enjoy a variety of wholesome foods year round. Some would agree with that statement but caution Americans not to become complacent when it comes to the food they consume. The sad truth is that wholesomeness is not the primary goal for many food manufacturers. Unfortunately, profits are paramount, and as long as consumers demand orange oranges and perfect round red tomatoes in January (not to mention salty, fatty, sweet packaged goods that keep for months on the shelf before being consumed), producers will continue using additives in ever-increasing amounts. If it is shown that consumers want more ingredients that are found in nature, and less that are concocted in a laboratory, manufacturers will fall in line and the quality of our food will improve.

Perhaps the most convincing argument for greater consumer activism regarding food additives is put forward by Ruth Winter, M.S., whose book *A Consumer's Dictionary of Food Additives*, published by Three Rivers Press, New York, is essential for the savvy food buyer. "The FDA's requested 1994 budget was $209,000,000 for food and cosmetics. Of the 1,854 field officers, 1,149 are assigned to consumer safety for food, drugs, cosmetics, and medical devices; 29 are toxicologists; and 20 are food technologists. They must cover the multibillion-dollar food, drug, medical-devices and cosmetics industries with their hundreds of thousands of products. The FDA

Who's in Charge?

It is often said that the responsibility for a child's diet must be split two ways: with the parent deciding what foods will be served, and the child deciding when he will eat, whether or not he will eat them, and how much he will eat. As any parent of a toddler will tell you, this is a tricky guideline to follow with the temptation always looming to serve less-nutritious foods simply to ensure that the baby doesn't go hungry. If she's neglected most of the healthy, appealing food on her lunch plate, try to trust that she's probably not hungry and will most likely make up for it with a nutritious mid-afternoon snack or at dinnertime.

personnel, while well-intentioned, do not have the resources to prevent all potentially harmful food additives from reaching the market. Your knowledge is your best protection."

Sweet Stuff: When Does It Mean Sugar on the Label?

Manufacturers often use several ingredients at once to boost the sweetness of their products. Sometimes this is because they know that people may not buy a product if sugar appears too soon in the list of ingredients, and using other sweeteners may allow sugar to appear later. All of these ingredients are forms of sugar:

- Brown sugar
- Corn syrup or sweetener
- Dextrose
- Fructose
- Fruit juice concentrate
- Glucose
- High fructose corn syrup
- Honey
- Lactose
- Maltose
- Mannitol
- Maple syrup
- Molasses
- Raw sugar
- Sorghum syrup
- Sucrose
- Sugar
- Syrup

Are All Sugars the Same?

Yes and no. All sugars are simple carbohydrates and are broken down by the body into glucose, which is the main source of energy for the body, to be used immediately or stored for later use as body fat. In that sense it is no better to use maple syrup or honey as a sweetener than regular table sugar. In some ways it's worse because liquid forms of sweeteners are more likely to coat and cause damage to tooth enamel. However, understanding differences between sweeteners that are used commercially and in the home is helpful to many parents.

Table sugar (sucrose) is refined from sugar beets or sugarcane and is composed of one molecule each of glucose and fructose. While the body quickly absorbs glucose, the absorption of fructose is slower. Sucrose comes in two forms: granulated or as powdered confectioner's sugar.

Corn Syrup is liquid sugar extracted from corn and is used both industrially and by home cooks. Sugar in liquid form is concentrated; it will taste much sweeter and contains about twice as many calories as table sugar. Because it is inexpensive to manufacture, it is used widely in the food industry, particularly for soft drinks.

Honey is also a liquid form of sugar, but it is made from a natural process by honeybees. Honey should not be given to babies before one year because of the risk of exposure to botulism. Like other liquid forms of sugar, honey is about two times sweeter than table sugar. It contains 990 calories per cup compared with 750 calories for sugar. Honey also contains very small amounts of phosphorous, potassium, and calcium.

Maple syrup is concentrated liquid sugar drawn from maple trees.

Molasses is a byproduct of the process for refining table sugar. It contains significant amounts of several nutrients such as calcium, iron, and potassium. Generally speaking, the darker the molasses, the more nutrients it contains.

Fructose is the sugar that naturally occurs in fruit. When it is consumed as part of whole fruit, it is the most nutritious option for a sweet treat. When fructose is used as an added sweetener, it adds no nutrients and is no better in this respect than regular sugar. However, fructose is absorbed more slowly by the body and therefore creates less erratic blood sugar swings. You can buy granulated fructose at the health food store and you can choose products that are sweetened primarily with fructose.

Feeding Your Baby in the Real World

"I do look at the labels. Anything with the number of ingredients with words I don't understand outnumbering basic ingredients—I just stay away from those."

—Leah, mother of Mira and Tano

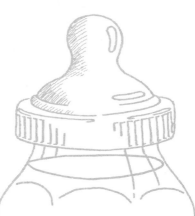

Enriched versus Fortified Foods?

An enriched food has nutrients added into the product that were lost during processing. For example, refined white flour loses nutrients when the germ and bran are removed during milling, so it may be subsequently enriched with B vitamins. On the other hand, a fortified food has vitamins or minerals added as a public health measure, as when vitamin D is added to milk.

Brown sugar is simply table sugar with a small amount of molasses added for color.

Raw sugar (also called turbinado sugar) may seem like a more healthy choice, but it is really only slightly less refined than table sugar. Raw sugar has slightly larger crystals and still contains a small amount of molasses. Otherwise, it is the same as white sugar.

Industrial sugars are used primarily in the food industry and are obtained from various sources: glucose, also called dextrose, is the simplest form of sugar and is even more refined; lactose is refined from milk; maltose is obtained from barley and other cereals; high fructose corn syrup has 40 to 90 percent fructose and is an inexpensive ingredient; mannitol is obtained primarily from seaweed; sorghum syrup is refined from sorghum grain.

Nitrates and Nitrites

The issue of using nitrates and nitrites in cured meat, bacon, some lunch meats, hotdogs, patés and canned meats, and some smoked fish is a complicated one. Potassium nitrate or nitrite is a combination of potassium and sodium used by humans for centuries to preserve foods for long periods and was once known more commonly as Chile saltpeter. It acts to preserve the red color in meats and serves to inhibit the growth of deadly *Clostridium botulinum* spores. Nitrates change into nitrites upon exposure to air. Nitrates are also naturally occurring in many vegetables, including spinach, beets, radishes, eggplant, celery, lettuce, and collard and turnip greens, especially if they are grown in soil naturally rich in nitrates or treated with nitrate fertilizers. Nitrates also appear in the water supply.

In the human digestive tract, nitrates and nitrites are converted to nitrosamines, which are known carcinogens. The presence of vitamins C and E in food containing nitrates, or consumed at the same time, has been shown to inhibit the development of nitrosamines. As a result, the USDA and the FDA strictly regulate the use of nitrates and nitrites in food manufacturing and require that processors also include sodium ascorbate and sodium erythrobate (vitamin Cs) in cured meats. Manufacturers of baby food voluntarily discontinued use of nitrates in their products early in the 1970s. Although efforts have been undertaken to ban the use of nitrates and nitrites in food processing, the FDA and USDA still classify them as GRAS. This is because they feel the health risk of nitrosamines is adequately addressed by limiting their use in manufacturing and the addition of vitamin C to certain products. They also feel that these health risks are outweighed by the ability of nitrates and nitrites to inhibit the growth of C. botulinum, which in itself poses another risk to the population.

So, what does all this mean when you are choosing food for your baby? Clearly, nitrates and nitrites should not be consumed in excess by anyone, and many experts feel that babies and children should not be exposed at all. Whether or not this is a practical solution for you is a matter of personal choice, since it can be very difficult to avoid nitrates completely, particularly when dining out. Certainly, very limited exposure to nitrates is not likely to cause harm, especially as your child reaches school age. Also, consuming a glass of orange or grapefruit juice at the same meal can help reduce risk. Some people choose to ban or nearly ban the following foods for their children: bacon, hot dogs, cured meat, salami, and bologna, which tend to contain the largest amount of nitrates and/or nitrites. Fortunately, there are also nitrate-free versions of many of these foods available, but be aware that they tend to have a less appealing dark brown color, and they must be handled with more care since they are more prone to spoilage.

Irradiated Food

Irradiated foods, such as fresh produce and raw meat, poultry, and fish, are treated with ionizing radiation produced by radioactive isotopes that kill potentially harmful bacteria and allow the food to remain fresh for up to several weeks longer than it normally would. The resulting food is not radioactive and many experts insist that irradiation provides many public health benefits by inhibiting food-borne illness

Irradiated Food Symbol

and allowing for less frequent use of toxic fungicides. Others are concerned that we don't know enough about the long-term effects on human health from eating irradiated food. The FDA requires that all irradiated food be labeled with an international logo resembling a flower in a circle.

Reading Nutrition Facts Panels

Nutrition Facts panels were first introduced in 1994, and many consumers are still learning how to read them. Nutrition facts are required on almost all packaged goods sold in the United States and are available at point-of-purchase for many fresh foods such as produce, meat, fish, and poultry. Exceptions include packaged goods that are sold or imported in a relatively small quantity. Products that are so small as to make including nutrition facts on the label impractical, such as tiny packages of gum or candy, are exempt as well. In this case, the consumer is given an address or phone number to call if they wish to see a nutrition facts statement. Nutrition Facts panels represent a tremendous leap forward in helping consumers choose more healthful foods by forcing manufacturers to present information in a straightforward, useful manner. Experts believe that Nutrition Facts panels will result in fewer diet-related diseases in the years to come.

Serving Size

Serving size is the first piece of information that appears on the Nutrition Facts panel, and is probably the most important. In response to consumer outcry, "realistic" standard serving sizes for many foods have been set by the FDA, but there is still some latitude the manufacturer can use in order to make a less nutritious product appear to be not so bad. In other words, by presenting information using a small serving size, the consumer may think that they are consuming less calories, fat, or sodium than they really are. Before you look at the rest of the panel, evaluate the serving size. On a 10-ounce package of snack chips, for example, the manufacturer might set a serving size as

"Use By" Dates

Many foods are required to display a "use by" or "best before" date. To get the freshest foods with the most nutrients and flavor, look for this date while shopping. Additionally, some foods, especially prepackaged deli items, will display a "packed on" date. If the date the food was packed on does not correspond with your idea of fresh, ask at the service counter if a fresher rotation is available.

1-ounce (10 servings per bag). If your child will be more likely to eat a quarter of the bag at once, adjust all of the nutritional information upward accordingly before deciding whether or not to buy the product.

Calories and Calories from Fat

Many people read only the calorie line in a Nutrition Facts panel. If they have not seen the serving size information, an uninformed decision is likely to be made at this point. This line tells you how many total calories are in a serving of the food, and how many of those calories come from fat (you do not add the two together to calculate total calories). This information is very valuable in deciding whether to buy a product or how much you should use. When you see that mayonnaise, for example, gets almost all of its calories from fat, you may decide to forego it or use just a little instead of slathering it on a sandwich for your little one. However, low calorie content does not always correspond to more healthful foods. In order to choose the most beneficial foods, you must read further.

Percentage of Daily Value (DV)

The information that follows (fat, cholesterol, sodium, carbohydrate, protein, and micronutrients) is listed with information including the quantity of each nutrient per serving and the percentage of the Daily Value (DV) this represents for an adult or child eating a 2,000-calorie diet. Daily Values are more commonly known as Recommended Daily Allowances (RDAs) and are set for adults and children older than four years.

Nutrition Facts

Serving Size 1 cup (228g)
Servings Per Container 2

Amount Per Serving

Calories 250   Calories from Fat 110

	% Daily Value*
Total Fat 12g	18%
Saturated Fat 3g	15%
Cholesterol 30mg	10%
Sodium 470mg	20%
Total Carbohydrate 31g	10%
Dietary Fiber 0g	0%
Sugars 5g	
Protein 5g	

Vitamin A	4%
Vitamin C	2%
Calcium	20%
Iron	4%

* Percent Daily Values are based on a 2,000 calorie diet. Your Daily Values may be higher or lower depending on your calorie needs:

		Calories	2,000	2,500
Total Fat	Less than		65g	80g
Sat Fat	Less than		20g	25g
Cholesterol	Less than		300mg	300mg
Sodium	Less than		2,400mg	2,400mg
Total Carbohydrate			300g	375g
Dietary Fiber			25g	30g

Nutrition Fact Panel

Total Fat and Saturated Fat

This line tells you how much of the fat that is contained in a serving is saturated fat (as with calories, the fat and saturated fat figures are not added to make total fat). In general, saturated fat should be limited as part of the total fat consumed. It can also be helpful to refer to the ingredient list to determine the source of saturated fat. If saturated fat is derived primarily from hydrogenated or partially hydrogenated oils, you may want to think again.

Cholesterol

Health officials are concerned about the amount of cholesterol consumed by Americans, because high cholesterol levels in the blood have been linked to coronary heart disease (CHD). However, a diet high in saturated fats but low in actual cholesterol consumption can also raise blood cholesterol above safe levels. If you want to limit cholesterol, you must also pay attention to the quantity of saturated fat and the source of that fat. Also, the Nutrition Facts panel makes no distinction between levels of HDL and LDL cholesterol. Many dieticians feel this is an oversight that should be addressed, because HDL cholesterol can actually reduce overall levels of cholesterol in the bloodstream, while LDL cholesterol is the actual culprit in the development of CHD.

Sodium

Sodium is another substance that health officials feel should be limited because of the risk of high blood pressure, kidney disease, and heart failure. The maximum amount of sodium that is recommended for adults and children older than four is a DV of 2,400 milligrams. Only 500 milligrams will meet our needs and will usually be supplied from naturally occurring sources without adding any table salt at all. A DV has not been established for infants and young children, but experts agree that added sodium is not beneficial to babies. Most Americans consume the equivalent of between one and three teaspoons (2,300 to 6,900 milligrams) of salt every day.

Total Carbohydrates: Dietary Fiber and Sugar

The total carbohydrate figure represents a combination of dietary fiber, added sweeteners, and complex carbohydrates, as well as some nondigestible additives like thickening agents and stabilizers per serving. The more nutritious a food is, the greater disparity there will be between the amount of sugar to the total amount of carbohydrates. A larger amount of fiber is also beneficial.

Protein

A DV for protein is not required on the Nutrition Facts panel because protein deficiency is rare in the United States, but the total grams of protein are listed. If you are concerned about protein intake, know that an adult should have between 50 and 75 grams of protein a day, and a baby should have approximately 14 grams per day at 6 to 12 months and 23 grams per day between 1 and 3 years.

Micronutrient Information

Vitamins A and C and the minerals calcium and iron are considered to be the most important micronutrient DVs to meet, and therefore are required on the label. DVs for other vitamins and minerals may be listed at the manufacturer's discretion.

Footnote

The footnote elaborates on the information that has gone before, stating the exact DVs that should be met within both a 2,000-calorie diet (which was assumed as the norm) and a 2,500-calorie diet for fat, cholesterol, sodium, and carbohydrates. A 2,000-calorie diet is used as a mean partly because it approximates the number of calories needed to maintain a healthy weight in post-menopausal women. This is the group within the population that will be most likely to attempt weight reduction. The footnote also confirms that the DVs for fat, saturated fat, cholesterol, and sodium are recommended *maximums*.

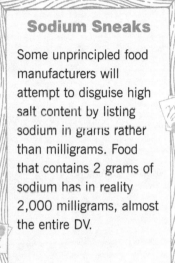

Sodium Sneaks

Some unprincipled food manufacturers will attempt to disguise high salt content by listing sodium in grams rather than milligrams. Food that contains 2 grams of sodium has in reality 2,000 milligrams, almost the entire DV.

Nutritional Claims: What They Really Mean

With all of the hype designed to make you think a product is healthy, it can be easy to be swept away thinking that something is good for you without understanding the true meaning of the terms used. In reality, law defines these terms, and a product must meet strict requirements before advertisers can use them.

- **Low fat**—contains fewer than 3 grams of fat per serving.
- **Low saturated fat**—a serving contains 1 gram or less of saturated fat.
- **Fat-free**—contains no more than a half gram of fat per serving.
- **Lean**—contains no more than 4 grams of saturated fat, 10 grams of total fat, and 95 milligrams of cholesterol per serving or per 100 grams of food.
- **Extra lean**—a serving or 100 grams contains 5 grams total fat and 2 grams or less of saturated fat.
- **Light or Lite**—contains more than one-third fewer calories or 50 percent less fat than the regular product. If the regular product contains more than half fat calories, fat content must be reduced by 50 percent or more.
- **Low calorie**—a serving contains 40 calories or less.
- **Reduced calorie**—contains 25 percent less sugar than the regular product.
- **Sugar-free**—contains no more than a half gram of any sugars per serving.
- **Low sodium**—a serving contains 140 milligrams of sodium or less.
- **Cholesterol-free**—contains no more than 2 milligrams of cholesterol and 2 grams or less of saturated fat per serving.
- **Low-cholesterol**—a serving contains 20 milligrams or less of cholesterol and 2 grams or less of saturated fat.
- **Good source of, Contains, or Provides**—will mean that a serving provides 10 to 19 percent of the DV (or RDA) of the named nutrient.

- **High, Rich in, or Excellent source of**—will mean 20 percent or more of the DV (or RDA) per serving of the named nutrient.
- **More, Fortified, Enriched, or Added**—will mean a serving provides at least 10 percent more of the DV (or RDA) than the regular product.
- **Natural flavors**—are flavorings extracted from nonsynthetic food or plant sources.
- **Healthy**—means that a serving contains no more than 3 total grams of fat, 1 gram of saturated fat, 60 milligrams of cholesterol, and 300 milligrams of sodium. There is no limit on sugar content. A serving must also contain 10 percent of one of these nutrients: vitamin A, vitamin C, calcium, iron, protein, or fiber.
- **Fresh**—Fresh foods must not be processed, cooked, or frozen. Produce may be washed and coated.
- **Fresh frozen**—Foods may be frozen using flash freezing technology, which may preserve fresher flavor.
- **Organic**—New national organics standards have recently been proposed by the USDA and could go into effect by the year 2002. Until this time, individual states and private organizations set organic standards for their regions. This means that to understand what "certified organic" means on a label, you must contact the certifying organization.

Genetically Modified Organisms

Products containing agricultural ingredients that are grown using genetically modified seed are not currently required to be labeled as such. Strong consumer reaction against the use of GMOs means that growers and manufacturers are not likely to label products containing GMOs unless they are forced to, since 80 to 90 percent of Americans say they would not buy GMOs if they were labeled as such. Many activists in Europe and the United States vigorously protest this policy (or lack thereof) on the part of the U.S. government. For more information about GMOs, see Chapter 5.

Health Claims

The FDA regulates the use of certain health claims linking nutrients found in or added to food to certain health benefits. This applies only to foods regulated by the FDA and therefore does not include fresh meat, poultry, or fish. Health claims can be made only in the following instances:

- A lower chance of developing CHD relating to low levels of saturated fat and cholesterol in the diet
- A high-fiber diet and cancer prevention
- Increased consumption of calcium linked to a reduction in the rate of osteoporosis
- A low-fat diet related to a reduced risk of certain types of cancer
- Consumption of fiber, especially soluble fiber, and a reduction in CHD
- Low sodium intake and a reduced risk of hypertension and high blood pressure

Bovine Growth Hormone in Milk

Bovine Growth Hormone (rBGH/rBST) is a genetically engineered hormone injected into cows, causing them to produce up to 25 percent more milk. Although products made from milk from treated animals are not required to be labeled, some producers will choose to label dairy items that do not contain BGH. No long-term tests of the hormone's health effects on humans have been conducted, but some preliminary studies link BGH with increased risks of breast cancer, colon cancer, diabetes, and hypertension. BGH-treated cows are more susceptible to disease, and as such are given higher quantities of antibiotics. Milk and other products from BGH-treated cows may contain less protein and higher levels of saturated fat. The use of rBGH/rBST is banned in the European Union, Canada, New Zealand, and Australia, so cheeses and other dairy products from these countries will not contain BGH. Goats and sheep cannot be treated with BGH. Organic cow's milk is always BGH-free.

Health claims made by food manufacturers may not exaggerate the effect of eating a certain food and must not imply that eating a certain food can be considered as a part of a druglike therapy.

CHAPTER TEN

Feeding Multiples—Special Circumstances

The number of multiple births has been skyrocketing in recent years, increasing by three times between 1980 and 1995. One reason is that many couples are using modern fertility drugs and other techniques, which often increase the likelihood of a multiple birth. Also, older women are having babies in increasing numbers, which increases the number of multiples born in two ways. First, women older than 35 are more likely to release several ova simultaneously at ovulation. Second, older women are also more likely to use fertility drugs.

Feeding a baby under special or difficult circumstances presents a variety of different challenges to new parents. Some undertakings are expected, as is usually the case with multiple births of twins, triplets, or the arrival of even larger broods. Other experiences, such as a premature birth or the birth of a baby with health problems or birth defects, are unexpected and often traumatic. Because premature birth, low birth weight, and medical complications often coincide with multiple births, parents of multiples may find more information that is of interest to them in this chapter. It is my intent to clarify some of the resources and techniques used by parents feeding their children under unique conditions.

Breastfeeding Twins

Although many mothers of twins worry that they won't be able to produce enough milk to nurse twins exclusively, this is often not the case. Mother Nature usually provides for the birth of multiples by increasing the mother's milk supply accordingly. This is because when a mother nurses her twins, she will either be spending twice as much time with a baby at her breast or, more frequently, she will have both babies at the breast at the same time. This increases the levels of the hormone oxytocin in her bloodstream, which sends the signal to her body to produce more milk. Nursing twice as much may also have a relaxing effect—an additional benefit for an especially tired new mother. Many mothers of twins feel that nursing is preferable to bottle-feeding because it saves time over sterilizing so many bottles and preparing formula for both babies.

Breastfeeding Higher-Order Multiples

Although nursing triplets and even quadruplets is possible, it cannot be done without a *lot* of help from others. Most women who breastfeed higher-order multiples (triplets, quads, and so on) do supplement with formula. However, remember that any time your babies spend at the breast is helpful to them, so don't hesitate to try nursing if that's what you want. You can find support for your efforts through La Leche League and many other parenting organizations who work specifically with parents of multiples (see Resources).

Tips for Nursing Multiples

- Talk to breastfeeding counselors and other mothers who have nursed more than one baby before your babies are born so that you will be more prepared for the challenge.
- You may want to begin by nursing each baby one at a time so that you have a chance to become comfortable, and switch to simultaneous feeding later.
- Make sure to have each baby alternate between your breasts so that you won't have any problems with unbalanced breasts if one baby turns out to be a more vigorous nurser than the other is.

Nursing Positions for Feeding Two Babies at Once

Many mothers find that one of these positions works best for nursing two babies. I encourage you to try them all, and to try each one again periodically. As your babies grow, they may be more manageable in a new position. Always make sure you are seated comfortably. Using a nursing stool is a good idea so that your legs provide extra support for your babies' wobbly heads and less pressure is placed on your back.

Modified cradle position. Using a U-shaped nursing pillow or several bed pillows for support, get one baby latched onto one breast in the cradle position. Then, put the other baby to the other breast in the same position. The babies' legs and feet will be draped across each other in your lap. You won't

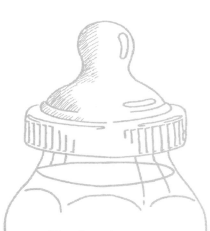

Having Trouble Keeping Track?

Nursing mothers of multiples frequently have trouble keeping track of which baby nursed at which breast last, or which is due for a bottle-feeding. One solution to this problem is to put a different colored band on each baby's wrist (one for the right breast, one for the left breast, and one for the bottle). After each feeding, switch the bands so you will know where to place each baby at the next feeding.

Modified Cradle Position

Modified Football Position

Combination Position

be able to get each baby in position without help until you have had a great deal of practice. This position is good if you like to sit cross-legged.

Modified Football position. Hold each baby at your side, propped on bed pillows or a nursing pillow with his or her feet facing the back of the couch or chair. Guide the babies to the breast one at a time until each is properly latched on. This is easier to accomplish without assistance at first than the modified cradle position.

Combination position. Hold one baby in the cradle position and one baby in the football position. In this case, the babies are lying in the same direction, with one baby's head near the other baby's feet.

Karyn, Scott, Max, and Josh

When I was researching the subject of feeding twins for this chapter I was lucky enough to be able to consult my friends, Scott and Karyn Miller, whose twin sons, Max and Josh, were born on Labor Day in 1999. Scott and Karyn were kind enough to share some of their story with me, and while no experience is typical (especially when raising twins), I thought some of their adventures would be interesting to new parents.

The twins were born by C-section five weeks early. Josh weighed in at five pounds, one ounce, and Max four pounds, six ounces. Despite their early arrival, both boys were in fairly good shape after the birth; breathing well on their own and in generally good health. Still, their doctors wanted them to stay for several weeks in the neonatal intensive care unit (NICU) until it was shown that they were gaining weight properly and that they would be able to regulate their body temperature. Lung immaturity is a danger to preemies, so the twins were monitored carefully for any sign of respiratory distress.

Nursing

The twins were able to nurse well from the start, and Karyn had no trouble getting them latched on, and had none of the trouble with engorgement and sore nipples she had heard so much about. After four days, Karyn was released from the hospital and was faced with having to go home without her babies, an experience no one could have prepared her for. Because she could not be with the twins day and night any longer, she went to the hospital at seven every morning and stayed with them until seven each night. She sat with them every moment and nursed them every two to three hours. The nurses in the NICU showed Karyn how to nurse both babies at once by sitting in the rocking chair with an extra large nursing pillow designed especially for twins. Karyn used the football hold with each and switched sides with every other feeding. This prevented the boys from developing favorites and helped them develop better eye coordination as they would gaze at her from both angles.

Because she could not be with the twins at night, Karyn continued to pump at home every three hours through the night. In order to help the boys gain weight more quickly, they were also given supplemental formula. In the end, Josh was sent home four days earlier than his brother. This was another difficult moment for Scott and Karyn, because they no longer had the comfort of knowing the boys were at least together, even if they could not be with them every moment. Once both boys were home, however, Scott and Karyn began their new home life as parents of twins. Thinking back, Karyn wonders now if the experience of having the boys in the hospital, however difficult it might have been, wasn't a blessing in disguise. As each day passed, Karyn learned so much from the incredibly dedicated nurses who worked in the NICU. Not only did she have invaluable help with breastfeeding, but she also learned a great deal about the care of babies. By seeing how the nurses expertly handled and cared for her tiny boys, she began to realize that they were not as fragile as they looked and began to gain confidence in her own ability to care for them.

Breastfeeding Multiples Takes a Lot of Energy

You'll need to eat an additional 400 to 500 calories per day per baby. Be careful not to allow yourself to become run down because you haven't had enough nutritious food. Be sure to eat lots of whole grains, dairy products, fruits, and vegetables to provide you with the energy you'll need.

Life at Home

Once Max and Josh were home, Karyn's sister came to stay for 10 days, which allowed Karyn and Josh to get at least a little rest. They quickly discovered that life with two newborn boys allowed for only about an hour's sleep each night. Once her sister went home, Karyn learned how to nurse both boys when she was alone by laying one on each side of her as she sat on the bed. Once the nursing pillow was placed around her waist, she would scoop each of the boys into one arm and hold them in the football position. This method worked well until the boys were about four months old, and they were simply getting too big to pick up with one arm. At this point, she resigned herself to nursing the boys one at a time, which took at least an hour. For night feedings, Scott would help her get the boys in position so she could get back to sleep sooner.

Throughout this period, the boys continued with one or two bottles of supplemental formula every day. They continued nursing until they were 10 months old. At this point, Max began biting Karyn and Josh just seemed to lose interest. The time to stop had come, but both Karyn and Scott look back fondly on the days, beginning at three months, when the boys would gaze into one another's eyes and hold hands while they nursed together. When this happened, their parents' hearts would melt, and the special relationship the boys will share all their lives began to show itself.

Besides ongoing help from Karyn's sister ("A saint!" says Karyn), they decided to hire a doula (a birth and baby care assistant), who came to help with the babies three days a week for about five weeks when they were one month old. At first, Karyn thought she would want the doula to help her get caught up with household chores, so that she could spend more time with the boys. After a short while, though, she realized that what she needed most was some time to herself to rest and recharge for the rest of the week.

Using More Than One Kind of Formula

Sometimes, different babies in the same set of multiples will need different kinds of formula. In this case, buy different-colored bottles for each baby so that you can keep track of prepared bottles.

Moving to Solid Foods

The boys began eating solid food at about four months, starting with infant cereal and a few varieties of jarred organic baby foods. As he began to see six to ten 60-cent jars of food fly out of the cupboard every day, Scott, a professional chef, resolved to make the boys homemade baby food. At first, the boys were taken aback by the richer flavors of homemade food, but they adjusted quickly. As their eating habits developed, it became increasingly apparent that the boys have very different styles when it comes to food. Although Scott wonders if this may be due to an unfortunate lemon experience Max had at six months, Max has definitely proven to be the more cautious of the two. As the smaller boy, Max seemed to have more difficulties in general, picking up more illnesses and being more likely to react adversely to new foods. Josh, on the other hand, must be watched to make sure he doesn't stuff so much food into his mouth that he chokes.

These days, the boys are happily eating a variety of foods: eggs, tofu, tomato sauce, rice, cheese, turkey, chicken, avocado, and eggplant are favorites. While Karyn reflects that the beginning of life with the twins was about 80 percent hard work and 20 percent fun, the tide has reversed as they approach their first birthday, and today it's about 20 percent work and 80 percent fun. Having twins, she says, is an incredible education in how different two kids can be, even if they are born on the same day and given the same parents and the same environment.

Multiple Survival Strategies

- Arrange for help ahead of time. Friends, family, hired babysitters and housecleaners, and even live-in hired help are all useful to new parents of multiples. Decide what sort of help you will need and what you can afford before the babies come so that you'll have one less thing to worry about when you get home from the hospital. Be realistic, talk to other parents of multiples to find out what sort of

Feeding Your Babies in the Real World

"I tried tandem nursing with the twins and doing one at a time but I was never comfortable with either. I wrote down when they nursed and on which side but it was very difficult, as I was exhausted. Once we were on formula I felt I had a better grip on whether they were getting enough, and my husband would feed one and I would do the other. After they got older, I would end up propping the bottle for one and feeding the other on my arms. I would put the one not being held in a carrier and would usually hold the bottle for her or give her some kind of physical touching and eye contact. I would then reverse the setup for the next feeding so they would get lots of snuggling!"

—Sonya, mother of twin girls

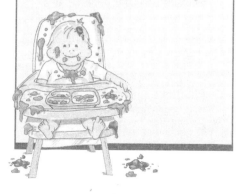

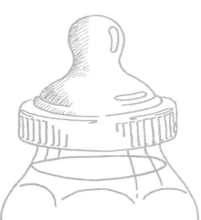

Feeding Your Babies in the Real World

"I tried to breastfeed my twins, but didn't produce enough milk, so went bottle. When the feedings were still frequent, I held one, and propped the other in the infant seat, then alternated positions for the next. (I was a single parent, so went it alone, but whenever a visitor came round, they got a bottle and a baby right away.) Lots and lots of bottles were a must. I used the concentrated powder that you mix with water for ease of preparation. My county has fluoridated water, so they also got the benefits of this: 14 years old, and not a single cavity in either of them."

—Sharon, mother of twins

help was the most useful to them and how long you should expect to need it.

- Make lists of household and parenting chores with schedules attached so that helpers can make themselves as useful to you as possible without disturbing you.
- Work toward having the babies on the same schedule if possible and if desired. This is especially useful for middle-of-the-night feedings. If you wake one baby when her brother has already woken for a feeding, you'll begin to teach them to expect feedings at certain times and hopefully get a little more sleep. Similarly, feeding them at the same times during the day will allow you to spend about half as much time feeding them as you would otherwise.
- Join a support group for parents of multiples. One may be offered through the hospital where you gave birth, or you can contact Twin Services at (800) 243-2276.
- Keep meticulous records of everything from feeding schedules to childhood illnesses to immunizations. With multiples, it's easy to lose track. Who took what amount at the last feeding? Who hasn't had a poopy diaper in a few days?
- Get plenty of rest. This is important whether you are breastfeeding, bottle-feeding, solid foods feeding, or just plain parenting.

Bottle-Feeding Multiples

When bottle-feeding multiples, you'll be stunned by the amount of bottles you'll need to have on hand and the sheer amount of work it is to sterilize them all, not to mention the time it takes to prepare the formula and give each baby her bottle. Most parents of multiples try and use every time- and labor-saving device they can afford. From fully prepared formula to bottle-sterilizing kits, parents of multiples are often willing to try anything. Parents of twins are encouraged to feed both babies at the same time by laying them down on either side of you on the couch or sitting between them while they are each in a safe baby seat. This will save you the time you would spend feeding them one after the other, and you will avoid having to prop the bottle. While bottle propping is not recommended, it becomes a necessity with multiples unless you have enough time to feed them all individually or you have a lot of helpers constantly on hand. If you prop the bottle, use a product specifically designed for that purpose; to prevent choking, never leave your baby unattended with a propped bottle, and always use some form of infant seat so that your baby is safely secured and not lying flat.

Solids Feedings and Multiples

When it comes time to introduce solid food to your babies, it will become even more apparent that you have brought multiple *individuals* into the world. While one baby takes immediately to rice cereal, another may literally gag at the sight of it. Baby A might gobble up strained peas for months, when baby B has long since moved on to table foods. Remember that this is not a contest. While it may be more convenient for you if your children fall into line and display similar abilities and tastes, don't get your hopes up. Allowing your child to set the pace never becomes so important as when other babies are present, which allows for too many opportunities for critical comparisons. This does not mean that parents of multiples shouldn't seek extra reassurance from their children's pediatrician that each child is growing properly according to his individual pattern.

Food Refusal and Multiples

I have read many accounts from parents of multiples in which one child's refusal to eat or misbehavior at mealtimes instigates the other child or children to do the same. This can be very frustrating and worrisome to a parent who is coping not only with one fussy eater but also a baby she knows would eat better if his sibling weren't such a powerful influence. Here are some ideas for coping

There Is Light at the End of the Tunnel

The first four months is generally acknowledged as the most difficult when rearing multiple babies. After this time, as your babies mature and as you become more proficient, parenting multiples should become much easier.

Keeping Up

If your babies have similar tastes and eating patterns, you'll find that it's difficult to spoon the food in fast enough. To save time, use just one bowl and one spoon unless one baby has a cold or infectious illness.

• • •

Birth-Weight Disparities

It is not uncommon for there to be disparity in birth weights among multiples, sometimes with one baby coming into the world several pounds heavier than his sibling(s). This may require that parents adopt different feeding strategies for each baby at first, but frequently a smaller baby will begin to keep pace with her sister in weight gain, even though she may never catch up entirely.

with this situation. Keep in mind, though, that neither baby will allow himself to go hungry for very long just because of his sibling's behavior.

- Start the less fussy eater with his meal slightly earlier so that if the food-refusal-instigator quits early, he'll have had a chance to consume more food.
- Try letting the babies feed each other. This creates quite a mess, but you may discover that more food is consumed as a result.
- If the babies are toddling, try letting them have snacks or less messy meals at their own child-size table. The change in venue may inspire both of them to eat more.

Preemies

Coping with the birth of a premature baby can be extremely difficult for parents, and the same medical technology that is now able to save many preemies who previously would have died can make parents feel as if they are unnecessary for the care of their infant. Nothing could be farther from the truth. Your baby needs you more than ever. For example, it is highly recommended that mothers of premature infants provide their baby with breastmilk if at all possible. Although your baby may not be able to suckle at the breast right away, the milk your body produces when she is born preterm contains even more irreplaceable nutrients and antibodies than it would if she was born on her due date. Additionally, breastmilk will place less strain on the baby's immature digestive system than formula will.

If you are able, begin pumping your milk as soon as possible using a breast pump provided by the hospital. If your baby is not yet ready to nurse, this milk can be saved and given to your baby by you or by a nurse through a feeding syringe or though a feeding tube when he is medically able to receive it. Some doctors do not recommend giving preemies a bottle because the constant sucking required to feed from a bottle uses too much of the baby's valuable energy. Once he is able to suck (which may be days or weeks away), it is better to try giving him the breast because the milk comes in bursts, allowing him to rest between the let-downs when the milk comes in the most copious amounts. For the first feedings, try to work closely with both a lactation consultant and a nurse experienced in the care of premature infants. Not only will these key people be able to help you get off to the right start under challenging circumstances, but they will help you evaluate whether or not your baby is ready to continue with regular breastfeedings. Once your baby is able to nurse on a regular basis, you may want to continue pumping for a time because your milk supply may have suffered due to early separation from your baby.

Although it can be difficult, nursing your baby may help you overcome the daunting emotional issues surrounding caring for a premature baby by allowing you to get on with the job of parenting even while your baby is still in the hospital. If, on the other hand, you are simply unable to nurse your baby for emotional or physical reasons, do not feel that you have failed. Premature babies are truly modern miracles and your job as a parent is only just beginning.

Babies with Birth Defects

For parents who discover in the delivery room that their baby suffers from a birth defect, the shock can be tremendous. However, many babies born with birth defects are not really that different from their "normal" counterparts just at birth. Their differences will become more apparent as they develop at a different rate from other babies. In most cases, breastfeeding is still best if it is possible for these special babies, but there are some considerations parents should be aware of.

If your baby is born with Down's syndrome, she may have difficulty getting started with breastfeeding because Down's babies frequently have poor muscle tone, which results in a weak or

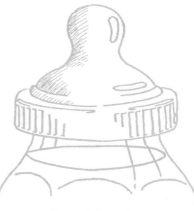

Freebies for Multiples

Many companies such as Gerber, Beechnut, or Carnation, offer coupons or freebies for baby food or infant formula to families with multiples. Offers come in a variety of formats, and I suggest you contact each company directly to learn the details of each offer. A list of baby food and formula companies with contact information appears in the Resources section of this book. Some companies will require a copy of your babies' birth certificates to qualify for special offers. Many parents are reluctant to send a copy of this sensitive document to a stranger, and they often find that a note from the babies' doctor verifying a multiple birth will suffice instead.

ineffective suck. This means that the mother and other caregivers will need to be extremely patient as the baby very slowly gets the hang of nursing. In the meantime, the mother can pump her milk and give the baby the sustenance she needs with the use of a feeding syringe. With persistence, however, many Down's babies eventually become competent nursers and benefit from breastmilk even more than other babies. Not only does breastmilk provide extra immunity against the colds and ear infections Down's babies are prone to, but breastmilk coats Down's babies' intestinal tracts with friendly flora preventing all-too-common intestinal infections. Down's babies also frequently suffer from constipation, and breastmilk has a laxative effect. Breastmilk has also been shown to help in brain development, which is particularly useful to Down's babies.

Breastfeeding a baby with a cleft lip and/or palate may be extremely challenging or even impossible, especially at first. Normal difficulties in getting a baby latched on to the breast during first feedings will be compounded by the malformation of your baby's mouth. In this case, it is very important to seek out the help of a mother or lactation consultant experienced in nursing babies with a cleft of the lip or palate. It is advisable to pump milk and feed your baby with a syringe as you try to teach him to feed from the breast. In many cases, babies with this birth defect are able to nurse, and the breastmilk they receive helps them to avoid some of the ear infections that often affect children with this condition. Surgery to repair a cleft usually occurs somewhere between one and two years.

Preemies Need Extra Iron

Unlike babies born at term, premature infants may not have the iron reserves that are usually stored in babies' bodies during the latter part of their time in the womb. For this reason, doctors will usually recommend an infant iron supplement from birth.

CHAPTER ELEVEN

The Family Meal

Including your baby in family meals is an important part of his social and emotional development. A baby learns by example, and his experiences eating with his family are sure to have a positive impact on his future eating habits. It's not necessary that every meal be shared (many parents prefer to eat together after the children have gone to bed), but eating with your young child whenever it is practical or convenient will be of lifelong value to him.

Meal-Eating Stages

Babies go through many stages of participation in the family meal. When our baby was a newborn, it seemed that the only way I could get an occasional quiet dinner with my husband was to nurse him while we ate. This might sound inconvenient, but for us it provided a quiet moment when we could sit down together as a family and truly relax. We even took advantage of this a few times when we went out to eat, and I would discreetly nurse him in his baby sling or front pack, while other diners continued with their meals, oblivious to the fact that a baby was in the restaurant. Integrating him into our lives in this way helped me to feel more at ease and confident as a new mother.

As your baby grows, there may be several intervals when it is impossible for everyone to eat at the same time. Some babies are incredibly active eaters, whether they are at the breast, the bottle, or while they messily slurp rice cereal while waving a sloppy spoon around. Clearly, handling this sort of situation requires too much of your attention to allow you to enjoy your own meal. Other babies have an uncanny knack for becoming extremely fussy just as the family is about to sit down to dinner (this is often reserved for holiday meals). I'll never forget when the fussies happened at Easter dinner, and Max began to wail just as our large family was about to sit down. I was starving (of course) and frustrated that he was fussy when I had just given him a lovely meal of strained carrots and applesauce for dessert. I was amazed, though, when my sister, who has four children of her own, held him happily on her lap while she ate her dinner. She lined up little bits of dinner rolls and pasta salad on the edge of her place mat for him to grab and eat while everyone ate and laughed around the dinner table. Clearly, I hadn't realized that he was ready for something more substantial, both in terms of food and social interaction.

As your baby enters the toddler years, he will increasingly become a social force to be reckoned with. Eating by himself will simply not provide enough stimulation any longer. If you already have other children, it will be easier to adjust to a family dinnertime. If this is your first child, you may have difficulty changing your eating patterns to accommodate your little one. This is especially true if you are accustomed to having dinner standing over the kitchen sink or sitting in front of the TV after the baby goes to bed. Eating earlier may not be an attractive option for many adults, but still it will be useful to sit with your child and participate in a family mealtime. Remember that family dining is a process, not an objective. Enjoy the different phases as much as you can, because none of it lasts. Soon, soccer practice, birthday parties, and piano lessons will make life so hectic that you will long for the days when you could sit down together every day.

When you have more than one child, the pandemonium is compounded, but so is the joy. In reality, having two or more children can make mealtimes go more smoothly in many cases. If a solid routine of family mealtimes has already been established, a new baby will quickly adjust to this as a natural part of her day. An older child may be delighted to "help" feed the baby by bringing her food to the table and doling out finger foods. Weekend pancake and omelet breakfasts will be particularly enjoyable even as you marvel at the fact that your baby is eating twice what her preschooler brother eats (babies often eat their older siblings under the table).

Feeding Your Baby in the Real World

"My husband and I both work full time, and our schedule is often crazy, with each of us working late several nights a week. It makes a big difference that we make sure the kids always have dinner with one of us at about the same time every night. I mean, everything else is so hectic, It's nice for all of us (especially the kids) to know there's one thing we can count on. I also think it helps the rest of the evening go more smoothly when the kids have had a good dinner."

—Andrea, mother of Joshua and Elizabeth

Including Your Baby in Holiday Family Meals

From Fourth of July picnics to Thanksgiving dinner with all the trimmings, babies make wonderful company at large family dinners. Whether you pull her high chair up to the table or hold her in your lap, these gatherings can be fun for everyone. Here are a few tips for making sure the holiday stays cheery.

- Keep wine glasses, sharp knives, hot dishes, lit candles, and other dangers out of your baby's reach. If there's a table-cloth, make sure it's weighted down sufficiently so he can't pull it off the table along with everyone's dinner.
- If your baby is in your lap, you may want to use a large dishtowel to protect your special occasion clothes from stains. Depending on how messy things might get, a bath towel on the floor to protect the rug might not be such a bad idea, either.
- Bring a basket to the table with toys and books for your baby to play with in case she gets bored with all the grown-up talk.

Choosing the Right Seating for Your Baby

As your baby becomes a toddler, his needs for seating will change. Expect that between 16 and 24 months, he'll become dissatisfied with the current arrangements. He may become frustrated with having to sit in the high chair (especially if he can't climb into and out of it himself), or he may simply desire a wider variety of seating options for different times of day. As always, safety should be your primary concern. Many families continue to use a high chair with safety straps for their baby well into the second year and include baby in family meals by pulling his high chair right up to the table. If the tray is at the right height to clear the tabletop, this can work beautifully. If not, try removing the tray to see if the table top itself will serve just as well. Otherwise, you'll want to shop for a safe booster seat or booster chair.

The Kid's Table

As soon as your toddler is able to feed herself, she can be introduced to the kids' table. This is the separate table where the kids, who usually range in age from 18 months to early teens, can all enjoy their meal together so the adults can have their boring conversations in peace. Usually reserved for family gatherings, I think the kids table should be used much more frequently. Having other friends with kids for dinner can be a nice social activity for young parents who feel like they never get out or see anyone, and letting the kids eat together can be fun for everyone. You may even be amazed at how advanced your child's self-feeding skills are when she is influenced by the behaviors of older kids.

Table Manners

Different families have different standards for proper behavior at the table. However, many children are taught not to play with their food, to say please and thank you when asking for anything, and to ask to be excused from the table when they are finished eating. Other families simply try to prevent bold misbehavior at the table—no hitting, shouting at, or teasing of siblings, and no gross behavior like chewing with your mouth open or picking your nose, for example. Old-fashioned table manners may seem a bit outmoded to young parents, but stop to consider that mealtimes are a perfect venue for introducing the idea that polite behavior is expected generally and especially at certain times. Also, having a child who already knows the rules of politeness can be a great relief if you are invited to the house of someone you don't know very well. In any case, at some point close to your child's second birthday, your baby will probably have the

awareness and competence to learn a few simple rules of behavior for mealtimes. Simply understanding that mealtimes are for eating and not playing is a big step at this age, and with gentle instruction and patience, she can slowly learn how to eat with others without being a disruption.

Six Easy Recipes for Both Children and Parents

Sometimes, it seems impossible that your mealtime will ever return to normal after the arrival of your baby. It's true, becoming a family means adjusting your eating habits to accommodate the little one(s), but that doesn't mean that you can't all enjoy the meal. In fact, you would be wise to use this opportunity to examine your own adult eating habits. It may be time to introduce more healthy foods into your own diet. Many people who never crossed the threshold of a health food store before becoming parents suddenly find they have become health food "nuts" who look and feel better as a result. Here are some ideas for healthy meals that will please both parents and children. The concept is simple: create meals that can be easily altered in the final preparations to suit adult tastes while pleasing youngsters as well. In the case of dishes that include meat, these recipes can easily be adapted for families who prefer a vegetarian lifestyle.

Homestyle Burritos

Burritos are great family food because they can include any number of healthy favorite ingredients as well as a wide variety of leftovers. I keep flour tortillas in the freezer for emergency midweek meals when I suddenly run out of ideas for what to cook. Although younger babies can't really eat a burrito until they are much older, they love the tortillas and quite a few of the other ingredients. I usually serve my son a tortilla with melted cheese and rice, beans, tomatoes, and avocado on the side. Burritos are great for older kids, because they can build their own. Feel free to vary the ingredients to suit your tastes and the contents of your refrigerator.

Serves two adults and as many children as there are tortillas.

Ingredients

3–5 large flour tortillas

1 (8-ounce) can of precooked kidney, pinto, or black beans, or $1/2$ cup of same, soaked overnight and boiled in a change of water for one hour or until soft. You can substitute refried beans if you wish.

1–1$1/2$ cups cooked brown or white rice

1 large avocado, mashed

$1/4$–$1/3$ pound of grated cheese, such as mild cheddar, mozzarella, monterey Jack.

$1/2$ cup chopped tomatoes (stew with a few tablespoons of olive oil and a dash of Italian dried herbs or fresh cilantro for 10 minutes for extra flavor)

Hot sauce (for older kids and grownups)

Instructions

1. Preheat oven to 300°F.
2. Heat beans in their water in a small saucepan over medium heat (5 minutes), or in the microwave. Use a slotted spoon when you add the beans to your burritos so you don't get any of the water in your burrito.
3. Heat tomatoes in a small saucepan over a medium-low heat, or in the microwave.
4. Sprinkle a small amount of cheese on one side of each tortilla (leave about two inches around the edges to keep cheese from melting out) and fold in half. Place tortillas between layers of fairly damp (but not soaking) clean dish towels and place in the oven for 5–10 minutes or until cheese is melted.
5. Take tortillas out of the oven and unfold them immediately while the cheese is still melted. The cheese may all stick to one side. This is OK. Turn off the oven.
6. Place a small or large amount (according to your favorites) of all the other ingredients in a small heap on one side of each tortilla. Your burrito will be small or large, depending on how much filling you use. Skip the hot sauce for any of the younger kids.
7. Fold one corner of the burrito just over the heap of fillings and fold in each side. Roll the resulting bundle over the rest of the tortilla at least once to make each finished burrito.

English Muffin Pizzas

Pizza is unbelievably popular with kids of all ages, and it's incredibly easy to make (who needs frozen or take out?). By using English muffins (you can even buy whole wheat), you can tailor each pizza to the individual family member. Toddlers and older kids can assemble their own. You can even make special animal faces with olive eyes and pepper mouths for toddlers and preschoolers. If you're feeling ambitious, you can make yeast-risen pizza dough from scratch. Individual pizzas are great served with a green salad. You may find that a regular weekly pizza night becomes a favorite family tradition.

Serve one to two individual pizzas per person.

Suggested Toppings, Mix and Match

Tomato sauce (I like a simple marinara, but anything will do)
Thinly sliced zucchini
Whole leaves of spinach
Ricotta cheese
Sliced button, crimini, or shitake mushrooms
Shredded mozzarella, or thinly sliced fresh mozzarella
Pitted olives
Raw or roasted red pepper strips
Sliced grilled chicken breast
Peeled, sautéed shrimp

Instructions

1. Move oven rack to one below the top position.
2. Preheat oven to broil.
3. Top each half English muffin with desired ingredients and place together on a baking sheet.
4. Put the baking sheet in the oven and broil for 5–10 minutes or until the cheese is bubbling and the ingredients are beginning to brown.

Pasta with Roasted Peppers, Baby Spinach, and Salmon

This is obviously a dish geared more toward adults (and why not?), but there are lots of elements here that a baby who has graduated from finger food will enjoy: pasta, salmon, and maybe even the vegetables. If you have a gas range, you can make the roasted peppers ahead of time and store them in olive oil in an airtight container in the fridge. Otherwise, you can buy a jar of roasted red peppers at the grocery store. All in all, an elegant, but simple to make, dish.

Serves two adults and one baby.

Ingredients

3/4 lb. hard wheat (durum) penne pasta
1/4 lb. baby spinach
1 sweet red pepper, or one small jar of roasted red peppers in oil
1 salmon fillet (8–12 ounces)

4 tablespoons extra-virgin olive oil
1 ounce grated Parmesan cheese
2 tablespoons any finely chopped fresh herb, such as tarragon, oregano, or thyme
1/2 teaspoon salt
pinch of black pepper

Instructions

1. To roast the pepper: On the stovetop, turn the gas flame on high and using heatproof tongs, place the washed whole pepper directly on the middle of the burner. Watching carefully and turning the pepper frequently, cook the pepper until all of the skin on the outside of the pepper has turned completely black. This may take five minutes or more. Turn off the flame and place the pepper in a clean paper bag to steam. After five minutes, remove pepper from the bag and, using your fingers, peel the blackened skin from the entire pepper. Once this is done, you can cut the pepper into strips, discarding the core and seeds, and put the strips in a dish. Sprinkle the pepper strips with the salt and black pepper. Cover the strips in the olive oil and marinate with a few cloves of whole garlic and a sprinkle of any fresh or dried herbs you may have around (rosemary is great). Let marinate for at least one hour, overnight is best.

2. To cook the salmon fillet: Sprinkle fillet with a little salt and pepper. Heat a heavy skillet over medium high heat and place the salmon in the dry skillet. Cook for about 3 minutes on one side and 2 minutes on the other, or until the center is no longer rare. (To check doneness, pry apart two layers of muscle with the tip of a sharp knife and check for bright pink, underdone spots.) Once the salmon is cool enough to touch, peel off any skin and crumble the meat into small pieces using your fingers. Using this opportunity to look and feel for any bones (especially fine, small pin bones), which should be removed. Set aside.

3. To cook the pasta: Bring a large pot of salted water to a boil. Put pasta in the water to cook. Once the pasta is done, drain it, saving about 3 tablespoons of the pasta water, and return the pasta to the pot it was boiled in.

4. To assemble: Toss the spinach, salmon, red pepper strips, olive oil, and fresh herbs in with the pasta. Add a little of the pasta water to the oil to make a sauce. Add salt and pepper to taste. Serve the pasta in bowls or plates and finish with another drizzle of olive oil and a sprinkling of the Parmesan cheese.

5. For the baby, you may want to cook the pasta a little longer, and he may enjoy his supper with a little more cheese.

Saffron Risotto
with Chicken and Peas

Saffron is a wonderful spice because it is subtle and luxurious enough to please adults, and innocuous enough to be overlooked by even the youngest family diner. (Also, it makes the dish yellow, which is a good kid-food color.) Rice, of course, pleases everyone. The key to making risotto is to have all of the prep work done ahead of time. Once you get started with the actual cooking, you'll be too pre-occupied to get any unfinished business out of the way. Risotto makes great microwavable leftovers and keeps well for one or two days.

Serves two adults and one baby.

Ingredients

$^3/_4$ lb. Arborio rice

6 cups chicken or vegetable stock (this is the same as a large 49-ounce can)

1 pinch saffron powder or 25–30 top-quality threads, soaked in 2 tablespoons warm water or stock

1 small, mild yellow onion, chopped

2 cloves garlic, minced

1 small boneless, skinless chicken breast half

1 cup fresh or frozen peas

2 tablespoons finely chopped fresh Italian flat-leaf parsley

2 tablespoons extra-virgin olive oil

4 tablespoons grated Parmesan cheese

Instructions

1. Cut the chicken into one-inch strips and sauté in olive oil in a wide-based, but not too deep, heavey pan, being careful not to overcook it.
2. In a medium saucepan bring the chicken stock to a boil, then cover and reduce to a simmer.
3. Heat the pan used to sauté the chicken to medium and sauté the onions and garlic until translucent.
4. Turn up the heat to high and add the rice, sautéeing for one minute, stirring constantly.
5. Begin adding the simmering chicken stock a little at a time using a ladle. Add just enough to immerse the rice, and stir the mixture constantly until most of the stock has been absorbed before adding more stock. Continue to stir.
6. When about $^3/4$ of the stock has been added, add the saffron with its liquid to the risotto and stir it in. Continue to cook.
7. Different varieties of Arborio may absorb slightly different quantities of stock. You will know that the dish is close to being done when the rice is soft but still a little chewy. If there is stock left over, or if you need to stretch out the stock with a little boiling water at the end, this is fine. As you add the last of the stock, salt and pepper to taste, being careful to make adjustments depending on how salty the stock is, and mix in about three-quarters of the chopped parsley. When the rice is almost done, add the chicken and peas. Turn off the heat and allow the dish to continue cooking for another five minutes. Total cooking time is about 20 to 25 minutes.
8. Serve with a sprinkle of fresh parsley and Parmesan cheese to garnish.

Risotto makes a good microwavable leftover for baby.

Whole Wheat Waffles
with Apple and Yogurt Sauce

I was introduced to this yogurt sauce when I visited with a German family in college. It was so delicious that I've included it in many weekend breakfasts since. My baby also loves it, and it makes the perfect accompaniment to hot waffles.

Ingredients for the Waffles

$1\,^3/_4$ cups whole wheat pastry flour
2 teaspoons baking powder
$^1/_2$ teaspoon salt
2 eggs
2 tablespoons melted butter
1 teaspoon honey
$1\,^1/_2$ cups milk

Instructions for the Waffles

1. Thoroughly mix together the dry ingredients.
2. Add the wet ingredients all at once, being careful not to overmix. If you want to make a lighter waffle, you can separate the eggs and fold the whipped egg whites in at the end.
3. If the batter is too thick, add a little more milk or water. If the batter is too thin, add a little flour.
4. Cook in a hot waffle iron.

Ingredients for the Yogurt Sauce

2 cups whole milk yogurt
1 small green apple, grated
1 teaspoon lemon juice
1 tablespoon toasted wheat germ

Instructions for the Yogurt Sauce

Mix together all the ingredients and serve with the waffles.

Classic Custard

This simple but fabulous dessert is a favorite from my childhood. It's also a great way to add a little dairy and egg nutrition to your toddler's diet, and it's so easy to make that it's ridiculous. In fact, this is an extremely forgiving dish—you can easily double or triple the recipe. You can also add coconut for extra flavor or use half cream, half milk to create a richer custard. If you prefer a firmer custard, add an extra egg.

Ingredients

2 cups whole milk
$^1/_3$ cup sugar or $^1/_4$ cup honey (note: babies under one year
   should not have honey)
$^1/_8$ teaspoon salt
2 large eggs, beaten
1 teaspoon vanilla
sprinkle of nutmeg or cinnamon

Instructions

1. Preheat oven to 325°F.
2. Whisk together all the ingredients very well and pour into a shallow glass baking dish. If you are substituting honey for sugar, mix the ingredients in a saucepan over a very low heat so that the honey will be well-incorporated in the mixture. Sprinkle with a dash of nutmeg or cinnamon.
3. Place the dish in a large pan of water or bain marie, so that it is three-quarters submerged.
4. Bake for approximately one hour (longer if you are using honey instead of sugar) or until a knife inserted near the edge of the dish comes out clean.

CHAPTER TWELVE

Baby Food and the Single Parent

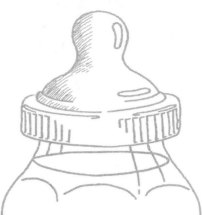

Custody and Breastfeeding

Unfortunately, cases where the father of a breastfeeding baby insists on overnight visitation are not that uncommon. This is not an issue that family court judges are always sensitive to, so be prepared to try and find a compromise. Perhaps you can explain that this period of nursing will be limited and agree to renegotiate custody terms after your baby turns one or after he is weaned. Try to maintain this special time for your baby and yourself, but be prepared for what may come.

As everyone knows, the rate of divorce has skyrocketed in the United States over the past few decades, creating millions of single-parent households. What many people don't realize is that the rate of single parents who choose to have babies without a spouse has also been climbing steadily. In 1998, 1.29 million babies were born to single mothers, accounting for almost 50 percent of births that year. The largest increases were seen in white, college-educated women, many with full-time professional jobs. These combined trends mean that the two-parent family is no longer the assumed norm and that the special needs these families have must be addressed by the larger society. Single parents, often with two, three, or more children to care for, face many challenges, and providing good nutrition for the kids can easily take a back seat. It is my goal in this chapter to address some of the problems single parents face in providing healthy foods for their babies, and to suggest easy, time- and money-saving ways to solve those problems.

Coping with Divorce

Most divorced couples remain more or less amicable, depending on the circumstances surrounding the divorce and the amount of time that has passed since the separation occurred. If the couple maintains some form of shared custody with the children, conflicts are not unusual, and conflicts around food are no exception. Any parent who is trying to set healthy standards for the food his or her child eats may consider an ex-spouse's perhaps different standards as a form of sabotage. Walking the tightrope between sticking to a program you feel is best for your baby's health and acknowledging that you can't really control what your baby eats when he is with your former spouse can be very difficult indeed. If you and your ex-spouse have wildly different viewpoints on what are healthy or appropriate foods for your child, try to take an approach that will serve the best interests of your baby. Pick your battles and work with your former spouse as best you can to come up with a list of foods that your child should simply not have. If you know that your former spouse feels that healthy eating is too much of an inconvenience, maybe you'll want to send some home-cooked frozen entrees with your child on his visits (or maybe not). Make suggestions for convenient restaurant options that you know provide more healthy choices, and specify by name restaurants you would prefer your baby not be taken to. Once the situation is resolved more or less to your satisfaction, try to adjust to the fact that your baby may be raised with two different standards of eating, as he is sure to be raised differently relating to other issues as well.

Feeding Your Baby When Time Is in Short Supply

Single parents are almost always working parents also. Without a spouse around to pick up the slack, they find themselves in charge of everything from dropping off and picking up the kids from school or day care, to doing all of the shopping and household errands, to doing (or overseeing) all of the household chores like the cooking, the laundry, and the cleaning. This description doesn't even begin to cover what a single parent does in a single day—it's exhausting. Yet, many parents accomplish this task with considerable skill, the key being organization. The refrigerator often becomes command central, and endless lists of things to shop for, things to do, and things to remember become as essential as water. How else could one person remember all this stuff? Fortunately, despite what the endless commercials for convenience frozen foods and fast foods would have you believe, healthy eating doesn't have to be inconvenient. Here are some time-saving tips for healthy family eating.

1. *Shop wisely.* Post an ongoing shopping list throughout the week, and try to cut back on emergency trips to the grocery store. Make sure you have all the ingredients you will need on hand for healthy family eating, including quick healthy snacks, fresh vegetables, eggs and dairy products, and dry goods such as pasta, rice, and bread. Create a permanent checklist for items you consider to be essential so you can run through it prior to going shopping in case you forgot to add something to your list. Try to shop at a time when your kids will be in a good mood and at a time when the market won't be too hectic, so that you can get in and out with as little fuss as possible. Organize your shopping list to roughly coincide with each item's location in the store. Put all the fruits and veggies on one part of the list, the dairy items on another part, and so forth.

2. *Limit eating out to special occasions, or save it as a special weekly treat.* Not only is eating out more expensive than preparing food at home, but it takes more time. By the time you get the kids in the car, drive to a restaurant, order, wait for your meal, eat, pay, get everyone back in the car again, and drive home, you've probably spent at least two hours getting a meal together that you could have done with usually healthier ingredients in 30 minutes. Plus, the more you cook at home, the easier it becomes. It really pays to break the habit of eating out every time you feel too tired to face making dinner. Try just making something simple like scrambled eggs, steamed frozen vegetables, and toast (15 minutes prep time maximum). Or, you could make burritos or individual English muffin pizzas. If you have a well-stocked pantry, refrigerator, or freezer, anything is possible on short notice.

3. *Try to have everyone eating the same food at the same time.* Life is complicated enough without learning to be a short-order cook. Single parents often institute family meals earlier and more frequently simply out of necessity, and usually the family feels better for it. You probably have so little time with your kids already that these meals together are precious. Also it's

probably better to put up with macaroni and cheese for the second time in a week than to prepare a separate meal for you and the kids. Single parents have even less time for picky eating behaviors than do couples. Try to offer a few different options within each meal. For example, if one kid doesn't want the vegetables, at least she can have the chicken breast. Kids will usually sense this and find ways to get the calories they need even if their doting parent isn't prepared to whip up another dinner in case the first is rejected.

4. *Cook in batches.* If you know you can count on a few hours each week (maybe an evening when your former spouse or a relative has the kids, or Saturday afternoons when an older child is at soccer practice and the baby is napping), try to use them to get ahead on some cooking. Cook simple hearty dishes like chicken soup, lentil or bean stew, casseroles, macaroni and cheese, and spaghetti sauce. Serve it that night for dinner and put some single-meal-sized containers in the freezer for later use.

This is time well spent because a quick, nutritious midweek dinner will give you the time and energy to get caught up on your regular chores and time with the kids as the week goes on. Also, if you can do this regularly, you'll get a stockpile built up that will come in handy several times each week. I've even heard of people who subscribe to a program for batch cooking only once a month. I personally can't imagine ever being that organized, but this would certainly save considerable time throughout the rest of the month.

Baby Food on a Budget

Single parents frequently struggle to support a family on only one salary, which can be very challenging. All of the tips aforementioned for feeding healthy foods to your family with a limited

Feeding Your Baby in the Real World

"I don't give my kids sweets (other than graham crackers or an occasional small cinnamon alphabet cookie) because I know that they'll learn about sweets soon enough from the rest of the world. I see no reason to accelerate the process by introducing them to candy and chocolate myself. Not only is this healthier for them, but it's great for me too because they don't ask me for these things. I can pass the candy counter at the checkout stand in the grocery store and they don't even pay attention to the stuff because they don't know what it is. That's one less headache for me, thank you!"

—Christina, mother of Christopher and Sophia

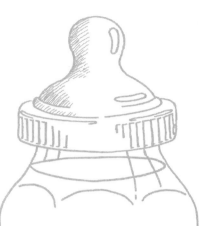

Be Prepared for Illness

Single parents are often caught by an unexpected illness, either their child's or their own. While many pharmacies can deliver medicines and other supplies, you can easily be stuck without food if you can't go out to the store with a sick child. One single mom I know had to eat microwave popcorn for three days once when her infant son was ill. Be prepared with food for both you and the baby. Canned soups, frozen food, and other staples are always good to have on hand. Also, keep a supply of pediatric electrolyte solution to prevent dehydration in the baby in case of vomiting or diarrhea.

amount of time, are doubly important if you are also trying to save money. Shopping wisely, limiting eating out, and cooking in batches are all particularly useful if you are feeding a family on a budget.

1. *Call the companies listed in the resource section of this book.* Ask if they have any special offers or coupons for parents of new babies.
2. *Look for special offers and promotions* in the newspapers and at the grocery store. There are new, healthy foods for babies appearing on the market all the time, and many companies offer free samples or two-for-one deals in order to entice people to try their product.
3. *Avoid junk food.* Junk food may sometimes be cheaper than healthy food, but it doesn't provide proper nutrition for your child's growth. When you are shopping for food on a budget, don't waste your money on empty calories. Also, your child's good health will save money on health care costs in the years to come.
4. *Cook with your kids.* Meals and treats gain added importance to a child when he helps in their preparation, and memories of time together in the kitchen last a lifetime. You may not have the money to spend on expensive toys and family vacations, but the time you spend with your kids is more valuable to them than any of that stuff anyway.

CHAPTER THIRTEEN

Baby Food on the Run

In the very first weeks after your baby is born, you may stay pretty much close to home. The idea of someone else taking her for a few hours so you can get some time may even seem foreign. And everything you would need to prepare for an outing makes staying at home sound like a much better option. However, these days will fly by, and before you know it you'll be whizzing around town, a seasoned parent, with or without your baby. And feeding your baby while you're away or while you're out with her will be a big part of getting on with the rest of your life. This may sound obvious, but it can be one of the biggest transitions for parents and babies to go through. If a nursing mom goes back to work, there's pumping and introducing a bottle to consider. Or, if an older child needs to be picked up at preschool every day at noon, when will your baby have his lunch? If your baby has food allergies, how will you ensure she won't be exposed in day care? Babies must eat, and coordinating feeding schedules and food choices with the rest of our daily routine takes consideration, flexibility, and a great deal of space in the brain of a harried parent.

Nursing Your Baby Away from Home

Many mothers become very comfortable with nursing in public under almost any circumstances. Indeed, putting your baby to the breast can often give you a chance to have an actual uninterrupted conversation at a cafe with your husband or even a good friend. As you and your baby become better at getting latched on, the process of lifting your shirt, unhooking your bra, and getting down to business becomes almost seamless. You can even tell yourself that no one will notice, although there's never a guarantee of that. Quite a few mothers come to the conclusion that flashing a little breast isn't a big deal. After all, that's what they're there for, and if somebody has a problem with it, he or she can just look away. Some mothers even become so comfortable that they perfect the skill of walking around with their nursing infant carried in their arms or in a baby sling or carrier.

If you are *not* one of those women who are able to put some modesty aside, don't beat yourself up about it. Everyone has a different sense of privacy, and everyone has different needs for intimacy with their baby. In fact, every baby is different. There are plenty of superactive nursers who can't keep their hands from lifting Mommy's shirt even higher or who are so distracted they pull off the breast every few seconds, repeatedly exposing Mommy's nipple. Such a baby has ruined many well-laid plans for discretion. If you find yourself needing more privacy, go ahead and indulge. You don't have to hide away in some smelly bathroom or sit with your baby in the car in a sweltering parking lot. It may take some thinking ahead and coordination, but try to enjoy your privacy and this special time you have with your baby. The more relaxed you are, the better your milk will flow. You can also give your baby a bottle-feeding of breastmilk or formula while you are out. For tips on keeping milk fresh and warming it before your baby drinks it, see the later section about bottle-feeding on outings.

Places to Nurse Your Baby Away From Home

- The ladies lounge at a nice downtown department store. Posh couches, deluxe changing tables, soothing music.
- The back corner of a quiet café or restaurant during the lull between service. Treat yourself to a snack and a cup of tea.
- Your car, parked in a shady spot, overlooking nice scenery.
- An unused den or the master bedroom at a friend's house. Find a comfy chair; go ahead and lock the door if you want.
- A quiet park bench in a shady spot. Your baby will love watching the sunlight dancing in the leaves, and you can relax and let the milk flow while you listen to the birds.

Feeding Your Baby in the Real World

"A couple of weeks ago I had a dental appointment and found myself stuck without childcare last minute. I had (my older daughter) Hannah come along to watch Sophie for me in the waiting room. During the appointment Sophie got quite cranky and Hannah ran out of steam, so I ended up nursing her in the dentist's chair while having my teeth worked on. The hygienist was a little flustered—clearly didn't have children, but at least I gave them something to talk about on their coffee break!"

—Jane, mother of Sophie and Hannah

The Bottle-fed Baby, Out and About

Once your baby is a little older, bottle-feeding him on outings will become easier because he'll probably be less likely to care if the formula is warm or not. In the meantime, there are any number of ways you can keep formula fresh but still have it warm for him to drink. If you prepare the formula ahead of time, you must keep it cool by using an insulated bag or ice packs. Be sure to adjust your method depending on how long it will be before your baby drinks the formula and the weather on a given day. If you are running a quick errand, an insulated bag will probably be sufficient unless it is the height of summer. If you plan to take formula for the whole day, be sure to use ice packs, regardless of the weather.

When it is time to warm the bottle, there are several gadgets you can buy for this purpose. These range from a preheated pack you wrap around the bottle to an electric device you can plug directly into your car's cigarette lighter. Our favorite method was to bring a thermos filled with hot water and a bowl, and warm the bottle in a hot bath (you can also use very hot tap water or water from a coffee or tea urn for this purpose). Some parents also have great success with keeping sterilized water warmed to the correct temperature in a thermos and adding it to a bottle with a premeasured scoop of formula in it. Many parents solve the problem of keeping formula fresh by preparing it only when the baby needs it. Bring a bottle of presterilized water with you and measure formula in when you need it. There are even handy formula storage containers you can buy for this purpose that will dispense a correct measure of formula directly into the bottle. This gadget is small enough to fit in a diaper bag. If you need to warm the prepared formula, you can use one of the methods just described, or, since the bottle will be closer to room temperature, your baby may not mind if it isn't warm.

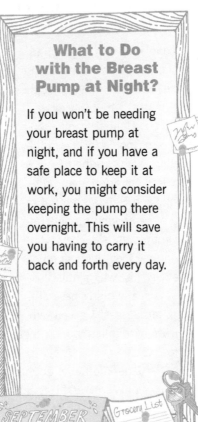

What to Do with the Breast Pump at Night?

If you won't be needing your breast pump at night, and if you have a safe place to keep it at work, you might consider keeping the pump there overnight. This will save you having to carry it back and forth every day.

The Nursing Baby in Child Care

When a nursing mother decides to go back to work, continuing with breastfeeding becomes more challenging, but many mothers accomplish it with patience and support. There are a number of factors that will impact how easily this transition occurs. You will need to decide whether or not and how frequently to pump your breasts, for example. You will also need to help your baby become accustomed to receiving feedings and other care from someone else. In order to anticipate your needs, ask yourself the following questions:

- How many days will you be working each week? If you are working only a few days at the beginning or for the longer term, it may be easier to make the adjustment to working. If, on the other hand, you go back full-time right away, the transition will be tough, but probably shorter.
- How many hours will you work each day? A brief separation of a few hours between feedings each day may mean that you can avoid pumping and bottle-feedings altogether. However, if you will be gone half or full days, pumping will become a fact of life if you wish to continue with exclusive breastfeeding.
- How old is your baby? If your baby is very young (six weeks to three or four months), he will probably make the adjustment to receiving feedings from a caregiver fairly easily if he has already been introduced to the bottle and has been taking regular bottle-feedings. If your baby is older, or is not accustomed to a bottle, things may get a bit more complicated. An older baby may be beginning to eat some solid food and drink from a cup, which will help the caregiver meet his needs. A young baby who has trouble accepting or who will not accept a bottle, on the

other hand, presents a very complicated challenge for parents and caregivers.

- How far away is work from home? If work is very close, you may be able to nurse your baby during breaks and lunch. You can either go home, or the caregiver can bring your baby to your work. A combination of the two may work also. However, if you will need to commute to work, don't forget to include this time as part of your total time away from the baby. Try to time pumpings and the feedings your baby gets from her caregiver so that both you and your baby are ready to nurse as soon as you are together again. Try to nurse just before you leave for work in the morning also.

- Where will you use a breast pump at work? If you have a private office or room that is yours or that can be made easily available to you at work, fantastic! Even better is a workplace where there are several women who are nursing or who have nursed. If this is the case, count yourself lucky. Where to pump may seem like a minor detail, but the lack of a private, comfortable place to use a breast pump has made continuing breastfeeding much less convenient or simply impossible for many women. This is a shame, because while many employers try to be sensitive to the needs of nursing mothers, they fail to understand all of the practical issues involved. Don't be shy about talking to your employer about your need for a private place to use a breast pump. Explain how frequently you will need to pump and how long you expect it to take each time. Don't accept a glib answer like, "You can use my office," however well meant it may be. Think critically about whether or not this will really work. Will your boss really be happy to vacate her office every few hours each day? By working out these problems ahead of time, you can avoid a lot of unpleasantness later. Above all, be creative about solving the problem, and don't give up until you feel as comfortable as possible with the arrangement. As more and more nursing mothers return to the workplace, these issues will become easier to solve.

Staying in Touch, Even While You're Away

Ask your baby's caregiver how your child liked his lunch and snacks every day. She will usually be happy to give feedback about what works and what doesn't. She may also share ideas from her own experience.

Feeding Your Older Baby in Child Care

Once your baby is well accustomed to solid food, you will be faced with a whole new array of choices when someone else is caring for her. Your arrangements for child care will be as individual as your own circumstances, and the way you feed your baby in these situations will vary as well. A lot will depend on the amount of control over your baby's diet you are willing to assert (or give up). Whatever you decide, remember that a variety of options is available to suit your needs. You may need to be assertive, though, if you want to ensure that specific standards are met. Lunch and snack routines are as likely to grow from your preferences as they are from the situation at hand.

Baby Food and the Baby-Sitter or Nanny

In some ways, maintaining your own standards for the food your baby eats is easiest if you have a regular baby-sitter or nanny who takes care of your baby in your own home. After all, you're probably the one who did the grocery shopping. Still, it can't hurt to be specific about your ideas of what is good for your baby. Write down your expectations and provide lists of acceptable foods for your baby. If you don't want your baby having sugar, for example, don't assume the caregiver will know this or that she will understand that not having sugar may also include hidden sugar in, say, ketchup or salad dressing. Most experienced caregivers will be accustomed to following specific instructions from parents, and younger baby-sitters will be grateful for any kind of guidance. Each of us comes to the task of caring for a baby with different standards and experiences. A nanny who is from a different culture may have very different ideas about feeding babies than you do. Take the time to find out what her ideas are, and you may find a few new menu items. Post a list of healthy foods your baby enjoys on the refrigerator, and update it as time goes by. Encourage the caregiver to add to the list as new discoveries are made. Some parents skip this process entirely by leaving prepared

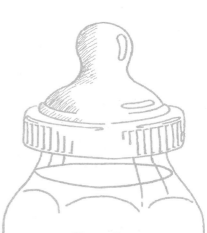

Keeping Breastmilk Safe

Follow the instructions in Chapter 2 for safely handling breastmilk. Make sure your baby's caregiver also understands how to handle breastmilk properly and that the milk should be used in the order of the earliest date first and the newest date last. If your baby is in day care, you should write his name on each bottle of milk.

snacks and meals for the baby each day, which is also fine, if a lot of work. By working together with your caregiver, however, you can both have a positive impact on your baby's nutrition. Also, if you are lucky enough to have a caregiver who will also do some of your shopping, you may want to provide her with a list that is fairly specific, including brand names when appropriate and other specifications such as "whole" milk or "whole wheat" bread.

Share Care

Share care is becoming an increasingly popular option, especially in cities where child care is more expensive and there are more families with young children living close together. In this case, two families will share a caregiver who takes care of two or three (sometimes four) children at once in one of the families' homes. Sometimes the families will switch between houses and sometimes share care happens at only one family's house or even at the caregiver's house. When you are considering entering into a share care arrangement with another family, it really pays to discuss your food philosophies. After all, if the other family thinks nothing of giving their baby fast food every day and you have decided to feed your baby only food made from organic ingredients, you are not likely to be compatible. Once this compatibility is established, work together on a list of foods that both babies can eat, so that the caregiver isn't stuck making different meals for each baby every day. Some families work out a weekly menu ahead of time and post it on the refrigerator, making sure all of the ingredients are available. Don't expect the caregiver to make anything complicated, though; he'll have his hands full just caring for the kids. If share care happens in only one family's home, you'll need to work out how to pay for the food the other family's baby will eat. Some people decide to bring the baby's lunch and snacks with them each day, or they may just drop off some extra groceries each week. A financial reimbursement may also be worked out.

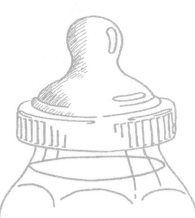

Traveling Abroad

In most cases, traveling abroad shouldn't present too many more challenges to maintaining a good diet than traveling domestically. However, if you are not familiar with the language of the country you are visiting, some extra homework will be helpful. Many guidebooks provide sections on vocabulary specifically relating to food, giving examples of menu listings and their meanings. Study these before you leave and give some thought to which foods will be the most appropriate for your child. In areas without modern water-treatment facilities, it is wise to drink only bottled or boiled water to avoid being infected with harmful waterborne bacteria.

Day Care

Most in-home and regular day care centers expect parents to pack a lunch, which can be a challenge with limited or no refrigeration capabilities. Some day care centers will prepare meals for all of the children to eat together, and many will prepare snacks. In this case, be sure that the day care staff is aware of any allergies your child may have. If an allergenic food causes an extreme or life-threatening reaction, you should remind the staff frequently about your child's allergy and stress how critical the situation is. A few day care centers have the added benefit of providing special meals for the children, perhaps made with organic ingredients or even to fit a vegetarian lifestyle. This can be extremely convenient for the parents, but the convenience comes at a price . . . and usually an expensive one. Weigh your choices based upon your and your baby's needs. If you feel your child will be eating food you approve of at a day care center that provides meals, and that the convenience is worth the expense, then the choice is obvious.

Shared Snacks in Day Care

Some day care centers ask parents to provide a snack for all the children each day on a rotating basis. The day care center then provides lunch. This is a nice compromise for many parents who dread packing a lunch every day but will happily provide a snack for the group once a week. Also, the children will get more of a variety than if the same person prepared their snack every day.

Food Allergies in Day Care

One day care center I spoke with asks parents to provide a long list of snacks (everything they can possibly think of) that their babies can and will eat, including brand names for packaged foods. The staff then compiles a final approved list of snacks for the children, consisting only of foods that all of the children can eat. Parents are given this list to use when shopping for shared snacks for the children.

Do Babies Eat Better in Child Care?

Of course, there's no straight answer to this question because situations vary so widely, but some parents swear that their toddlers eat more heartily at day care than they do at home. Maybe this is because there is less pressure to eat well when the caregiver isn't watching as closely as Mom and Dad do. Or, maybe babies respond to the fun social aspects of eating in a group.

Packing a Daily Lunch for Your Baby

Many times, by choice or necessity, parents engage in a daily struggle to come up with creative ideas for lunch for their baby or toddler. This can be extra challenging when no refrigeration is available, and many parents fall into a rut of preparing similar meals every day.

Tips for Packing Healthy Lunches Without Refrigeration

- Pack a reusable ice pack to keep fresh dairy products, meat, and fish cold. Tape a note that says, "Please Save!" on the ice pack so that you can use it again.
- Use an insulated bag to keep food cool.
- Pack food that is frozen but that will defrost by lunchtime.
- Pack warm (not too hot!) soup, stew, or macaroni and cheese in a short wide-mouthed thermos.

Great Packable Lunches and Snacks for Your Baby

Baby Foods

The young baby who is still eating mostly pureed foods is the easiest one to pack a lunch for. In my case, it meant throwing in a few jars of baby food (and some cereal when he was ready for that) along with a few bottles of breastmilk. When I was feeling really ambitious, I would include some homemade food I had stored in small containers in the fridge. Parents who make their own food and store it in ice cube trays in the refrigerator will often pop out a few varieties of frozen food into a plastic container. The frozen cubes can slowly defrost in an insulated bag (although refrigeration is probably safer) to be ready in time for lunch.

Finger Foods

Although the pureed baby food phase was easy, most parents are happy to begin adding some finger foods to their baby's lunches around the first birthday. Some good ideas are:

- Whole wheat pasta tossed with mixed pureed vegetables (anything made with sweet potatoes or a similar starch sticks on really well).
- Crazy sandwiches (little babies don't know they're different and nutritious). My baby's favorite was almond butter with milled cooked broccoli or carrots on whole wheat bread. Nut butter makes the sandwich stick together well; slice the bread very thinly (you can cut a regular slice in half if you have a very sharp bread knife and if you're careful).
- Rice crackers with hummus for dipping.
- Sliced bananas, ripe peaches, or other soft fruits.
- Hard-boiled egg (after one year).

Spoonable Lunches

Your baby will be anxious to practice her newfound spoon skills not only at home. Make sure to adjust what you send for her lunch as well. Try to make sure the foods are thick enough to stick well to the spoon, but not so thick as to hinder her ability to get them on the spoon.

- Macaroni and cheese (get used to this one!)
- Brown rice mixed with pureed vegetables or tomato sauce
- Mashed avocado mixed with yogurt
- Taboule (buckwheat salad with parsley, lemon, and olive oil)
- Couscous mixed with refried beans and cottage cheese
- Applesauce

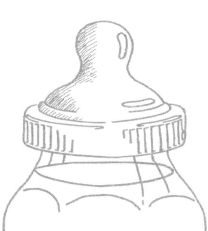

Keeping the Ideas Fresh

Keep a running list of your child's favorite lunches and snacks so that you can shop and plan accordingly. That way you won't stand around groggily in the morning trying to think of something to pack. Some parents even plan a menu before the week begins, so that they don't have to throw something together at the last minute.

Toddler Foods

As the two-year mark approaches, you'll find that both your baby's ability to eat different foods and his likes and dislikes have changed dramatically. Although he may be able to eat more foods, his repertoire may seem to have shrunk considerably as the food-phobic toddler years have begun. For the first time, he is also influenced by what other babies around him are eating. Don't be surprised if he suddenly likes foods he's been exposed to at day care.

- Thinly sliced vegetables (carrots, celery, peppers) and yogurt with chopped fresh dill for dipping
- Macaroni and cheese
- Thin sandwiches: peanut butter and jelly, egg salad made with yogurt, turkey
- Raisins and other dried fruits
- Sliced apples and almond butter to dip
- Rice and beans

Snacks and the Family on the Go

Snacks are important, indeed critical, for the family that can't stay still. Busy parents need to (and often love to) bring their babies with them on trips to the grocery store, to pick up older children at school, and to meet a friend for coffee. Babies have very small stomachs, so smaller, more frequent meals are generally best. The actual amount eaten at each meal can vary tremendously from day to day and week to week. This is why any seasoned parent will tell you that it's important to be prepared to feed your baby while you are out and about. Indeed, an on-the-go snack can help the entire day go more smoothly. Fitting your life in around naps and early bedtimes is hard enough without having to stay home for every meal.

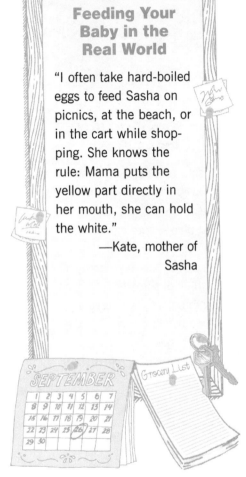

Feeding Your Baby in the Real World

"I often take hard-boiled eggs to feed Sasha on picnics, at the beach, or in the cart while shopping. She knows the rule: Mama puts the yellow part directly in her mouth, she can hold the white."

—Kate, mother of Sasha

Traveling with Baby

Planes, Trains and Automobiles: How to Eat Well on the Road

Family vacations are one of life's greatest pleasures, until your baby vomits the back seat of the car one hour into a four-hour trip en route to a week-long summer (hot) trip?! Yuck! Or, how about in your lap just after takeoff during a five-hour flight? This is the unpleasant reality of parenthood. When this happened to me on a recent trip, I found I could only laugh with chagrin while my husband helped to mop up the mess. The man across the aisle from me shook his head and said, "I've been there." Thinking back, I'm pretty sure we had been feeding our baby Max too many snacks as a way to keep him pacified during a long period (in toddler terms) while we waited for the plane to take off. So, there's one thing to avoid when traveling.

Many people see vacations as a time to relax eating standards that they would normally follow at home. This is only natural, as many of the circumstances you encounter while traveling or visiting with relatives fall outside of your child's normal experience. Try to remember that this can be a good thing. Special local dishes can be just as enriching for your child's vacation as they are for yours, and they will broaden his horizons. For some children, however, a sudden dramatic change in routine can be disorienting, a time of increased suspicion. In this case, foods they would normally gobble up with glee are suddenly refused, which can make providing a balanced diet challenging, to say the least. Added to this is the limited number of options associated with airline food and roadside diners.

Tips for Happy and Healthful Eating on the Road

*   Bring lots of snacks and plenty of water, juice, and/or milk. Three or four jars of baby food are good for younger babies. Crackers, hard-boiled eggs, dried fruit, yogurt, and bananas are good for toddlers.

Great Baby Snacks to Take Along

Think about potential mess when deciding which snacks to bring along. Since these snacks will often be consumed while riding in the car seat or stroller, make sure your baby is old enough to eat the snack safely without direct assistance from you. As always, keep a close eye on your child in case of choking. Your baby may enjoy having her own little plastic zipper bag of treats. She will be less likely to spill this than an open container.

*   Rice cakes and puffed corn
*   Healthy dry cereal with raisins
*   Whole-wheat fig bars and fruit-juice-sweetened animal crackers
*   Dried fruit
*   Sliced apples

- When traveling by plane, order a special vegetarian or children's meal. These are usually brought early in the serving, which can be a lifesaver. If there is a choice of entrees, order one of each for you and your partner so that there will be more possible options for the baby.
- When traveling by train, don't expect to find too much more than hotdogs (if that) in the dining car. Pack a picnic lunch.

Feeding Your Baby at Someone Else's Home

When staying with relatives or friends, it really helps to plan ahead for feeding your baby. I usually find it very helpful to ask my host to pick up a few things for me at the grocery store before I arrive. You may worry about being a burden when you do this, but consider that your host may have already thought to buy a few things for the baby and might be grateful for a little guidance. A complete list of everything you may want during your stay isn't necessary, just enough to get you through a few meals before you can do some shopping.

Of course, you wouldn't want to appear rude by asking someone to change their habits to accommodate your family. Be sensitive to others and try to think of ways to keep your child well fed without offending your hosts. Claiming that you don't want your baby to "spoil her supper" is a classic excuse to keep indulgent grandparents from offering yet another piece of chocolate. Conversely, quietly preparing a simple, quick meal for your child before sitting down to a Midwestern meat-and-potatoes spread might be a good idea.

Staying at a Hotel or Bed and Breakfast

When staying in hotels, finding good food for your baby can be much more challenging, since you will usually be obliged to eat out at every meal. If you are staying in a city, take the opportunity early in the visit to find a market or corner store where you can buy a few staples such as milk, yogurt, fruit, bread, and cereal. Store the perishables in the hotel room minibar if there is one. Ask the concierge for his or her best recommendation for local restaurants that welcome babies.

A Word about Well Water

If you are staying with someone whose house is supplied with well water, you should use store-bought distilled water to make your baby's formula or as drinking water. Sometimes well water has nitrate levels that are unsafe for babies, and boiling only concentrates nitrate levels.

• • •

A Quick Shopping List for Hosts

- Plain whole milk yogurt
- Eggs
- Fruit juice
- Bananas
- Rice
- Whole milk (for older babies)
- Whole wheat bread

Small inns and bed and breakfast accommodations are sometimes (but not always) the most welcoming for families with small children. Often the operators have raised children of their own and they may be willing to provide you with small, but valuable, amenities like the privilege of keeping a small amount of personal food in the kitchen refrigerator or providing unseasoned portions of some of the breakfast entrees for your baby.

Resorts and Cruises

Couples who would have never considered a resort or cruise as an option for a vacation, sometimes reconsider after they have children. One factor is that all of the meals are included in the package, which is one less thing to worry about if you want to focus on relaxing as a family. However, you should be aware that while the food is a big draw for most people who choose a cruise or resort, it is almost always geared toward adult tastes and is rarely designed for health. Luxury is often the order of the day, with fatty, salty hors d'oeuvres and heavily seasoned, complicated dishes. On the other hand, when resorts and cruises want to attract families, they will frequently offer junk foods like unhealthy pizzas and french fries. Fortunately there is almost always a salad bar option, and there is usually such a huge selection of different dishes that you will be sure to find something that you consider healthy and that your baby will like.

Providing Safe Seating for Your Baby While You Are on the Road

Most restaurants provide high chairs or booster seats to families upon request, and there's no harm in asking for one, even if you're not sure your baby will sit in it. If you question the safety of a high chair that is provided, don't use it. You may even want to mention the fact that you feel doubtful of the chair to the host/hostess, and why. Most babies will be just as happy sitting on Mommy or Daddy's lap. For smaller babies you can also bring an infant car seat into the restaurant with you. Toddlers may be willing to sit on their knees for about the same brief period of time that they would have been able to sit still anyway.

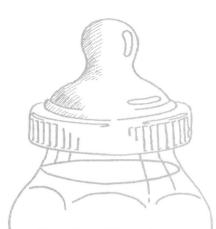

Feeding Your Baby in the Real World

"I take store-bought prepared food that doesn't need to be heated, such as Earth's Best peach/apricot muesli and their yogurt breakfast (because it doesn't have to be refrigerated). Now that Christopher is older and has teeth, I also take a jar of chicken or turkey sticks, string cheese, Cheerios, graham crackers, Goldfish crackers, and always a sippy cup of water. It's easy to buy yogurt while traveling and use that as a food staple. Fresh fruit too."

—Christina, mother of Sophia and Christopher

Food and Safety for Traveling

These are some choking and poisoning hazards that you should look out for while traveling or visiting other people's homes.

- Airline peanuts or snack mixes
- Hard candy, enticingly displayed in a dish on a low side table
- Medicines in a nonchildproof container in a purse or jacket pocket
- Cleaning chemicals stored in an area where your child can reach them, such as beneath a kitchen or bathroom sink or in the laundry area or garage

If you are traveling by car, you may want to bring along your own booster seat. There are two kinds of portable booster seats—those that are secured to a regular chair and those that hook directly onto the table. These seats can easily be brought to friends' houses and even restaurants. However, neither type will work in every situation. Some hook-on booster seats cannot be secured safely if the table has a skirt beneath the table top, and chair booster seats cannot be secured properly to stools or chairs that do not have a level seat. In this case, it is tempting to use the old telephone book trick you may remember from your childhood, but this is not really wise. Besides the obvious fact that phone books do not come with safety straps, they do not really provide that much height and so must be stacked in a very precarious manner to bring a child to the right height. At the home of friends or family, your toddler will be delighted with a child's table improvised from a coffee table and cushions or pillows placed on the floor.

A Special Note about Allergies and Traveling

If your child suffers from severe allergies, you should take sensible precautions when traveling. For example, if your child has a severe reaction to peanuts, be vigilant about avoiding airline peanuts. In rare cases, simply touching a peanut can cause a reaction in an allergic child. Parents of such children are wise to be prepared with written instructions from their child's doctor about what to do in case of an attack, and with a small kit containing an inhaler or prescription medicine. Take two of everything, one for carry-on bags and one for checked luggage. Your child's doctor may prescribe an injector for administering epinephrine in case of an emergency. If possible, get a referral for a physician in the area you are visiting before you leave. If you are traveling abroad, learn all of the foreign words for an allergenic food and ask restaurant servers if dishes contain them before ordering.

Parents of a child who seems to have no allergies should also be prepared in case she encounters an allergen for the first time far from medical help. Learn how to tell the difference between symptoms of an allergic reaction and a regular illness. Inquire about the proper dose of liquid antihistamine for your child's weight, and pack a bottle just in case.

CHAPTER FOURTEEN

Dining Out As a Family

DIAPE
BABY II
PAPER I
FORMUL

Dining Out with a Very Young Baby

Although not foolproof, eating out with a baby younger than three or four months of age can sometimes be the easiest. Coordinate your outing for a time when you're fairly sure your baby will be sleepy (preferably right after a feeding). If you drive to the restaurant, the baby will probably go to sleep on the way, and unless she is one of those babies that wakes up at any change in her sleep environment, she will most likely remain sleeping while you carry her car seat into the restaurant. Choose a table that is out of the way of traffic to and from the kitchen, and order quickly.

Choosing the Right Restaurant

It doesn't take a genius to realize that your local establishment of haute cuisine might not be a great place to take your 16-month-old, but what kind of restaurant *is* the right place? Bringing a baby to a restaurant was uncommon 5 or 10 years ago, but today's families are more accustomed to eating out, and interesting trends are emerging as a result. What follows is a brief summary of the pluses and minuses of several different dining options, and some of the issues you may want to think about when dining out. In our family, we always preferred eating at small, neighborhood family-owned restaurants, whatever their stripe, because we usually felt most welcome there.

Family Style

Bit "family-style" chain restaurants may seem to be the most obvious choice, but surprisingly, fewer and fewer young families are choosing to eat at them. One reason is that the menu usually emphasizes meat and potatoes, rather than fresh vegetables, rice, pasta, and other foods suitable for babies. Also, traditional American food may not be as appealing to young parents who are used to more interesting fare. When dining at a family-style restaurant, be sure to take advantage of the salad bar if there's one available. There are usually some finger foods for toddlers like cherry tomatoes (cut in half to avoid choking) and celery or carrot sticks.

Also, salad dressing makes a great dippy sauce. Avoid low-fat salad dressings, which are usually loaded with fillers, sugar, and sodium. If you've never examined the "heart healthy" portion of the menu, now is the time. Your baby will be likely to prefer the plainer fare, and you can usually order steamed vegetables, grilled fish or chicken, and other foods suitable for babies. It's also a good idea to ask for any dressing, butter, and other condiments on the side, so that you can control the amount used.

Family-Style Weekend Morning Treats

Family-style restaurants can be great fun for an occasional weekend breakfast. Morning is undoubtedly the best time of day for most babies. For parents, a weekend morning to relax and catch up on the funny papers, while your baby soaks in the bustling environment, and flirts with a friendly waitress, can be a welcome relief after a hectic week. Also, babies love many breakfast foods such as scrambled eggs, fresh fruit, waffles, and pancakes. Forego or go easy on the syrup, which is mostly high fructose corn syrup at these places. Bacon and sausage are *not* good food for babies, because they have too much sodium and nitrates. It's true that family-style restaurants (especially the chains) are not known for the high quality of their ingredients. They generally don't use whole grains, much of the food is fried in hydrogenated oils, and fruits and vegetables are likely to come from a can. However, if you choose wisely, you can eat at the family-style chain restaurants of the world occasionally without compromising your baby's healthy eating habits.

Good Family-Style Menu Choices for Babies and Toddlers

- Salad bar fresh vegetables like pepper strips, celery, carrots, and so on, with a French dressing dippy sauce
- Scrambled eggs, which can often be ordered at any time of day (Ask your server that they be prepared with as little oil as possible.)
- Mashed chickpeas or red beans from the salad bar mixed with cottage cheese

Thai Treats

- Tasty drinks with papaya or mango nectar and coconut milk
- Fresh veggies and potatoes in a (very) mild curry and coconut milk sauce, served with steamed rice
- Broccoli and tofu in mild black bean sauce, served with steamed rice
- Grilled fish of the day, served with steamed vegetables and rice

• • •

Chinese Stars

- Steamed vegetarian potstickers
- Moo shu pancakes filled with steamed veggies
- Chicken and broccoli, served with steamed rice
- Chow mein with vegetables
- Don't forget the fortune cookies!

- Whole wheat toast with butter and jam on the side
- Steamed vegetables
- Fruit cup
- Pancakes or waffles with cut-up banana

Ethnic Food

Ethnic cuisine of all types is a great choice for families. Chinese, Thai, Japanese, Mexican, Middle Eastern, and Indian restaurants all use rice in copious amounts, which most babies love. Asian food is also frequently prepared to order using mostly fresh vegetables, so it is usually easy to request steamed vegetables with little or no seasoning. Fresh fish is also an important part of most Asian cuisine. Many Asian restaurants proudly proclaim that they do not use the highly allergenic MSG, a flavor enhancer that should be avoided. Babies love fresh Indian naan bread, Middle Eastern pita bread, and Mexican tortillas. Be careful of spicy food and dishes that feature complicated sauces. Ask your server if a dish is hot and spicy, and explain that the food is for the baby. He will most likely understand and be able to guide you expertly. He may even have raised babies on this food himself.

One of the greatest things about ethnic food for parents is that it's almost always ready to take out. Often Mom (who's starving) simply can't cook after a draining day with a little one, and Dad can pick up Chinese on the way home from work. Other times, a planned evening out dissolves into disaster after your toddler realizes he won't be allowed to play with the little mermaid in the restaurant fish tank. Why not change your order to go instead? You'll probably all be happier.

Let's Do Italian!

Italian restaurants are wonderful for babies who love noodles in any form. Filled fresh pasta such as ravioli can be especially nutritious when stuffed with cheese and vegetables like spinach or squash. Italian cooking also uses plenty of olive oil, which is one of the healthiest oils. If your child is allergic to nuts, be very careful to ask your server if any are used in the dish you are ordering. Pinenuts and walnuts are commonly used in many Italian sauces, especially pesto, and are often ground up so that you wouldn't notice them in the dish.

Three Good Reasons to Avoid the Take-Out Pizza Rut

Unfortunately, many American families fall into a rut of ordering delivered pizza once, twice, or more times a week as a way of getting dinner on the table after a hard day at work. Endless commercials for big chain pizza restaurants (not coincidentally scheduled during children's programming) encourage kids to repeat the pizza habit. Don't be fooled. Take-out pizza is fine occasionally, but it is definitely not a healthy option for regular family dining.

1. Poor-quality ingredients. Most pizza joints use tomato sauce with too much salt and sugar added, way too much cheap processed mozzarella cheese, nitrate- and sodium-laden pepperoni, and canned vegetables.
2. They'll get plenty of take-out pizza later at school, birthday parties, and at other kids homes, without having it once or twice a week at home.
3. You can make much healthier pizzas at home *very* easily, and have tons of fun doing it.

Fast Food

Fast food should be a last resort for family dining. True, school-age children in America seem to exist on fast food, but consider the impact of condoning these eating habits on your child's future health. Fast food menu items most popular with kids are loaded with hydrogenated oils, saturated fats, and sodium. This is bad enough for adults, but for babies, especially, every bite counts, and these bites provide nothing for a child to grow on. If you do find yourself stuck with fast food, try to choose wisely. Use the salad bar, and order fish or chicken or even a plain burger. Choose grilled or baked items over fried. Opt for any fresh

Spanish Sensations

- Tortilla (omelet with potatoes and cheese)
- Fresh crusty bread rubbed with fresh tomato and drizzled with olive oil
- Vegetarian paella (a rice dish served with sweet saffron and vegetables)
- Sheep cheese with membrillo (sweet quince paste)

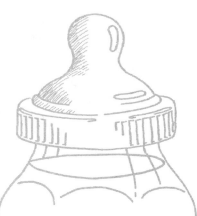

vegetables or fruit that are available. Recently, several fast food chains that offer all-you-can-eat cafeteria-style dining and enormous salad bars have become popular. This is great news because there are quite a few healthful choices at these restaurants, but it is wise to keep a close eye on trips to the dessert bar where an independent toddler is concerned.

Special Orders

Patience is not the strong suit for most babies. The first thing you should do when you are seated is to get something for your baby to eat or play with as soon as possible. Many restaurants bring bread, which is perfect. If not, a handy snack that you have brought along can be useful. You may want to peruse the menu while you wait for a table, and order a quick appetizer from the hostess as you are being seated. Also, more and more restaurants will provide crayons and paper to color with, which is fantastic when you are trying to entertain a restless toddler. You can also request a package of Saltines or soup crackers.

For a baby that still eats mostly strained and pureed foods, a jar of baby food or a small plastic container of homemade baby food brought along may be all that's necessary. Feeding an older baby or toddler can be a bit trickier. Not only are his eating habits more fussy, but more heavily seasoned adult foods may simply be unsuitable. Think about an entrée you can order for yourself that includes something your baby will like. For example, most babies love mashed potatoes, cottage cheese, small bites of grilled fish, or raviolis. Think of what you can order that could be fork-mashed or that would make suitable finger food. It is rarely necessary to order a separate entrée for your baby or young child. He couldn't possibly eat that much, and unless both Mom and Dad are very big eaters, there's usually plenty to share, especially if you order a few appetizers and/or side dishes. Ask the waitress for an empty dish, or bring your own unbreakable baby dish to use for the baby.

Encourage Your Baby to Try New Foods

Sometimes, a new environment is just the place to try a new menu choice. After all, according to toddler logic, food offered by parents is not nearly as delicious and enticing as food on someone else's plate. When dining out with friends, this curiosity may peak, and your child may show an interest in a food your friend is eating that you never thought your baby would try. Unless the food is simply unsuitable and if your friend is amenable, let your baby try it. Never say, "You won't like that!" because you may be very surprised.

Keeping the Peace

Dining out with children and especially babies was once an uncommon occurrence, and parents were viewed with suspicion. Fortunately, this situation has changed dramatically, and young families are welcomed by many restaurant owners and fellow diners alike. It is important to remember, however, that we are still on probation, and a certain finesse is required to carry off dining out successfully with a baby. Plenty of parents have spoiled the experience for everyone else by ignoring obvious signals that the meal is not going as planned. Flexibility is a key trait in all successful parents. Know your baby, know her tendencies, and know when to cut your losses. There may be brief (or long) periods during your baby's development when dining out with her is simply not a practical option. Maybe your young baby has a 6:00 P.M. bedtime or your toddler is going through an especially difficult phase. At these times, it would seem wise to get a baby-sitter and go out on your own (which is what you probably deserve anyway) or to get take-out.

Baby Etiquette: The Do's and Don'ts of Dining Out with Baby

*   **Do:** bring an extra favorite snack, just in case the menu just doesn't appeal.
*   **Do:** bring toys, books, and games to keep your child entertained during the meal.
*   **Do:** include the baby in the fun of eating out. Let her make friends with your server. Let her dip bread in olive oil, "like the grownups."
*   **Do:** go early. Most babies are fussy in the evening. Have an early dinner, or better yet, go for lunch or breakfast.
*   **Don't:** expect the server to clean up soggy crumbs and sloppy messes, especially if they are made with food you brought along. Use wipes or paper towels from your diaper bag to clean up at least the messiest bits.

Indian Luxuries

*   Fresh naan or chapati breads
*   Very mild curries with potatoes, vegetables, and steamed rice
*   Mango nectar
*   Raita yogurt dipping sauce with chopped cucumber

• • •

Japanese Treats

*   Soup with chicken broth, fresh veggies, and thick flour Udon noodles
*   Vegetable tempurah served with a dipping sauce
*   Steamed tofu with fresh veggies, served with steamed rice
*   Caution: No raw fish for babies!

- **Don't:** let your baby kick against a two-sided booth. The person sitting on the other side will not appreciate it. Use your best judgment about your baby making friends with that person. You can usually tell whether or not he or she minds the interruptions and know when to cut it short.
- **Don't:** subject other diners to the whining or wails of your overtired toddler. Maybe it's time to go home.
- **Don't**: sit in or near the smoking section. Second-hand smoke is especially dangerous to babies.

Avoiding Food-Borne Illness

Unfortunately, food-borne illness (or food poisoning) has become an ever-increasing concern for the American public, largely because of several tragic cases of serious illness and death from food-borne illness that have occurred over the past few years. Often, the most vulnerable victims are children, who do not have enough immunity defenses to ward off harmful pathogens. It is important to stress that cases of serious food-borne illness are quite rare. Still, there is never a guarantee that you or your baby will not contract a food-borne illness even with the maximum amount of vigilance (and even in your own home). However, these are some signs that I look for that help me feel reassured that the restaurant we are dining in is fairly safe. These tips may not be very scientific, but after over a decade in the food business, I have gained a sense for food safety that is above the norm.

- I always instinctively feel better dining in a family-owned and -run business. People whose livelihood depends on the success of their business are naturally more motivated to ensure that the food they serve is safe. One case of food poisoning or one temporary closure by the health department is enough to destroy a small business. Also, I figure a small-business owner is more likely to care about her customers' health than the employees of a large company or corporation are.

- When I see a food service employee wash their hands or use a clean damp towel to wipe off a table or counter, I feel incredibly reassured. Nothing turns me off faster than having my table wiped down with a nasty, sour-smelling towel I just know hasn't been rinsed out throughout the service. Other turnoffs are gum-chewing, nose blowing, coughing on bare hands, and employees who habitually touch their faces or run their fingers through their hair.

- Although some local health officials are beginning to require food service workers to wear plastic, rubber, or latex gloves when handling food, I personally don't find gloved hands a particularly reassuring sign. This is because I believe that properly washed hands are a much more effective tool for preventing cross-contamination of bacteria from humans to food, from raw to cooked food, or from one food to another than gloves are. The reasons are just practical. It's simply much easier and cost-effective to wash one's hands with hot soapy water than it is to get a new pair of gloves every time you handle raw food, poultry, or fish. I can't tell you how many times I've seen a prep cook or deli worker who is wearing gloves handle poultry immediately after touching fish or observed some other cross-contamination nightmare. How long are these gloves worn without being changed? I suspect the answer in some cases is all day.

- This may sound silly, but I always make a judgment based on how a place smells. If it smells like fresh cooking food like toasted bread, sautéed onions, and brewing coffee, I always feel better than if it smells like sour milk, rancid oil, or strong cleaning chemicals.

- This is another somewhat strange observation, but if the restroom is nice and clean, I always feel very good about eating in a restaurant. The restroom doesn't need to be fancy, just clean. I've used some frankly rustic facilities that were as neat and clean as a pin in many of my travels, and I've seen restrooms in very fancy restaurants that were absolutely trashed. My theory (never proven) is that restaurant management will probably pay equal attention to the cleanliness of their restroom as they do to the cleanliness of their kitchen.

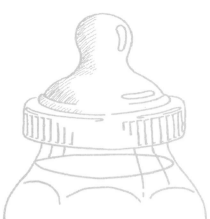

How about Brunch?

Trying to fit dining out with visiting friends or relatives around a baby's nap and sleep schedule can be awkward. You don't want to cramp someone else's style by declining an invitation to a nice restaurant, but you don't relish the idea of trying to soothe a fussy, overtired baby while everyone else is lingering over after-dinner coffee, either. A weekend brunch can be the perfect solution. Many good hotels and restaurants feature over-the-top brunch buffets, and the timing for brunch is perfect for many babies, as it is less likely to interfere with either the morning or afternoon nap.

CHAPTER FIFTEEN

The Equipment Parade

G et ready for baby! It seems that everything about your new baby has some kind of equipment you can buy to make life easier, and feeding is no exception. The following is a review of most of the products and equipment you can buy, their purpose, and some available alternatives. Manufacturers would like you to believe that you can't live without some of these items, but remember that your baby is unique, and so are you. Trust your instincts, and be skeptical about what might work for you.

Nursing Supplies

Nursing pads These are usually essential in the first few months of nursing, and some women need to use them the entire time they are lactating. The pads slip inside your bra and soak up leaking milk before it stains your shirt. Disposable and washable breast pads are both fine (washable pads are much less expensive in the long run). Be sure not to buy breast pads with "leak-proof" plastic inside the pad. This type of pad traps moisture next to your skin, where bacteria can multiply. If you've received hand-me-down pads, cut one of them open to check that it doesn't have a plastic insert. Avoid pads with any scratchy seams or fabric. You will need at least six pairs of washable pads (probably more), and you should expect to change them at least once a day.

Nursing bras Most nursing bras have more support than regular bras, which women usually need desperately (often day *and* night) in the early months of breastfeeding. Nursing bras also provide quick access to the breast, which newborn babies vigorously demand. Regular bras with a front closure do not work very well for nursing because you need two hands to fasten and unfasten them, and new mothers rarely have both hands free. It is a good idea to buy one bra before your baby is born, and you should expect to increase one cup size and one band size in girth. After the baby is born, start shopping for one or two other bras (you'll need to wash them often). You'll have a much better idea at this point about what works for you. Be sure to try the bras on, and think critically about the decision you are making. Does a snap closure or a hook-and-eye closure work best for you? Is the bra at all scratchy? I recommend all cotton for this reason. How much support do you need, and where? Having a comfortable nursing bra can make all the difference. After all, you may be wearing a bra 24 hours a day for the first few months.

Breast pumps These can be a lifesaver if you need to be away from your baby, or if your baby skips feedings for another reason and you need to express excess milk or keep your milk supply up. Most hospitals, many diaper services, and good baby supply stores offer electric breast pump rentals to mothers, and it is a good idea to try out a rental first. A few women have trouble using a breast pump, and it would be a shame to find this out after making a big investment (breast pumps are not returnable). Some women find they have no trouble expressing milk manually and don't need a breast pump.

There are two kinds of breast pumps: electric and manual. Manual breast pumps are very inexpensive but can be a chore to use. You may be given one by your midwife or doctor at the hospital, so it can't hurt to see if a manual pump works for you. Most women, however, quickly switch to some kind of electric or battery-operated pump. There is also one kind of pump operated with a pedal. There are dozens of models of electric breast pumps, ranging in price from $40 to $300, and it pays to shop wisely. If you plan to stay at home with your baby, you may not want to invest in a very expensive pump. On the other hand, some of the more affordable pumps do not provide a lot of suction power and/or speed and so don't work well for some women. The most deluxe breast pump models have attractive, discreet carrying cases, insulated pockets and ice packs for storing fresh milk, and even have an attachment that allows you to plug the pump into your car's cigarette lighter (believe it or not, this came in quite handy in my own experience!).

Nursing pillows Specialized pillows are definitely not necessary but can be very nice to have. Using regular pillows to prop up aching arms and shoulders works pretty well, but you find yourself spending a lot of time arranging pillows without complete satisfaction. A nursing pillow slides around your body as you sit, and you

Breast Pumps to Avoid

There is one type of manual pump operated by squeezing a bulb similar to a bicycle horn. Many lactation professionals recommend *against* using this type of pump for expressing milk you will later feed to your baby, because milk can easily back up into the bulb, which is difficult to sterilize properly.

can rest your arms at the right height. Some nursing pillows double as a place where your baby can lie comfortably, and where your baby can be propped up when she is learning to sit. Other pillows have deluxe features such as a pocket for storing a magazine, snacks, or even a portable phone and can be strapped close to your body to use while standing. Nursing pillows also work well for bottle feedings. Nursing pillows don't work for everyone. Many large-breasted women find they only get in the way.

Nursing bibs/canopies   These are gadgets designed to allow you to nurse in public without exposing your bare breast. While this may seem like a good idea, using a canopy tends to draw more attention to what you are doing rather than less, and is not particularly convenient. Most women are surprised to discover that their usual modesty is suspended during the time they are nursing. Also, people's attitudes toward a mother nursing in public are beginning to relax as more women refuse to feel ashamed for doing something so natural.

Nursing clothes   It is wise to consider your choices in clothing during the time you are nursing. There are specially designed nursing dresses and blouses with convenient flaps allowing quick and discreet access to the breast. Most women wear loose-fitting, waist-length T-shirts, blouses, and cardigan sweaters (unbutton from the bottom for best effect), and find that getting the baby's head under the shirt is very quick and just as discreet as when they are wearing nursing clothes. Your regular dresses will probably stay in the closet, even if they have buttons in front, because unbuttoning from the collar down can leave you feeling very naked.

Baby Bottles and Nipples

If you are bottle-feeding your baby, be prepared to spend some time (and money) finding the right kind of bottle and nipple for your baby. There are several brands that offer a system for bottle-feeding your baby, and most make various claims about reducing colic and gas. The truth is that each baby will have *several* types of bottles and nipples that work well for her, and finding those types is a

Breast Pump Options

Type of Beast Pump	Possible Options/Features	Advantages	Disadvantages
Manual	Adjustable suction	• Low cost • Very portable • Fewer parts to clean • Good choice for occasional pumping	• Can only pump one breast at a time • Pumping may take a long time • Not a good choice for women who have any trouble with pumping • Not a good choice for frequent use
Battery-operated pump	• Adjustable suction • A/C Adapter (typically adds quite a bit to the cost)	• Relatively inexpensive, but much more expensive than a manual model • Very portable • Doesn't need to be plugged in • Good choice for pumping several times weekly or for women who have little trouble pumping	• Can pump only one breast at a time • Pumping may take longer than with electric models • Continuous suction may not be as comfortable for some women • Does not have as much suction power as electric models, and suction power diminishes as the battery wears out • Batteries wear out quickly
Small electric pump	• Adjustable suction • Possibly adaptable to pump both breasts at once • Small carrying case with insulated compartment for storing collected milk	• Not as expensive as an automatic pump • Many models are small enough to fit in a diaper bag • Good choice for daily pumping for women who have little trouble pumping	• Not as efficient as an automatic model • Continuous suction may not be as comfortable for some women
Automatic electric pump	• Adjustable suction. • Able to pump both breasts at once • Attractive carrying case • Insulated compartment with ice packs for storing collected milk • Car cigarette lighter adapter	• Build-and-release suction style more similar to a baby's suck, which is more efficient and more comfortable for many women • Frequently available to rent • Good choice for women who will be pumping every day, as when they go back to work	• Highest cost • These pumps are typically larger and heavier than other pumps and are therefore not as portable

process of trial and error. You may settle on a suitable bottle right away, but be patient if you don't. The wrong type of nipple is often a source of problems. Most nipples are designed to coincide with a baby's stage of development, with small holes for younger babies and larger holes for older babies who need to drink more and can cope with a faster flow. There are also nipples made of rubber (which a majority of babies prefer) and nipples made of silicone. Additionally there are several nipple shapes, some of which mimic the shape of a mother's nipple in the baby's mouth. Don't make a large investment in any type of bottle-feeding system until you are sure you like it. Most brands are designed to the same size specifications and you can mix and match parts between brands, but some brands have unique sizes, which can lead to greater expense if they don't work for your baby.

Bottle Cleaning/Sterilizing Equipment

Good hygiene and the importance of sanitation of baby-feeding equipment cannot be overemphasized. Serious illness can result from exposure to bacteria due to improper cleaning and sterilization of equipment, or contamination of the equipment after sterilization. For more information about sterilizing bottle-feeding equipment, see Chapter 1.

Baby bottle/nipple brushes are an inexpensive essential item and are available at most baby stores, pharmacies, and supermarkets. Milk and formula dry very quickly in the bottom of a bottle and in the nipples and cannot be properly cleaned off with just hot water or a regular sponge (which may harbor unwanted bacteria). Avoid gimmicky brushes that rotate, which are a waste of money. Be sure to store your brush so that it dries thoroughly (hanging is best).

Bottle-drying racks can be quite useful but are not essential. They prevent bacteria from growing in small amounts of water that collect in the bottles if they are drying on a flat surface or tipped at a shallow angle. They come in a variety of styles and are not particularly expensive ($4 to $12). You can improvise your own drying rack if you are handy, with dowels inserted into a wooden base. Consider how much counter space you have available before purchasing or making a drying rack.

A dishwasher basket is another handy item that doesn't cost very much. The basket holds nipples and small parts of bottles in the dishwasher, preventing them from being lost (or melted). It is very easy, and much cheaper, to make your own basket from two discarded plastic berry baskets fastened together with plastic twist-ties (paper-coated twist-ties disintegrate).

Bottle-sterilizing sets come in a variety of models and are not necessary because bottles can be easily sterilized on the stove in a large pot you probably already own. However, some parents do find the features of a set convenient. The most common set is a complete sterilizing kit for the stove top that includes a large (and very cheaply made) pot, several baby bottles, nipples, lids, a lift-out tray, tongs, and a bottlebrush. Buying all of the components together may save you a little money. Other sets are designed for use in the microwave (usually you need a 500-watt unit) and sterilize a few bottles very quickly. This set costs about $30, and many parents find it convenient to use. An electric steam sterilizer is the most expensive (about $60 to $70), and after your baby has grown, it usually becomes another obsolete appliance.

Miscellaneous Bottle Supplies

Insulated bottle bags have become very popular in recent years and for good reason. It is important to keep formula and breast-milk cool until it is consumed, and these bags are useful for this purpose, especially if you are going any distance in the car (for

The Modest Nurser

No matter what you wear, there will probably be a moment when you feel uncomfortably exposed, especially when you are just getting started. If this bothers you very much, you may want to try a nursing bib, or you can learn to nurse your baby while holding him in a sling or front pack baby carrier.

storage requirements and perishability of breastmilk and formula, see Chapters 2 and 3. Some even have reusable ice packs, which makes them even better. There are many other kinds of insulated bags and coolers available, however, and you may already own something else that will do the job just as well.

Electric bottle warmers are useful for midnight feedings and usually do the job fairly quickly. Warming a bottle in very hot tap water usually works just as well, however. Some warming appliances are quite deluxe, with cooling chambers in addition to the warming unit. This type of warmer falls into the expensive-and-obsolete category when you are through with it.

Portable bottle warmers are a good invention because they allow you to warm a bottle anywhere (these are especially useful when you are on a trip). The warmer is a sleeve that holds a hot pack heated in the microwave or in boiling water. The hot pack stays warm for many hours and can be used several times. Some warmers also serve as an insulated cooling bag. An alternative is to carry a thermos filled with hot water and a bowl to warm the bottle in. You can also use hot tap water or hot water from a coffee or tea urn. This may not be quite as convenient, but it works just fine.

Powdered formula dispensers, depending on what kind you get, can be a little silly but useful nonetheless. There are several different types. The simplest is a snap-on lid that fits on the container with a spout you can open to pour the formula out, saving the "mess" of scooping. Slightly more useful is another lid-type dispenser with a premeasured receptacle in the spout, which saves the time of using the measuring scoop. The best is a small portable container designed for storing premeasured portions of powdered formula to be used at the time your baby wants her bottle. This is great because you can take it with you anywhere and drop the formula right in the bottle filled with water when you need it, so you don't have to worry about the formula spoiling before it is drunk.

"Hands-free" feeding kits are a perennial item in most baby stores but are not as popular as you might expect. Most parents enjoy time spent feeding their baby, and the time before the baby learns to hold his own bottle is much too short. Still, there are times when "hands-free" feeding is an attractive option. This is especially true if you are caring for more than one baby at the same time. There are basically two types of products to serve this purpose. A bottle holder is a simple device that props the baby's bottle in the correct position. Other self-feeders use flexible tubing that siphons the liquid from the bottle to a nipple in the baby's mouth. The tubing must be very carefully cleaned and sterilized in this type of device. Remember that babies should always be closely supervised during their feedings.

Bottle straws are designed to draw liquid from the bottom of the bottle right up to the nipple, and their manufacturers claim that the result of less air and an upright feeding position will reduce the occurrence of ear infections. If your child does not suffer from chronic ear infections, there is little reason to use this product. If he does, you will probably be ready to use anything that might help him feel better. It may not work, but it's worth a try.

High Chairs/Infant Seating

After all the equipment you've had to purchase for your baby, spending $100 or more on a high chair might seem a bit much. Some parents are lucky and get a wonderful high chair as a hand-me-down. If this is the case, be sure the high chair meets current safety standards and that it has a crotch strap. If it doesn't, you should purchase a strap at a baby supply store. To find out if the manufacturer has recalled a used high chair, you can write the Consumer Product Safety Commission or log on to *www.childrecall.com* (see the Resources section at the end of the book).

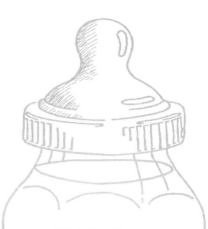

Think Ahead

Experienced parents will tell you that you may (*may*) get more use out of a high chair if your baby can climb into and out of it easily during the independent toddler years. Although this may be difficult to imagine now when your baby is still so helpless, he will become quite nimble in the coming years. Maybe you could bring a toddler with you to the store for experimentation purposes.

Making an investment in seating for your baby is a very important decision. However, the amount you spend may have very little to do with how satisfied you are with your choice, and there are several other much more important factors to consider. For example, the configuration of your home is critical. Do you have room for a traditional high chair? Some models can be folded easily and put away—a must in a small house or apartment. Or, maybe your baby is a *very* messy eater. In this case, ease of cleaning will be a priority for you. Some parents like to feed their babies at the table from the beginning, and in this case a booster seat or hook-on seat may be right for you. Different seating options are as follows:

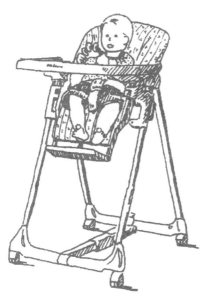

Traditional high chairs are usually wooden or metal and have a tray that lifts over the baby's head or slides and hooks onto the armrests. Be sure the chair has a stable base and won't tip over as your child gets bigger and more active. Some models (especially older metal chairs) can be difficult to keep clean because there may be lots of seams and corners where food will get stuck. Also, make sure that a metal chair is not rusting. If you are concerned about your baby sitting on a hard surface, you can purchase a seat cushion and/or backrest that will fit in most traditional high chairs. Make sure this is washable. People usually choose traditional high chairs for aesthetic and nostalgic reasons. More than that, these chairs have a tried and true design and construction, which is why they are so often handed down from generation to generation. If you are purchasing your high chair new, you should expect to spend $80 to $150 or more. Used models may cost considerably less. Antique high chairs, which are often quite beautiful, can be very pricey.

Modern high chairs are distinguished from traditional high chairs by their added features. Many chairs have an adjustable seat that can be set at different heights or may even recline at different angles. The chair itself is often designed to hold your baby more comfortably and snugly in a seated position, which can be very helpful if your baby is younger or especially wiggly.

You could spend $40 on one of these chairs, or up to $200, but be aware that you get what you pay for. Pay attention to the construction of the chair. If the chair folds for storage, are the hinges sturdy? Try folding and unfolding it in the store, especially if you plan to fold it after each use. If it is awkward or heavy you may want to consider another chair. How does the tray attach to the chair? Is it easy for you to use? Most of these chairs have a fabric seat cover. Make sure it removes for washing, and that the fabric is durable and won't show stains. Ease of cleaning is another factor to consider. Are there crevices where food can fall? Are the surfaces washable?

Booster seats are generally designed for older children to use while sitting at the table, but many models provide a suitable and inexpensive high chair alternative for younger babies who are confident sitters. Look for a booster seat that has an attachable tray, a seat back, and sturdy straps for securing the child in the seat and securing the seat to a chair. You can attach the seat to a regular chair or a taller chair but only if it has a *very* stable base (many tall chairs have a narrow base, which can tip). No booster seat is guaranteed to attach properly to all chairs, so don't hesitate to take the seat back if you discover it won't attach safely. Some booster seats fold for traveling, which can be handy, but this feature can also make the seat much harder to clean. The best reason to buy a booster seat instead of a high chair is that they are very inexpensive, usually around $20 (keep in mind that they are also usually made entirely of plastic and will never become a family heirloom). You can also use the seat throughout your child's development and when she is ready to join the family at the table. There are some booster seats that recline for feeding an infant who cannot yet sit up. Generally, babies are sitting within a short time of beginning solid food, so this feature is not useful for very long. Try feeding the baby while he is in your lap until he can sit well.

Hook-on seats are very cleverly designed and hook directly onto the tabletop, bringing the baby to the right height for

Feeding Your Baby in the Real World

"We really like the convertible high chair we have. It works as either an inclined chair for infants, a regular high chair with a tray, a booster seat on a stand, or strapped into a regular dining room chair. It travels okay, but it's bulky."

—Greg, father of Zula and Moses

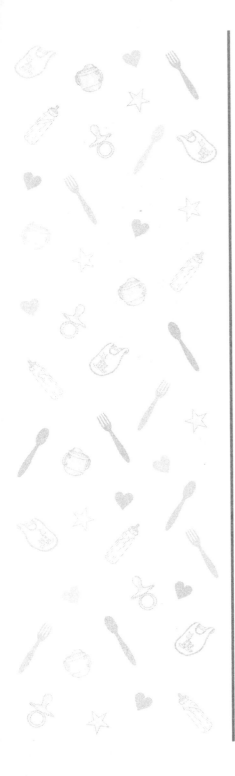

eating at the table. If you feed your baby at the table exclusively, you may want to use a hook-on seat as an alternative to a high chair. Be aware that a hook-on seat should be used only if your baby is already a confident sitter. Hook-on seats are great for traveling and dining out because they are very portable, and many families own one in addition to a high chair. Hook-on seats fit on most tables, but if there is a skirt under the tabletop, the chair might not lock properly. If this is the case, return the chair or use another sturdy table. Hook-on seats generally cost $25 to $40, and you can find them used. Check carefully for damaged and/or missing parts before purchasing a used hook-on seat. Also, when using a hook-on seat, be sure that no other chairs or table legs are within reach of your baby's feet. Otherwise, he could easily boost himself up and dislodge the chair.

Stand-alone booster chairs are built similarly to a regular chair but have a higher seat for toddlers and young children. This is a popular option for families with several children, because you can buy a booster chair when one child grows out of the high chair and know that it will be passed down to the next child. A booster chair is also frequently the most attractive option.

A high chair helper is a contoured cushion designed to prop up a baby that is not a confident sitter. As with a reclining booster seat, it probably won't be very long before your baby will not need this device. However, if your baby is very small and the high chair is large with hard surfaces, you may want to invest in the helper. Also, some models can be used for safely seating your infant in a grocery cart.

Solids Feeding Supplies

A baby food nurser should not be used by parents. A baby food nurser is essentially a bottle that's nipple has been enlarged to allow dilute cereal to pass through. If you are tempted to use this product, your baby is probably not ready for solid food. In the past, parents commonly used this type of feeder for younger infants (sometimes less than one month old) because of the mistaken belief that eating solid food helps a baby sleep through the night. Eating from a spoon is an important developmental stage that can be delayed, but not skipped. Your baby does not need to transition through this step by using a baby food nurser.

First feedings spoons and bowls. Spoons for early feedings should have a small bowl because your baby does not yet know to open her mouth wide for this unique experience. However, she may learn quickly, and a special spoon for first feedings may not be useful for very long. You may have a very small spoon already that will work well, or you can even give your baby food on the tip of your finger, which some babies prefer. There are also bowls designed with a hole for your thumb that are usually sold with a spoon as a set. This is a little gimmicky (a regular bowl isn't very difficult to hold), but it's nice to get as a gift.

Feeding spoons come in a variety of forms, and you'll probably have quite a few before you're through. The most popular kind has a long, slender handle and a rubber-coated bowl. The long handle makes it easy to feed your baby without getting your hand too close to his face, which most babies don't care for, and the rubber-coated tip protects sore teething gums from a hard surface. Some spoons have a rubber coating that will change color if the food is too hot, which is a nice safety feature.

As your baby grows, he will begin to want to feed himself with the spoon. Then it is time to begin the transition to a shorter-handled spoon with a bigger bowl, so that he can have a better chance of getting the food into his mouth. Some spoons are designed with a grip that helps the baby hold the spoon at the right angle. Using a spoon takes a lot of practice, so this sort of spoon may be very helpful to your baby. There is a variety of utensil sets made for toddlers that have cheerful

---

Shop Smart

Whatever high chair you choose, try it out at the store if you can (leave the rice cereal at home). Stand and sit in front of the chair. Is the reach comfortable? Is the chair the right height for you? Is the tray the right height for your baby? Take your time. After all, you'll be spending a lot of time feeding your baby.

colors or characters on the handles. These colorful forks and spoons do help make mealtimes more fun, but some utensils have very little use beyond their novelty. If an airplane spoon is difficult to hold, or has an impossibly small bowl, a toy airplane might be more fun for your child.

Bibs are a baby essential and may even be useful long before your baby begins eating solid food, especially for drooling and spitting up. Believe it or not, you can spend a fair amount of money on a bib (over $10!), but you certainly don't have to. Very expensive bibs are made to last, out of heavy-duty plastic-coated material or molded hard plastic. There's usually a pocket or trough to catch drips and crumbs, which comes in handy. All bibs have a variety of closures. Velcro fasteners can be quick to fasten and unfasten, but if your baby decides to remove his bib mid-feeding and throw it on the floor, there will be little you can do about it. A snap or tie fastener will prevent this. Some parents purchase inexpensive bibs in quantity, planning to throw them away after a couple of months' service.

Baby bowls and plates are available in an incredible array of shapes, sizes, and materials. Choosing these wares can be governed by your sense of practicality, your sense of fun, or both. If you are blessed with one of those children who always throws her bowl down on the floor, a china dish is not practical no matter how pretty or fun it may be. Bowls and plates with a suction cup on the bottom might be a better choice, but if your baby is determined to throw the bowl on the floor, the suction cups won't stop her. Older babies and toddlers might appreciate a plate with sections to keep the peas from contaminating the potatoes, and most delight in a cheery picture or "all gone" message to reward a well-cleaned plate. Generally, unbreakable plates and bowls are always better for children, and you should

The Cheapest Bib Option of All

If you find yourself stuck without a bib, try using a dishtowel fastened with a clothespin. Indeed, some parents never buy any bib at all and use something like this instead. Some toddlers also feel that this is a much more "grown up" option.

be aware that some older pieces of pottery may contain lead and should be avoided.

A *baby-safe feeder* is made with a mesh bag attached to a handle and is designed to allow infants to teethe on harder foods like apples or carrots. As the baby gnaws on a harder food, it is strained through the mesh, preventing any pieces that may cause choking from being eaten. I have heard some parents praise this device, but it is difficult to find, and, I suspect, not very popular.

Baby food carousels/organizers are by no means necessary but may be useful to you. If you are short of counter space, you can use the carousel to keep the food organized, but keeping it in the cupboard may work better for you. Organizers come in a variety of designs, but usually revolve on a lazy Susan-style carousel and have measured sections for storing jars of baby food, cans of powdered formula, and sometimes bottles and other equipment. Many models have several levels for maximum storage capacity.

A *high chair mat* is a plastic drop cloth that might make your life easier, especially if you are feeding your baby in a carpeted area. Otherwise, you'll have to wipe up the mat the same as you would the floor. The advantage of a mat is that you can throw it in the washing machine if things get really messy.

Sippy Cups

Training cups simply have a snap-on lid with a spout for easier drinking by small children. These cups are not a good choice for taking drinks with you on an outing because they are not spill-proof and the lid might pop off. Inexpensive and convenient for home use, most families find they have quite a supply of these cups on hand as their child grows, and they are useful until your child learns to be responsible with a regular cup.

Feeding Your Baby in the Real World

"I have a dish . . . that has three compartments and a huge rubber suction cup on the bottom. This is the best invention for me because it sticks so well to the tabletop or high chair tray that Christopher can't flip it over. You can also put hot water into it (like a canteen) to help keep food warm. That was helpful when I fed him baby food, but he no longer cares what the temperature of his food is, so I don't use that feature anymore. I take this plate with me to restaurants because he'll actually eat instead of playing with his bowl and spilling all his food out onto the floor."

—Christina, mother of Sophia and Christopher

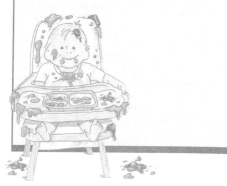

Tippy cups are similar to training cups, except they have a weighted bottom that keeps the cup upright (most of the time). Tippy cups usually also have two handles for the baby to grasp, which some children seem to like. If your child is prone to throwing his cup down, this cup can be useful in preventing some (but not all) spills.

Spill-proof cups usually have a screw-on lid and a plastic lid insert that prevent all spills but allow the baby to suck out the liquid. These cups tend to be sturdier and are very useful for traveling. The lid insert is very effective but can get lost.

Straw cups have a silicone straw that bends and retracts when a hood is pulled over it. This kind of cup is very useful for traveling, but only for an older baby who has learned how to suck through a straw. Be careful if your child is teething because the straw, while more durable than the regular variety, cannot withstand constant chewing and may even become a choking hazard if chewed on too much.

Graduated training cups are advertised as "systems" and are generally part of a bottle-maker's line of merchandise. They usually include a softer, more nipplelike spout, a harder spout, and a straw insert, and all of these fit onto a baby bottle. The idea is that your baby will learn how to drink from a cup and a straw in stages, and that if you already have the bottles, you will save money by buying the new spouts. Realistically, most babies learn how to drink from a cup more easily than you expect them to (after all, training cups didn't exist at all until just a few years ago), and if purchased as a set, these systems are really quite expensive (as much as $15). If you do already use the bottles made by the manufacturer, however, the new attachments purchased separately can be a great choice, and usually you'll have a few bottle tops that make the new cup convenient for traveling.

Bibs for Messy Eaters

As your baby gets older and is ready to eat more challenging foods like soups and stews and other messy items, you may want to occasionally use a long-sleeve bib or artist's smock (try to find one with a wide pocket in front for catching stuff).

CHAPTER SIXTEEN

What to Expect in the Years to Come

Once your baby has reached his second birthday, he is a full-fledged toddler. Preschool and kindergarten are just around the corner, and the school years will have begun. Then, of course, you'll have a teenager on your hands . . . Well, you get the picture. In any case, many would argue that the most effective time for teaching your child about good nutrition and enjoying food together is just ahead. In the preschool and early school years, many children are more open to trying new foods and can understand fairly complicated concepts. Toddlers and children are also still very much attached to their home and parents and will welcome any involvement in household tasks like meal preparation and shopping. Remember that everything you can teach your child about healthful eating now will have to last through the often rocky years of adolescence and young adulthood, when your influence may take a back seat to that of peers and mass culture. Plenty of anecdotal evidence suggests that this approach can really make a difference, not just in your child's future eating habits and health, but in his social skills as well.

How Will My Child's Diet Change?

First of all, at some point between two and five years, a child no longer needs about 50 percent of her calories from fat. Now, her needs are more similar to those of an adult—about 30 percent of calories should come from fat—with a maximum of one-third of those fat calories coming from saturated fat. As if they understand this instinctively, many kids will begin to turn up their noses at whole milk during these years, asking instead for the 2 percent or low-fat milk their parents use. With this shift, you can continue giving your toddler and preschooler 16 to 24 ounces of milk each day, if she can and will drink it. You should try to increase her calcium intake if she doesn't drink milk. Half of her calories should now come from carbohydrates: ideally, the whole grains, legumes, rice, and potatoes you've been feeding her all along. You should also remain aware of good sources for iron in her diet, to

Talking to Your Toddler About Healthy Eating

While toddlers and preschoolers may not be able to understand the finer points of nutritional science, they are interested in learning just about anything. Getting them to understand that food is what helps them to grow up to be strong and healthy is the easy part. Teaching them to appreciate which foods are healthiest (and tastiest) just takes a little imagination.

- Foods with different colors contain different kinds of vitamins and minerals, all of which are essential for proper growth and good health. This is an idea young children can easily understand. Help your child to pick as many different colors as possible for her meals. For example, a selection of different veggies like yellow and red bell pepper, carrot sticks, and celery served with a dippy sauce can be a fun way to "eat your colors."

- Teach your child about what different animals eat. While dog food may not be a great example, eating leaves like a bunny, drinking milk like a kitten, or noshing on bananas like a monkey may be enticement enough for many children. Take your child for feeding time at the zoo, and see what new foods he learns to appreciate.

- Be frank with your child about why your family makes certain food choices. "We don't eat candy very often because it's too sweet and won't help you grow if you have too much in your tummy," might be a helpful explanation when given by parents who are trying to limit sugar. I vividly recall a recent trip to the market where I saw a mom and her two young daughters, who were eagerly seeking out foods made with organic ingredients. Every few minutes, one girl or the other would cry out, "Look, Mom it's organic!" as they discovered one healthy treat after another.

prevent anemia. Other important nutrients to remain aware of are: vitamin A, vitamin C, folic acid, and vitamin B6, which are available in whole grains, fruits, dairy products, eggs, vegetables (particularly deep yellow, orange, and dark green vegetables), meat, poultry, and fish. Although children require more protein for their size than adults do, the typical American receives so much protein that this requirement is rarely a concern.

Involving Your Toddler in Mealtime Preparations

Toddlers often love to help in the kitchen and in the garden as well. While their "assistance" is really not a big timesaver for you, the time you spend performing these tasks, which are of basic importance to our cultural experience, will be of lifelong value to him. I really believe that cooking with your child is as important as reading with him and playing with him are.

Harnessing Your Little Helper

Your toddler and young child is often eager to help in the kitchen (see the sidebar on page 285 for ideas). When assigning tasks, consider your child's age and abilities. Remember that while his motor skills may be up for the challenge, his patience and attention level may not be. Don't forget to praise him for a job well done, and try to overlook the uh-oh's.

Fun Mealtime Ideas for Toddlers and Young Children

- Host a picnic. With a playmate or with Mom and Dad, a picnic will be a fantastic way to enjoy a satisfying lunch. A picnic or tea party is equally fun in the backyard, at the park, or on the kitchen floor. Serve fun picnic foods like corn on the cob, potato salad, and a cold chicken drumstick. Don't forget to invite the teddy bears!

- Have an un-birthday party. Un-birthdays are traditionally celebrated on the six-month anniversary of your child's actual birthday, but I never subscribed to that belief personally. Un-birthday parties are appropriate whenever the child or parent needs a pick-me-up. Keep it short. Pretend presents should come first (toys your child already owns are good) and then lunch with finger sandwiches and maybe special rice pudding with a candle stuck in it for dessert.

- Bread baking is an exciting activity for most toddlers, and if you start a loaf rising first thing on a weekend morning, you can usually finish baking it in time for lunch. Toddlers love to get messy and help with kneading and pounding the dough. And when a hot, crusty loaf is pulled from the oven and slathered with fresh butter, it makes the perfect accompaniment to a bowl of split pea soup.

- For the child who just cannot sit still right now, put out a plate of snacks with fresh cut vegetables, a tasty dipping sauce, and crackers at her little table. She'll eat when she's hungry and when she can fit it into her busy schedule.

The Slapdash Art of Food Decoration

A toddler can really appreciate subtle differences in food presentation. This can be infuriating when she refuses to eat peas that have come within a micrometer of the mashed potatoes, or it can be endearing as she joyfully gobbles up a bowl of oatmeal embedded with a sloppy happy face constructed out of raisins. Some parents get really involved in wild and creative food construction projects, carving out melon bowls with intricate designs meant to look like ships, or molding seafood croquettes to be shaped like stars or fishes. This can be really fun but is not necessary. Something as simple as cutting slices of toast in triangles instead of squares can

Help in the Kitchen

- Tearing lettuce for salad
- Snapping string beans
- Washing produce while using a stepstool
- Counting out eggs, cups, and tablespoons for recipes
- Pouring in ingredients as they are needed
- Cutting soft foods like banana or avocado with a dull table knife
- Setting the table
- Stirring mixtures
- Tossing salads
- Kneading bread dough
- Shaking up the salad dressing (make sure the lid is on tight!)
- Tasting and critiquing a work in progress—does it need more oregano or basil? (Be sure to teach your child to wash the tasting spoon *before* returning it to the food.)
- Clearing the table
- Loading the dishwasher

be enough to create a strange, if enchanting, glee. And the more your child is involved in the process of creating these edible masterpieces, the more she will enjoy eating the fruits of her labors.

Simple Tools for Creating Food Art

- Melon ballers of different sizes can be used to scoop out frozen yogurt, baked sweet potatoes, jicama, and, obviously, melon.
- Tiny cookie cutters (used for cake decoration) can be used to make interesting shapes for thin slices of salad vegetables. Then you can say, "Don't forget to eat your stars!" instead of "Eat your carrots!"
- Egg slicers create perfect, thin slices of hard-boiled eggs, which are appealing to the toddler's developing sense of aesthetics.
- A pastry bag can be used to squeeze out any kind of pureed food, especially mashed potatoes or yams, to make neat rows of dots or crazy designs on the plate.
- Toothpicks are great for making little stacks of yummy foods like tiny cherry tomatoes stacked with cheese and cucumber slices.
- Using squeeze bottles for condiments like mayonnaise, mustard, and maple syrup can make food decoration quick and easy for pancakes, open-faced sandwiches, and so on.

Special Cookbooks for Kids with Food Art Recipes

These cookbooks aren't just for the food art enthusiast, they're for parents who've simply run out of new ideas for what to feed their kids and ways to get them involved with preparing food. Think of food art as a craft project that happens to be nutritious.

Cooking Art: Easy Edible Art for Young Children by MaryAnn F. Kohl and Jean Potter. (Gryphon House Books, 1997).

This book was written by two early childhood educators who focus on helping parents to learn how to get their children involved in the cooking process. While most of the projects are designed for children who are three or older, there are many fun ideas for appealing dishes for toddlers, and helpful tips for introducing even a very young child to food preparation.

First Meals by Annabel Karmel. (DK Publishing, 1999).

This book has many recipes for dishes for babies and children of all ages. The beautiful pictures may provide you with inspiration to create mini pizzas with animal faces, or seafood meals with a whole undersea theme. This book isn't for everyone, though; I had one mother tell me she was ready to burn it, thinking that the beautiful depictions of food set an impossibly high standard. Even if you don't want to follow each recipe to its extreme conclusion, there are lots of nifty tricks for making dishes to spark the imagination of most toddlers.

Handling Outside Influences

Experts in child development agree that the more forbidden an activity or food, the more desirable it becomes to the child. It's wonderful to decide that your child will eat only healthy foods, but you must also be aware of outside influences that can undermine your efforts. If you stifle your child's natural curiosity in the face of these influences, you can easily find yourself back at square one. If your preschooler comes home from a play date exclaiming about a fast food lunch you neither knew about nor condoned, don't waste your energy getting mad. Ask him what he had to eat and how he liked it, the same as you would for any other source of excitement. Treat the event as no big deal and continue with your regular routine. This sends the truthful message that each family is slightly different, and not just in what they eat. Although you might not be thrilled by the fast-food stop, this approach will pay off in spades when your child comes home from visiting with another family that practices a cuisine from a different culture. The key to handling

Help in the Garden

Here are some tasks your little one can do in the garden with you.

- Tilling the soil with a small spade
- Sowing seeds
- Daily watering
- Weeding
- Harvesting

outside influences is not to shield your child from them, but to remain consistent in the direction of your own influence. If and when your child begs to visit the fast-food chain again, be honest about why you choose to limit eating out there and at similar restaurants. You might explain that it's OK to go for fast food once in a while (or never, depending on your viewpoint), but that it's too fat and salty and that the food there isn't healthy for Mom, Dad, or the kids.

In the early years, your influence on what your child eats is at its most powerful. Parents of picky eaters would often like to discount this fact, but it is true, and the AAP agrees. It should be you, not your child, who decides what food is served and when. Your child, on the other hand, has the ultimate authority over whether or not she will eat the food and how much she eats. This is the unavoidable power-sharing arrangement between the parent and child that is the source of so much trouble. The wise parent will use her authority wisely, choosing a healthy variety of foods that are appealing to her little one and offering them at intervals that suit the child's age and temperament. When your child is very young, you are in complete control of what foods are available in your home. Since most of her meals will be taken at home, your influence is at its most powerful. Take advantage.

Still, those outside influences will inevitably begin to creep in around the edges. The following is an overview of some of the most troublesome problems, and strategies for dealing with them.

Sweet Spoilers

The sweet spoiler is a worry for parents who have decided to limit sugar, and a walking nightmare for parents who are attempting the difficult task of eliminating sugar completely. Let's start by saying that I believe it's impolite to offer a child food without asking permission from the parents. Still, that doesn't stop many people. If the spoiler is a casual acquaintance, say, a neighbor, you might feel rude saying that you don't want your child to eat the food being offered. Try instead to find ways to mitigate the impact of this unplanned snack. If the treat is juice and cookies for example, you might say, "That's so nice of you, but only one or two, I don't want him spoiling his dinner (lunch)." The spoiling-of-the-dinner excuse works nicely in a variety of situations, as any experienced parent will tell you. Also, you could try eliminating the double sweet whammy of cookies and juice by saying, "Actually, he just had juice a little while ago. Do you have any water or milk?"

Spoiler grandparents and baby-sitters are another story entirely. Not only may your child see them more regularly, it may be more difficult to discuss the topic of food with them as well. After all, people have many different ideas about what is good for children, and they sometimes genuinely feel that limiting sweets to children is unkind. If you have a fast and hard rule about sugar, this may take quite a bit of explaining, out of earshot of the child. Offer alternative treats you know your child will enjoy such as fruit, or share an easy recipe for sugar-free cookies or homemade fruit-juice ice pops. Ideally, the spoiler will be convinced to respect your wishes. Also beware of the candy dish that is ever present in many grandparents' homes. Once your independent young child gets wind of this innovation, it may be difficult or impossible to stop him from going back again and again. Better to anticipate this problem before your child even notices the dish is there. Get the dish yourself, and take it to your host, saying, "You know how kids are. Once he gets sight of this, he won't stop until there's a temper tantrum. Can we just put it out of sight?"

Older Siblings

Many parents find that they have relaxed their standards by the time the second or third child comes along. While it's true that your baby will likely be "corrupted" by candies, cakes, and other less desirable foods much more quickly because his older sister has been exposed to them, this does not mean that all is lost. In fact, by having the mystery of these forbidden pleasures debunked, your baby will think less of their novelty when many of his peers are just discovering them. While your kids are still little, you are in control of the foods that enter your house and the activities your kids participate in, so take advantage.

Lunch Box Day Traders

Because of the potential for serious allergic reactions, many schools have imposed an outright ban on lunch box trading. Whether or not this is truly effective doesn't change the fact that one day you'll probably start hearing, "All the other kids get candy bars and potato chips in their lunches. Why do I always have to get fruit?" Try to realize that maybe she has a point, though the problem may not be so much the lack of candy bars as the lack of variety. There are so many tasty healthy options that kids love, you should have no trouble finding suitable alternatives: granola bars, fruit snacks, healthy puddings, fruit yogurt, and healthy snack chips, just to name a few. If you shop in a natural foods store, it's easy to get your child involved in selecting healthy treats for her own lunch. With a bounty of choices, fresh fruit and vegetables will be as welcome as any other part of her lunch.

The School Cafeteria

Many parents are dismayed with the lack of healthfulness of cafeteria school lunches. With enormous budget restraints and limited resources, some schools have even contracted with fast-food chains to supply meals. However, there is some good news. Beginning in 1996, schools receiving federal subsidies for school lunch menus are required to participate in the National School Lunch Program. This means that lunches must conform to current health standards put forward by the USDA, and steps must be taken to serve foods from all five food groups, including more grains, fruits, and vegetables. Additionally, menus must be varied to include more ethnic cuisine and vegetarian dishes and less fried food and red meat. Many schools will publish a weekly menu so you can make a decision about whether or not to send your child to school with a bag lunch. If you are not satisfied with the healthfulness of the foods served at your child's school, write a letter to the school's administrators, offering concrete suggestions for improvements, or get involved through the PTA.

Television, Mass Media, and Manipulative Product Placement

Junk food is cheap. It's made with cheap ingredients and manufactured in mass quantities at the lowest cost possible. This leaves plenty of money to spend on slick advertisements and product giveaways geared toward children. Manufacturers even pay money to grocery store chains for coveted child-height shelf slots. Even after all this money is spent, junk foods geared toward children typically have some of the highest profit margins in the food industry. Children are particularly vulnerable to these business tactics because they generally don't have the experience to know they are being manipulated. But children do have the capacity to understand the importance of good nutrition through explanation, experience, and the good example set by their parents. Don't fool yourself into believing your kids will never try these foods. They will, and you will simply have to trust that their previous experiences with healthful eating will give them an instinctive understanding that these foods are simply not as satisfying as those they are used to.

The Special Nutritional Needs of Teens

Adolescents have just as critical a need for healthful eating as young children. However, the influence of parents frequently wanes during these years, giving way to pressures from television, peers, and shopping malls. Besides the added need for healthful eating to help their bodies grow and develop, many teenagers need extra healthful calories because they are more active in sports and other activities now than they ever will be again in their lives. Other teens, anxious to fit in with their peers, may begin a struggle with their weight that may plague them throughout their young adulthood or even their whole lives. Many parents, thankful if their children are doing well in school and if they stay out of trouble, are content to let the issue of nutrition slip into the background. This is a mistake. Hopefully, the good work you have done so far will help to

Vending Machines

Many schools have made big changes to their vending machines and are now providing more healthy choices for students. Instead of candy bars, kids find granola bars or energy bars; instead of soda, they find water, juice, and milk. Kids use vending machines because they are hungry. Why not offer them food that will provide them with sustained energy?

mitigate some of the harmful influences on your child's diet, but be aware of potential danger signs.

- Does your teenager spend too much time watching television, playing video games, or sitting in front of the computer? Organize more family activities so he can get outside and enjoy some exercise. Encourage him to become more involved in activities at school or in the community. He doesn't have to be an athlete to be active.

    Encourage him to join a hiking, camping, or acting club at school. Becoming part of a community or church youth group may provide many more opportunities for physical activity than he currently enjoys. You may even want to consider adding a dog to your household so that your son and the rest of the family has an excuse to get out of the house several times a day for walks.

- Does your adolescent daughter pay a lot of attention to her weight? Are family meals becoming a battle over what she will and will not eat? She may be showing early signs of an eating disorder, and the time to act is now, before the problem becomes more serious. Encourage your daughter to pursue a physical activity that will help her maintain a fit physique, such as running, yoga, or team sports. Enlist the support of her pediatrician in creating a diet that will trim fat while caring for her nutritional needs.

- Your 13-year-old is overweight. His grandmother says it's just baby fat and that he'll grow out of it the same way his father did. In reality, you know that your husband has always struggled with his weight after losing 50 pounds on a crash diet as a teenager, and you want to save your child from the same experience. You are right that a crash diet is not the answer. While your son may be prone to the same genes that have caused his father's struggle, his experience with controlling his weight need not be so traumatic. Talk to his pediatrician about your concerns and take steps now, while he is still growing, to include more low-fat foods such as whole grains, fruits, and vegetables in his diet. It is not

Fun Kids' Books That Encourage Healthy Eating Habits

I Smell Honey by Andrea and Brian Pinkney. (Harcourt Brace & Company, Red Wagon Books, 1997).

This is a lovely book about a child preparing dinner with his family, and it will be appropriate when your baby is a little older. The pictures are great, and the message is clear and simple: Preparing and eating good food is what families do together, bringing lots of pleasurable sights, sounds, smells, and tastes.

Charlie the Chicken: A Pop-up Book by Nick Denchfield and Ant Parker. (Harcourt Brace & Company, Red Wagon Books).

In this book, Charlie the chicken comes to life in hilarious pop-up fun. As you read about all the good things Charlie eats, your child will understand that food is important for helping her grow up to be big and strong like Mommy and Daddy. Even though this is a pop-up book, it's sturdier than most, so it might even stand up to use by a toddler (for a little while at least).

It's Snacktime by Ant Parker. (Harcourt Brace & Company, 1996).

This book is wonderful because it represents what the ritual of snacktime is really like for a small child, down to the bib and sippy cup. Your baby will be able to relate to the fun and yummy foods he eats every day at snacktime, and it reinforces healthy eating habits as part of his understanding of the world.

What Does Maggie Like to Eat? by Lieve Baeten. (Barrons Juveniles, 1997).

This is a super fun lift-the-flap book, in which your child is asked to decide which foods are the right ones for eating. Are socks or pancakes more appropriate for breakfast? Babies love to lift the flap to see if they have the right answer!

The Very Hungry Caterpillar by Eric Carle. (Philomel Books, 1994).

One sunny morning, a caterpillar pops out of an egg, and he is *very* hungry. This story explains how the hungry caterpillar eats more and more each day (and then too much!) until one day he becomes a beautiful butterfly. The pictures are interesting and gorgeous, so you won't mind reading it over and over.

The Carrot Seed by Ruth Krauss and Crockett Johnson. (Harper & Row, 1993).

A classic children's book, first published in 1945, *The Carrot Seed* tells the story of a little boy who learns to be patient while waiting for his seed to grow, and teaches all children where food comes from. This is a great book to get if you plant a garden, and will help your baby understand that growing food takes time.

Eating the Alphabet by Lois Ehlert. (Harcourt Brace & Company, Red Wagon Books, 1993).

This is a beautifully illustrated book, with many examples of fruits and vegetables starting with the different letters of the alphabet. There are so many kinds, both common and a little more unusual (ever heard of the xigua fruit?). As your baby gets closer to his second birthday, you can make a game of identifying all of the different foods he has tried, and hunt for some of the more unusual varieties at the market.

wise to restrict your son's intake of healthy foods, but you should definitely keep high-fat, high-calorie junk foods out of your house and family activities. By combining this approach to food with an active lifestyle, including stimulating family and after-school activities, your son will be able to grow into his weight and avoid problems in the future.

- Your son is 15, a good eater, and is very involved in athletics. Despite this, he is quite thin and not particularly developed for his age. His friends have told him about a high-protein diet with supplements and a rigorous workout routine that might help him build more muscle, and he wants to try it. In reality, this type of diet can be harmful, and there is little evidence to show that it will significantly help in development. Your son is better off continuing to exercise regularly and to participate in team sports, while following a sensible diet as outlined by the Food Guide Pyramid. While he may always be thin, he will catch up in development soon enough.

Adolescence and Iron Deficiency

Teenagers (especially girls) have a greater need for iron than adults do. This is because a teen's blood volume dramatically expands during adolescence in response to growth and the body's increasing need for oxygen. Oxygen is supplied to the body through the bloodstream by iron rich hemoglobin cells. Iron deficiency is of particular concern for teens that are very active in athletics and for menstruating girls, and can lead to fatigue, increased susceptibility to infection, and anemia. To combat iron deficiency, make sure your teen has plenty of iron-rich foods in her diet such as meat, fish, poultry, legumes, dark leafy vegetables, dried fruit, or iron-fortified breads and cereals. Because only about 5 to 20 percent of iron from food sources are absorbed by the body, you can boost iron absorption by serving iron-rich foods from animal sources and vegetable sources at the same time, or by serving iron-rich foods from vegetable sources with foods that also contain vitamin C.

Vegetarianism

Your 11-year-old daughter comes home from school one day with the announcement that she is now a vegetarian. Eating animals is disgusting, she says, and she steadfastly refuses to eat nonvegetarian dishes any longer. Depending on whether or not your home is populated by confirmed meat eaters, this sudden shift may be difficult to adjust to. True, for many children, vegetarianism is a passing phase, but some kids stick with it for many years or through their whole lives. However, a vegetarian diet can be perfectly healthy. Many would say it is even healthier than a diet that includes meat. This does not mean you should merrily go about your business and assume that if your child skips the meat portion of each entrée, she'll be well fed. At the same time, preparing separate entrées for your new vegetarian isn't expected either.

In order to respect your daughter's wishes, ask her to take some of the responsibility for helping you to adjust to her new eating habits. Ask her to get some books about different kinds of vegetarian diets from the library so you can read them together and discuss what changes to make to ensure that she is getting a healthy diet. Perhaps you'll find recipes for hearty grain-based side dishes. Legumes are also an excellent source of nutrition for vegetarians, and there are many tasty recipes for side dishes using them. Maybe you can make pasta more frequently, either as a vegetarian entrée or with grilled chicken or sautéed shrimp added separately at the end. If your daughter will eat fish, include that as a more regular option each week. In the end, your whole family may eat better as a result of her decision.

Teen Smoking

Every day, 6,000 teens and children try a cigarette for the first time. It is estimated that about 1 in 10 children in middle school smoke. A teen whose friends smoke is 13 times more likely to take up smoking. Seventy percent of teenagers who currently smoke 1 to 5 cigarettes a day will still be smoking in five years. Cigarette smoke contains over 4,000 chemicals (43 of them known carcinogens) including carbon monoxide, DDT, arsenic, and formaldehyde. Long-term smokers are

Choosing Positive Influences for Your Child's Health

There are so many fun and interesting ways to expose your child to healthy food throughout her life. Some of these ideas have been mentioned many times in this book but bear repeating.

- Cook together.
- Grow a garden or window box with vegetables and/or herbs.
- Visit a vegetable farm.
- Play games about food. Create a pretend restaurant menu and discuss the healthfulness of each item. Make some of the dishes for dinner and take turns pretending to be the diner and host or waitperson.
- Visit a bread bakery or pretzel factory.
- Visit a fruit orchard or pick-your-own strawberry patch.
- Visit a dairy farm and cheese plant.
- Visit an ethnic grocery store.
- Visit the farmers' market.

Teen Girls and Soft Drinks

A recent study conducted at Harvard University discovered that adolescent girls who reported drinking soft drinks regularly were three times as likely as their peers to have broken a bone, and physically active girls who drank soft drinks were five times as likely to suffer fractured bones. Whether the problem is that soft drinks somehow prevent calcium absorption, or simply the fact that soft drinks have replaced milk in these girls' diets remains to be shown. Indeed, another study showed that fewer that 13 percent of girls 12 to 19 years of age receive the recommended daily allowance for calcium.

2 to 3 times more likely to die from heart disease and 20 times more likely to develop lung cancer. More Americans die each year from smoking related illnesses than died in World War II and the Vietnam War combined. These statistics are shocking, yet parents continue to feel helpless in the face of peer pressure and tobacco advertising (not to mention the fact that many teenage girls take up smoking in an effort to stay thin). Yet, parents are far from helpless, and their influence extends far beyond their expectations. Knowing that children as young as eight years old are regularly offered cigarettes, parents should begin early to talk with their children about their views on smoking. Even a brief conversation about why you would choose to sit in the nonsmoking section, or how you feel about the sight of cigarette butts on the ground, or your concern about the smoking habits of someone your child comes into contact with send a powerful message to him. If you smoke yourself, send the most powerful message of all—quit.

Junk Food Junkies

Adolescents frequently subsist on a diet of empty calories: soda, fried snack foods, processed baked goods, and candy bars. Hopefully, good eating habits learned early in childhood will help prevent your teen from falling into this dangerous trap. However, teens are notoriously influenced by their peers, and you may be horrified to see your former health food junkie transformed into a junk food junkie. If this is happening to your child, take action!

- Enroll your teen in cooking classes so that he can learn how easy it is to prepare healthful meals.
- Since poor eating habits are frequently a result of stress and a too-hectic schedule, help your teen evaluate her current list of activities. She may be trying to do too much, or she may need help in learning how to better manage her time. Set goals for attendance at healthful family meals.
- Encourage your teen to become involved in activities that tend to invite healthful eating, like camping or working on a farm or at a farmers' market or health food store.

Resources

Parenting, Breastfeeding, and Baby Food Web Sites

www.lalecheleague.org

La Leche League International's official Web site is an essential Web site for mothers who want extra support or need answers to breastfeeding questions. Not only does it give current information about contacting a group or La Leche League counselor in your area, but many questions can be answered in a comprehensive Frequently Asked Questions (FAQs) section of the site. This site is especially recommended for nursing mothers who face special challenges such as breastfeeding multiples or breastfeeding a baby with special needs. The site includes a complete listing of La Leche League periodicals and publications and also hosts live online chats, in which you can get real-time answers from accredited LLL group leaders during scheduled chat sessions.

www.medela.com

The official Web site for Medela, a well-known manufacturer of breastfeeding supplies. You can use this site to find everything from breast pumps to nursing bras to nursing supplementation devices. The site also features answers to common breastfeeding questions as well as live online chats with lactation professionals. You can also contact Medela by phone at (800) 435-8316.

www.nal.usda.gov/fnic

The Food and Nutrition Information Center's site provides a lot of good information about using the USDA's Food Guide Pyramid and has some great information geared toward preschool and school-age children. However, there isn't much pertaining to feeding babies.

www.mothers.org

Mother and Others for a Livable Planet is a nonprofit organization devoted to health and environmental issues, particularly those affecting children and families. There is information available relating to organic agriculture, GMOs, bovine growth hormones, and PVC in children's toys, as well as many other topics. The site provides opportunities for you to e-mail members of Congress and other people who can make a difference in issues that may concern you. Some parts of the site are accessible only to members, but most of the information is available to anyone.

www.naturespath.com

This site is operated by Nature's Path, an organic cereal manufacturer. There is some good information for the consumer about organic agriculture and GMOs, as well as links to other sites focusing on these topics.

www.drkoop.com

Dr. C. Everett Koop, a former U. S. Surgeon General, operates this site as an information-based commercial venture. The site contains good information about infant and toddler nutrition, including sample menus, suggestions for snacks, and information relating to the introduction of solid food.

www.fda.gov

This is the official site for the FDA, where you can look up the government's stance on many issues affecting the safety of foods you give your family. Because of the Freedom of Information Act, thousands of documents are available to the American public and are accessed through the site's search engine. The site also provides information for parents about infant nutrition

www.kidshealth.com

This site is operated by the Nemours Foundation, a charitable organization founded by Alfred du Pont and dedicated to improving the health of children and elderly persons. There are separate sections of the site for parents, children, and teenagers. The parents' section has comprehensive infant and toddler nutrition information, which includes age-specific guidelines and information on a variety of topics including vegetarianism, food safety, and eating disorders.

www.ccof.org

The California Certified Organic Farmers (CCOF) is the most recognized certification for organic foods in the country and is the oldest organization promoting sustainable agriculture. This site is valuable to consumers who want to learn more about the specific practices and benefits of organic agriculture, and also includes information for farmers who are interested in transitioning to organic practices.

www.breastfeeding.com

This is an informational site for nursing mothers. It features a very active message board on which you can solicit advice from other mothers on a variety of topics. Breastfeeding.com's site is more fun and less professional than La Leche League's site.

www.consumerreports.org

This is the online offshoot of the popular *Consumer Reports* magazine, offering comprehensive reviews of thousands of products, including baby gear. Most of the information on the site is available only to online subscribers, but if you are buying a lot of baby equipment or a new or used car, it may be worth subscribing for a few months. Occasionally, you may find free information that is useful.

www.childrecall.com

This site focuses on child safety and houses a database of recalled products. If you are considering buying any used baby gear, I suggest you check this site first. There is also a section for consumer complaints about specific products that may or may not have been recalled. The site includes a lot of great safety information. Users can sign up for an e-mail newsletter with current updates of recently recalled baby products and a variety of safety tips.

www.imaternity.com

Imaternity is a huge online retailer, offering a large selection of things you might want or need for your baby. There is a section for feeding and nursing supplies that includes many brands of baby bottles, feeding spoons, breast pumps, and so on. There is also a section of the site devoted to customer reviews of products. This may be extremely useful when you are considering making a purchase, because other parents' experiences with a product will help you make an informed decision.

www.nutritionforkids.com

Although Nutrition for Kids's site does not have much to offer parents of babies, the information about healthy eating for children is valuable. The site promotes a book written by dietician Connie Evers called *How to Teach Nutrition to Kids*. Although the topics addressed on the site are serious, the information is presented in a fun way, and there are many suggestions for getting your kids involved in healthy eating. There is also a free online newsletter with nutrition information and suggestions for fun healthy foods to feed your kids.

www.zerotothree.org

This is an outstanding site committed to helping parents and child care professionals understand child development. There is some excellent information about feeding babies and children (to three years) from a child development and child/caregiver relationship perspective. I would recommend this site to all parents, especially those who are struggling with feeding difficulties or who experience an unusually large amount of stress around food or feeding their babies. The parents' resource section provides names, addresses, and Web site/e-mail information for a large variety of organizations that provide services to parents.

www.parentsoup.com and *www.parentsplace.com*

These are channels in the ivillage.com network. They feature extensive and active message board for parents in every conceivable situation from parenting special-needs children to single parenting to breastfeeding difficulties to family health issues. Although the information presented on the message boards is strictly anecdotal, you may find it useful, and if you post a question you're likely to get lots of advice and support. One note: It's easy to become lost in the boards because they're so incredibly extensive, and some subjects may overlap. If you post a message, make a note of exactly where you left it (which site, which category, which specific board) or you may never find it again.

www.twinsmagazine.com

You'll have to subscribe to use this Web site, but parents of twins may think it's worth it. I visited the site and it featured a message board discussion relating to feeding twins with differing eating habits (one picky, one not), which I thought was helpful.

www.drweil.com

Dr. Andrew Weil is considered by many to be the health food guru of the moment. Actually, he is a Harvard-educated M.D. who has written many popular books about health. His approach combines conventional medicine and research with up-to-date information about natural foods and supplements, and his style is appreciated by many people who struggle with issues relating to food and health. I find myself frequently visiting this site when I am online, and often find useful information relating to organics and links between diet and disease. The site has a farmers' market finder, which is a great feature. The user plugs in the name of their city and state and a list pops up with all of the local farmers' markets, including addresses, dates, and times and whether or not the market features organic produce.

www.the-childrens-society.org.uk

The Children's Society is a charitable organization located in Britain that focuses on the needs of children. I mention this site because there is a good pamphlet available there for parents whose babies or young children have serious feeding problems. The brochure is available in pdf format, and you will need Adobe Acrobat Reader or a similar program on your system in order to download it.

www.nomotc.org

The National Organization of Mothers of Twins Clubs is a great resource for parents of multiples. There is a small section with tips on feeding multiples, but more important, this site will help you to contact other parents of multiples in your area.

www.aap.org

This is the official Web site for the AAP and serves both parents and physician members of the organization. You can access the section of the site meant for parents by clicking on "You and Your Family." There you can order books and brochures published by the organization, several of which address family nutrition specifically. The organization also publishes a long list of public health brochures, which your child's pediatrician may be able to supply to you.

www.drgreene.com

This site focuses on providing answers to parents' questions and concerns from a pediatrician. The site is useful for a number of different subjects and provides guidance relating to feeding and nutrition.

www.fitnesoft.com

This site offers a software program that includes a database listing nutrition information for 13,000 common foods, including many brand name products and menu items from some nationwide restaurant chains. The user enters everything eaten over the period of several days, and the program will automatically calculate the nutrient value of the foods consumed and compare this against an ideal diet based on the Daily Values recommended by the USDA. The program may be downloaded and used for 30 days on a free trail basis.

www.healthykids.com

You can find a lot of great information on this site relating to health and nutrition for your kids. You can register as a user according to your child's age and get age-specific advice relating to a variety of topics. The site also offers updated recall information from the Consumer Product Safety Commission.

www.babycenter.com

This is a commercial site and you can shop for thousands of products, but there is also a strong informational component. You can search the extensive site according to your child's age, post messages, join chats, and so on.

www.eatright.org

The American Dietetic Association sponsors this Web site for its members. Regular users can use the site to find a registered dietician in their area. There is no specific information on the site relating to children.

www.100topparentingsites.com

There are new Web site appearing on the Internet every day, and portal sites like this one help users keep track of new and undiscovered sites in a special area of interest.

www.motherwear.com

This is a Web retailer providing nursing clothing (including bras), infant clothing, and maternity clothing. The selection isn't huge, but if you don't have a great maternity clothes shop in your area, you'll find many necessities.

www.littlekoala.com

This is a Web retailer with an online gift registry, parenting resources, and a good selection of maternity and nursing clothing.

www.justbabies.com

This is a Web retailer offering nursing clothing and supplies, as well as information for new parents.

www.nncc.org

This is the Web site for the National Network for Child Care, a nonprofit organization providing all kinds of information to parents of babies and young children, including a great list of articles relating to infant and child nutrition. To access this part of the Web site, go to the infant and toddler care section in the "Information Station" and click on Nutrition. There are tons of great information on this site, much of it written directly for parents and caregivers. You can spend hours reading all of the topics listed.

www.allergywatch99.com

This site offers parents badges, buttons, stickers, and other items to help them keep others aware that their child has a severe allergy or chronic illness such as diabetes. The items are fun to wear and help in the constant battle to communicate this critical information to others.

www.epinions.com

This site has millions of customer reviews for a huge variety of products, including detailed reviews of baby foods, formulas, nursing supplies, high chairs, booster seats, and feeding supplies. For each product you research, product information is provided along with a link to the manufacturer's Web site and a shopping link so you can order the product online. I highly recommend visiting this site before making purchases, as it will allow you to think about all the factors that will affect your decision, whether or not you end up buying the product online.

Manufacturers of Baby Food and Infant Formula

Earth's Best Organic Baby Food: *www.earthsbest.com* (800) 442-4221.

Baby Fine Organic Baby Food: *www.babyfinefood.com* (212) 579-3194.

Gerber Baby Food: *www.gerber.com* (800) 4GERBER.

Beech-Nut Baby Food: *www.beechnut.com* (800) BEECHNUT.

Ross Laboratories, makers of Similac and Isomil Formula: *www.welcomeaddition.com* (800) 227-5767.

Carnation, makers of Good Start formula: *www.verybestbaby.com* (800) 284-9488.

Baby's Best Formula: *www.babysbest.com* fax: (954) 788-8984.

Mead Johnson, makers of Enfamil formula: *www.meadjohnson.com*

Nature's One, makers of Baby's Own Organic Toddler Formula: *www.naturesone.com* (614) 898-9758.

Parent's Choice formula: *www.parentschoiceformula.com* (800) 272-5095.

Bibliography

Dietz, William H., M.D., Ph.D., F.A.A.P., and Loraine Stern, M.D., F.A.A.P., eds. *The American Academy of Pediatrics, The Official Guide to Your Child's Nutrition.* New York: Villard Books, a division of Random House, Inc., 1999.

Duncan, Alice Likowski, D.C. *Your Healthy Child.* Neskowin, OR: Sanicula Press, 1995.

Eisenberg, Arlene, Heide Eisenberg Murkoff, and Sandee Eisenberg Hathaway, R.N., B.S.N. *What to Expect the First Year.* New York: Workman Publishing, 1989.

Firkaly, Susan Tate. *Into the Mouths of Babes, A Natural Foods and Nutrition Guide for Infants and Toddlers.* Cincinnati, OH: F&W Publications, Inc., 1995.

Fortier, Kristene. *The Whole Family Cookbook: Two-Tiered Meals to Please Both Parents and Their Kids.* Secaucus, NJ: Carol Publishing Group, 1998.

Gordon, Jay, M.D. *Good Food Today, Great Kids Tomorrow.* Studio City, CA: Michael Wiese Productions, 1994.

Hodgman, Ann. *One Bite Won't Kill You.* New York: Houghton Mifflin Company, 1999.

Huggins, Kathleen. *The Nursing Mother's Companion.* Cambridge, MA: Harvard Common Press, 1995.

Jones, Katina Z. *The Everything Get Ready for Baby Book.* Holbrook, MA: Adams Media Corporation, 1998.

Karmel, Annabel. *First Meals.* New York: DK Publishing, Inc., 1999.

Kimmel, Martha, and David Kimmel. *Mommy Made and Daddy Too: Home Cooking for a Healthy Baby and Toddler.* New York: Bantam Books, 1990.

Knight, Karin, R.N., and Jeannie Lumley. *The Baby Cookbook*, rev. ed. New York: Morrow and Company, Inc., 1992.

La Leche League International. *The Womanly Art of Breastfeeding.* Plume, NY: 1997.

Lansky, Vicki. *Feed Me, I'm Yours*, revised and expanded. Deephaven, MN: Meadowbrook, Inc., a division of Simon and Schuster, Inc., 1994.

Leach, Penelope. *Your Baby and Child, From Birth to Age Five.* New York: Alfred A. Knopf, Inc., NY: 1997.

Roberts, Susan B., Ph.D., Melvin B. Heyman, M.D., with Lisa Tracy. *Feeding Your Child for Lifelong Health.* New York: Bantam Books, 1999.

Robertson, Laurel, Carol Flinders, and Brian Ruppenthal. *The New Laurel's Kitchen.* Berkeley, CA: Ten Speed Press, 1986.

Sears, William, M.D., and Martha Sears, R.N. *The Baby Book.* New York: Little, Brown and Company, 1993.

Sears, William, M.D., and Martha Sears, R.N. *The Family Nutrition Book.* New York: Little, Brown and Company, 1999.

Watson, Susan. *Sugar Free Toddlers: Over 100 Recipes.* Charlotte, VT: Williamson Publishing, 1991.

Weil, Andrew, M.D. *Eating Well for Optimum Health.* New York: Random House, Inc., 2000.

Wilkoff, William G., M.D. *Coping With a Picky Eater: A Guide for the Perplexed Parent.* New York: Fireside Books, a division of Simon and Schuster, Inc., 1998.

Winter, Ruth, M.S. *A Consumer's Dictionary of Food Additives.* New York: Crown Publishers, Inc., 1994.

Yaron, Ruth. *Super Baby Food.* Archbald, PA: F. J. Roberts Publishing Company, 1998.

Yntema, Sharon. *Vegetarian Baby: A Sensible Guide for Parents.* Ithaca, NY: McBooks Press, 1991.

INDEX

We Have EVERYTHING!

OVER TWO MILLION EVERYTHING. BOOKS SOLD

Everything® **After College Book**
$12.95, 1-55850-847-3

Everything® **Angels Book**
$12.95, 1-58062-398-0

Everything® **Astrology Book**
$12.95, 1-58062-062-0

Everything® **Baby Names Book**
$12.95, 1-55850-655-1

Everything® **Baby Shower Book**
$12.95, 1-58062-305-0

Everything® **Baby's First Food Book**
$12.95, 1-58062-512-6

Everything® **Barbeque Cookbook**
$12.95, 1-58062-316-6

Everything® **Bartender's Book**
$9.95, 1-55850-536-9

Everything® **Bedtime Story Book**
$12.95, 1-58062-147-3

Everything® **Bicycle Book**
$12.00, 1-55850-706-X

Everything® **Build Your Own Home Page**
$12.95, 1-58062-339-5

Everything® **Business Planning Book**
$12.95, 1-58062-491-X

Everything® **Casino Gambling Book**
$12.95, 1-55850-762-0

Everything® **Cat Book**
$12.95, 1-55850-710-8

Everything® **Chocolate Cookbook**
$12.95, 1-58062-405-7

Everything® **Christmas Book**
$15.00, 1-55850-697-7

Everything® **Civil War Book**
$12.95, 1-58062-366-2

Everything® **College Survival Book**
$12.95, 1-55850-720-5

Everything® **Computer Book**
$12.95, 1-58062-401-4

Everything® **Cookbook**
$14.95, 1-58062-400-6

Everything® **Cover Letter Book**
$12.95, 1-58062-312-3

Everything® **Crossword and Puzzle Book**
$12.95, 1-55850-764-7

Everything® **Dating Book**
$12.95, 1-58062-185-6

Everything® **Dessert Book**
$12.95, 1-55850-717-5

Everything® **Dog Book**
$12.95, 1-58062-144-9

Everything® **Dreams Book**
$12.95, 1-55850-806-6

Everything® **Etiquette Book**
$12.95, 1-55850-807-4

Everything® **Family Tree Book**
$12.95, 1-55850-763-9

Everything® **Fly-Fishing Book**
$12.95, 1-58062-148-1

Everything® **Games Book**
$12.95, 1-55850-643-8

Everything® **Get-A-Job Book**
$12.95, 1-58062-223-2

Everything® **Get Published Book**
$12.95, 1-58062-315-8

Everything® **Get Ready for Baby Book**
$12.95, 1-55850-844-9

Everything® **Golf Book**
$12.95, 1-55850-814-7

Everything® **Guide to Las Vegas**
$12.95, 1-58062-438-3

Everything® **Guide to New York City**
$12.95, 1-58062-314-X

Everything® **Guide to Walt Disney World®, Universal Studios®, and Greater Orlando, 2nd Edition**
$12.95, 1-58062-404-9

Everything® **Guide to Washington D.C.**
$12.95, 1-58062-313-1

Everything® **Herbal Remedies Book**
$12.95, 1-58062-331-X

Everything® **Home-Based Business Book**
$12.95, 1-58062-364-6

Everything® **Homebuying Book**
$12.95, 1-58062-074-4

Everything® **Homeselling Book**
$12.95, 1-58062-304-2

Everything® **Home Improvement Book**
$12.95, 1-55850-718-3

Everything® **Hot Careers Book**
$12.95, 1-58062-486-3

Everything® **Internet Book**
$12.95, 1-58062-073-6

Everything® **Investing Book**
$12.95, 1-58062-149-X

Everything® **Jewish Wedding Book**
$12.95, 1-55850-801-5

Everything® **Job Interviews Book**
$12.95, 1-58062-493-6

Everything® **Lawn Care Book**
$12.95, 1-58062-487-1

Everything® **Leadership Book**
$12.95, 1-58062-513-4

Everything® **Low-Fat High-Flavor Cookbook**
$12.95, 1-55850-802-3

Everything® **Magic Book**
$12.95, 1-58062-418-9

Everything® **Microsoft® Word 2000 Book**
$12.95, 1-58062-306-9

We Have

EVERYTHING KIDS'! ®

Everything® Kids' Baseball Book
$9.95, 1-58062-489-8

Everything® Kids' Joke Book
$9.95, 1-58062-495-2

Everything® Kids' Money Book
$9.95, 1-58062-322-0

Everything® Kids' Nature Book
$9.95, 1-58062-321-2

Everything® Kids' Online Book
$9.95, 1-58062-394-8

Everything® Kids' Puzzle Book
$9.95, 1-58062-323-9

Everything® Kids' Space Book
$9.95, 1-58062-395-6

Everything® Kids' Witches and Wizards Book
$9.95, 1-58062-396-4

Available wherever books are sold!

For more information, or to order,
call 800-872-5627 or visit everything.com

Adams Media Corporation, 260 Center Street, Holbrook, MA 02343

Everything® is a registered trademark of Adams Media Corporation.

Available wherever books are sold!

Everything® **Money Book**
$12.95, 1-58062-145-7

Everything® **Mother Goose Book**
$12.95, 1-58062-490-1

Everything® **Mutual Funds Book**
$12.95, 1-58062-419-7

Everything® **One-Pot Cookbook**
$12.95, 1-58062-186-4

Everything® **Online Business Book**
$12.95, 1-58062-320-4

Everything® **Online Genealogy Book**
$12.95, 1-58062-402-2

Everything® **Online Investing Book**
$12.95, 1-58062-338-7

Everything® **Online Job Search Book**
$12.95, 1-58062-365-4

Everything® **Pasta Book**
$12.95, 1-55850-719-1

Everything® **Pregnancy Book**
$12.95, 1-58062-146-5

Everything® **Pregnancy Organizer**
$15.00, 1-58062-336-0

Everything® **Quick Meals Cookbook**
$12.95, 1-58062-488-X

Everything® **Resume Book**
$12.95, 1-58062-311-5

Everything® **Sailing Book**
$12.95, 1-58062-187-2

Everything® **Selling Book**
$12.95, 1-58062-319-0

Everything® **Study Book**
$12.95, 1-55850-615-2

Everything® **Tall Tales, Legends, and Outrageous Lies Book**
$12.95, 1-58062-514-2

Everything® **Tarot Book**
$12.95, 1-58062-191-0

Everything® **Time Management Book**
$12.95, 1-58062-492-8

Everything® **Toasts Book**
$12.95, 1-58062-189-9

Everything® **Total Fitness Book**
$12.95, 1-58062-318-2

Everything® **Trivia Book**
$12.95, 1-58062-143-0

Everything® **Tropical Fish Book**
$12.95, 1-58062-343-3

Everything® **Vitamins, Minerals, and Nutritional Supplements Book**
$12.95, 1-58062-496-0

Everything® **Wedding Book, 2nd Edition**
$12.95, 1-58062-190-2

Everything® **Wedding Checklist**
$7.95, 1-58062-456-1

Everything® **Wedding Etiquette Book**
$7.95, 1-58062-454-5

Everything® **Wedding Organizer**
$15.00, 1-55850-828-7

Everything® **Wedding Shower Book**
$7.95, 1-58062-188-0

Everything® **Wedding Vows Book**
$7.95, 1-58062-455-3

Everything® **Wine Book**
$12.95, 1-55850-808-2

Everything® **Angels Mini Book**
$4.95, 1-58062-387-5

Everything® **Astrology Mini Book**
$4.95, 1-58062-385-9

Everything® **Baby Names Mini Book**
$4.95, 1-58062-391-3

Everything® **Bedtime Story Mini Book**
$4.95, 1-58062-390-5

Everything® **Dreams Mini Book**
$4.95, 1-58062-386-7

Everything® **Etiquette Mini Book**
$4.95, 1-58062-499-5

Everything® **Get Ready for Baby Mini Book**
$4.95, 1-58062-389-1

Everything® **Golf Mini Book**
$4.95, 1-58062-500-2

Everything® **Love Spells Mini Book**
$4.95, 1-58062-388-3

Everything® **Pregnancy Mini Book**
$4.95, 1-58062-392-1

Everything® **TV & Movie Trivia Mini Book**
$4.95, 1-58062-497-9

Everything® **Wine Mini Book**
$4.95, 1-58062-498-7

Everything® **Kids' Baseball Book**
$9.95, 1-58062-489-8

Everything® **Kids' Joke Book**
$9.95, 1-58062-495-2

Everything® **Kids' Money Book**
$9.95, 1-58062-322-0

Everything® **Kids' Nature Book**
$9.95, 1-58062-321-2

Everything® **Kids' Online Book**
$9.95, 1-58062-394-8

Everything® **Kids' Puzzle Book**
$9.95, 1-58062-323-9

Everything® **Kids' Space Book**
$9.95, 1-58062-395-6

Everything® **Kids' Witches and Wizards Book**
$9.95, 1-58062-396-4

Everything® is a registered trademark of Adams Media Corporation.

For more information, or to order, call 800-872-5627 or visit everything.com

Adams Media Corporation, 260 Center Street, Holbrook, MA 02343